NEVER GIVE UP ON A KID.

*The Chronicles of the Life and Career of Emilio "Dee" DaBramo,
Educator/Humanitarian Extraordinaire.*

By David E. Hennessy

authorHOUSE®

AuthorHouse™
1663 Liberty Drive
Bloomington, IN 47403
www.authorhouse.com
Phone: 1-800-839-8640

© 2012 David E. Hennessy. All rights reserved.

No part of this book may be reproduced, stored in a retrieval system, or transmitted by any means without the written permission of the author.

Published by AuthorHouse 10/17/2012

ISBN: 978-1-4772-6088-3 (sc)
ISBN: 978-1-4772-6087-6 (hc)
ISBN: 978-1-4772-6086-9 (e)

Library of Congress Control Number: 2012917352

Any people depicted in stock imagery provided by Thinkstock are models, and such images are being used for illustrative purposes only.
Certain stock imagery © Thinkstock.

Because of the dynamic nature of the Internet, any web addresses or links contained in this book may have changed since publication and may no longer be valid. The views expressed in this work are solely those of the author and do not necessarily reflect the views of the publisher, and the publisher hereby disclaims any responsibility for them.

FOREWORD
BY
DR. RICHARD KEELOR

Former officer of The President's Council for Physical Fitness and Sports who served as Director of Federal/State Relations and Director of Program Development from 1972 through 1982 under Presidents Nixon, Carter and Reagan.

It is my honor to have been asked to express my sincere thoughts regarding my dear friend and former colleague Emilio "Dee" DaBramo in the Foreword of this book.

> *"The key to Dee's professional career, and what he stood for, was empathy, audacity and enthusiasm. Yes, he knew his subject and had all sorts of academic credentials, but experts are a dime a dozen. Dee's legacy will be the extent to which he changed the lives of the people and organizations he unselfishly served. They are legions. Dee's most endearing quality is his love of all people --regardless of race, religion, ethnicity or their physical or mental abilities."*

Dedicated to:
The children of Emilio "Dee" DaBramo

Debbie DaBramo Buckley
Jim DaBramo
Michael DaBramo
Shelly DaBramo O'Malley

In Memory of:

Celeste Cannizzo DaBramo
Aida DaBramo Stevens
Josephine DaBramo
Michael DaBramo Sr.
Sarah (Sadie) DaBramo Casey

TABLE OF CONTENTS

Preface xi

CHAPTER 1	The Immigrants from Compobasso 1
CHAPTER 2	Life in Stone House 11
CHAPTER 3	School Begins................................... 29
CHAPTER 4	The War Years................................... 45
CHAPTER 5	Homecoming................................... 109
CHAPTER 6	A New Beginning 127
CHAPTER 7	Back to the Real World 177
CHAPTER 8	Scarsdale, a Time of Stability 207
CHAPTER 9	Mamaroneck 213
CHAPTER 10	The Special Olympics 281
CHAPTER 11	Life after Mamaroneck 295

Postscript.. 321
Acknowledgements..325

PREFACE

During our country's 1976 Bicentennial Celebration of the Declaration of Independence the National Endowment for the Arts sponsored the production of a series of ten documentary films entitled Destination America. These films, which aired on public television during the year-long celebration, told the story of the great late 19th century and early 20th century migration of immigrants to the United States, most of whom were European. As I viewed each and every one of these films, I was struck by the producers' candid portrayal of the struggles of each ethnic and religious group of immigrants that landed on the shores of the United States. They did not find streets paved with gold, as advertised. In reality, what they did find was greed and exploitation, not only by the establishment, but by their own kind that had preceded them to America. The one positive offering that was universally available to all immigrants that came then, and is still offered to today's arrivals, is *opportunity*. Throughout my adult life it has been my observation that arriving immigrants recognize opportunities more quickly than resident Americans. Author Howard Fast in his book, The Immigrants, Houghton Mifflin, Boston, 1977, emphasized this trait of the immigrants. Why is this so? Having worked most of my adult life in developing countries where there is little or no opportunity for the average citizen, and those opportunities that do exist are reserved for the well-heeled establishment, it is easy for new arrivals to the United States to recognize an opportunity when it is presented to them. There are thousands of examples in the American immigrant story that clearly illustrate this fact. There are two examples that stick in my mind. The first is the story told in the documentary film, *A Place in the Sun*. It tells the story of how the Italian immigrants that settled in San Francisco at the beginning of the twentieth century, working as fishermen and garbage collectors, established their own bank. At the time, none of the prejudiced, establishment banks, would loan an Italian money. The bank they established is known today as *The Bank of America*, one of the largest in the world.

The second story is told in the documentary film, *On a Clear Day You Can See Boston*, which documents the plight of the Irish immigrants arriving in Boston during the great potato famine in Ireland in the 1850s and later. The Irish were so badly treated by the Boston Yankee establishment that the Irish immigrant leaders vowed to, first, take over the politics of Boston by electing an Irish Mayor and later, elect an Irish Catholic President. They accomplished their first goal by out-populating the Boston Yankees, thus voting them out of office, and later, in 1960, electing the first Irish Catholic President, John F. Kennedy.

The topic of immigration today is fraught with controversy and contradictions, not unlike it was in America during those earlier days. But beyond the controversy and contradictions, there are two facts of history that cannot be denied –immigrants bring an infusion of new ideas to the melting pot, and they are highly motivated to succeed, which has played a leading role in the development of America as we know it today. One of my interests in the life story of Emilio DaBramo stems from the fact that it embodies both of these characteristics of the early immigrants that came to America –poor in material wealth but rich in spirit and character, and highly motivated to succeed. This led Emilio "Dee" DaBramo to succeed way beyond the dreams of his Italian immigrant parents, and his dreams as well.

I first met Dee on July 3, 1998, when my friend Arnold Rist and I were engaged in a 1000-mile bike ride through the State of New York, to raise funds for scholarships for students attending our alma mater, SUNY Cortland. Arnold had planned a scheduled rest stop at Dee's house over the 1998 Fourth of July weekend. His home is located in the Catskill Mountains of southeast New York State. On the third of July we rode from Utica, N.Y. to Norwich, N.Y., via the very scenic Route 23. At the quaint little crossroads town of Grand Gorge, N.Y. that was comprised of a gas station/convenience store, the American Diner operated by a Polish immigrant couple, a small bank, a hardware store and a small motel, we stopped at the gas station to ask directions to Dee's home in Conesville.

"Who yah lookin' fur in Conesville?," the gas station attendant asked.

"Dee DaBramo," I replied.

"Oh, everybody knows Dee," he answered me with a pleasant smile.

He gave us precise directions, and we snaked our way along the Catskill mountain roads to Gilboa, N. Y., then past the Schoharie Reservoir to Conesville, which is so small it went by almost unnoticed. From Conesville to Dee's place was about a mile or so. Dee had indeed chosen a very remote location for his retirement home in Schoharie County.

We arrived late in the afternoon, and found Dee sitting alone on the back porch of his quaint, primitive 230-year-old hand-hued log cabin. The cabin, which had been refurbished and added-onto, sat on eighty-eight acres of mostly forested mountain land. Dee was observing several female deer grazing not more than a few hundred feet from where he sat.

Up until this meeting, the only comment Arnold had made to me regarding Dee, was that I would find him to be a very interesting guy. Upon their meeting, the two unabashedly embraced each other with a traditional Italian hug. Arnold introduced me to Dee, and Dee shook my hand and made the remark that, "any friend of Arnold's is a friend of mine."

Dee's Conesville, New York home in summer. (Courtesy of Peter Fox)

"Make yourself at home, my friends," he said as he escorted us into the kitchen and offered us a cold drink. At age seventy-five, his athletic five foot seven-inch frame appeared to be in good physical condition, and his quick wit defied his age. We sat down at the kitchen table, and Arnold opened the conversation by explaining our mission to Dee. Dee asked me about my training program and how, at age 68, I was holding up. I told him I was ready for a few days rest, and he agreed that was a sound idea.

First meeting of author David E. Hennessy and Emilio "Dee" DaBramo on the Fourth of July weekend 1998. (Courtesy David E. Hennessy)

Then he turned the conversation to Arnold, and the two of them immediately began to badger each other with friendly comments and innuendos dating back to their college days in the 1940s when they were classmates, fraternity brothers and soccer teammates at Cortland State Teachers College. None of it registered with me at the time, but they enjoyed it immensely. Dee, seemingly, was enjoying his retirement years, living alone in a most remote and serene setting.

While Dee and Arnold reminisced in the kitchen over their cold drink, I took Dee at his word and, with my drink in hand, meandered into the living room to survey the log cabin. The living room led directly off the kitchen and was the most inviting space in the cabin. It housed a massive fieldstone fireplace that extended from floor to ceiling and took up most of the outside wall, which was constructed from thick square hand-hued logs. On the opposite interior wall, a staircase led to the upper level of the cabin. At the foot of the stairs was the front door, and to its left and right windows that exposed a view of the driveway leading to the house and the county road that marked the boundary of Dee's front yard --a good distance of at least a hundred feet. To the right of the front door was an open doorway that led to an adjacent room. Upon entering this room, I discovered that it housed an old desk and wooden chair and some other wooden cabinet furniture, all of which appeared to me to be Dee's den or study. The interior of the cabin is as pioneer-looking as one might imagine it to be.

What excited me most about the living room and the den were not the stone fireplace or the hand-hued log walls, but rather the memorabilia hanging from the walls. After making a cursory round of the two rooms, I turned my attention back to the memorabilia. The first picture to catch my eye was that of Rafer Johnson, the gold medal winner of the decathlon at the 1960 Rome Olympic Games, where he beat out his UCLA track teammate, Yang Chuan-Kwang, in the final event of the competition, the 1500 meter run. Yang was representing Taiwan at the games, and took the silver medal. Next to the Rafer Johnson photo was a photo of Dee dressed in a tuxedo, sandwiched between the matriarch of the Kennedy Family, Rose Kennedy, and Eunice Kennedy Shriver, with one arm around each of their shoulders. There was a second photo with Dee, Eunice Kennedy Shriver and Ethel Kennedy, widow of the late Robert Kennedy. My curiosity was heightened even more when I discovered, hanging on the wall leading up the steps to the upper level of the cabin, a photograph of twenty-one-year-old Technical Sergeant Emilio DaBramo being presented with the Distinguished Flying Cross by an Army Air Corps Colonel. And, next to that, hung the printed citation and the medal itself incased in a glass covered frame. The obvious conclusion that I reached from this was that Dee had fought in World War II and was a medal holder. These were just a few of the many offerings. Not wanting to appear rude to Dee and Arnold, I returned to the kitchen and joined in the conversation as best I could. My attention, however, was not on the conversation, but on the plethora of memorabilia I had discovered in the other two rooms. The question which kept repeating in my mind was "who the hell is this guy, Dee DaBramo?" I was anxious to return to the living room and inspect them further.

At about 6 p.m., Dee invited Arnold and me to have dinner with him. Since he knew the way to the restaurant, we took our places in his red

Ford Cobra sports car and we drove off in the roar of its engine. Upon entering the parking lot at the restaurant, it was obvious to us that it was a popular place. We discovered that our assumption of its popularity was valid, since most of the tables were occupied and there were several couples ahead of us waiting to be seated. No sooner was Dee recognized by the hostess, an attractive middle-aged woman, when she extended her arms to him and planted a kiss on his cheek. Dee reciprocated with a kiss of his own on her cheek. He introduced us to her, and jokingly made some disparaging remark regarding our character, to which she laughed, and discarded it as not possibly being true. As she guided us to a corner table in the dining room, Dee was greeted by everyone he met. It seemed to me that he stopped to chat or joke with everyone in the spacious dining room. My impression was that everyone knew him and loved him. Arnold and I followed the hostess to the table and seated ourselves, while Dee arrived about ten minutes later. During dinner, Dee's friends and acquaintances stopped by, in what seemed like an endless procession, to inquire how he was doing. Again the question came to my mind, "Who the hell is this guy?"

After dinner, we returned to Dee's mountain home and sat in the living room chatting away. Dee never seemed to run out of ways to tease Arnold, telling jokes or reminiscing about their many years of friendship. I listened carefully in an effort to pick up clues as to what Dee was all about. At about eight o'clock that evening, while we were chatting, a knock came at the front door. Since I was closest to the door, I got up from my seat and opened the door to greet the visitor. Standing in the doorway was a pretty young lady, who I surmised was of high school or college age. She appeared surprised to see me, since she was expecting to be greeted by Dee. She quickly regained her composure, and before I could utter a word, she asked, "Is Dee home?" The summer sun had not yet set, and Dee caught sight of the young lady framed in the doorway and shouted out her name, greeting her. She smiled as he approached the doorway, and I retreated back into the room. Her conversation with Dee went something like this.

"Dee, the seniors are having a graduation party on the Fourth of July, starting at about eight o'clock. We all would like you to come," she said pleadingly, "if you can make it," she added in an attempt to soften her demand.

She mentioned the location at which the party would take place, and again extended the invitation to Dee. Dee did not hesitate to accept her invitation, but not until after adding a joking caveat to his acceptance.

"I'll come," he responded without hesitation, "if my two old fogy friends here can come along with me," he quipped, nodding his head in our direction. She laughed and willingly accepted his counter-offer. Upon closing the door, Dee turned to me and said, "Dave, please remind me on the evening of the Fourth about the party, because I don't want to miss it."

I confirmed that I would do just that. The hour was approaching 11p.m., and I asked to be excused to hit the sack, since I was tired after having ridden my bike about sixty miles that day. Dee, of course, could not resist the opportunity to admonish me, in a joking manner of course, for not being man enough to handle the physical activity of the day, in spite of the fact that he knew I was sixty-eight years old. Arnold, too, was tired, and he sided with me. Dee led us to our rooms in the upper floor of the cabin, which, much to my surprise, housed three bedrooms. The coziness of the cabin and the clutter of memorabilia adorning the walls made it look deceivingly smaller than it really was. The room I was offered had a skylight directly above the middle of the bed, and I had a magnificent view of the starlit sky that shown above the darkened Catskill Mountains. I slept like a log that night.

I awoke the next morning at about 8:30 a.m. Dressed in my pajamas and with my clothes and shoes clutched in my hands, I headed downstairs toward the bathroom to shower and shave. I could hear Arnold and Dee talking in the kitchen, which was but a few feet from the bathroom. I poked my head through the doorway to the kitchen and greeted them. Dee, turned to Arnold and remarked, "your new-found friend likes to sleep, doesn't he?"

Arnold added his bit of sarcasm in agreement with Dee, and I left them both laughing as I turned toward the bathroom. By now I was used to Dee's sarcastic humor. After dressing, I joined Arnold and Dee in the kitchen where I found them finishing off their breakfast. Dee made some disparaging remark about me being late for breakfast and that the cook had already left. Arnold just laughed, indicating his agreement with his long-time buddy. Dee set a fresh brewed cup of coffee in front of me, which I accepted without hesitation, and then offered to fry me a couple of eggs. I settled on some cornflakes and milk instead, and served myself. While I ate my cornflakes, Dee outlined the plan-of-the-day. First, he would show us around his place. This, of course, was for my benefit since I had never visited his home before. Then he planned to give us a driving tour of the local countryside, which included a view of the Schoharie Reservoir and Mine Kill State Park. Then he mentioned that his neighbor across the street had invited us all to a big barbeque to celebrate the Fourth of July. It was during Dee's tour of his homestead that I got my first inkling of what he was about. He began his tour by escorting me to a large outbuilding, a hundred or so feet from the rear of his cabin. I estimated the size of the building to be about two and a half garage doors wide and about 60 or 80 feet long. Its present use was to house his prized red Ford Cobra sports car, his maroon Ford Ranger pickup truck, two tractors that he used to mow his large expanse of lawn and hayfield, plus a plethora of tools and other equipment. In general, it was a workshop and storage space of sorts. A closer examination of the ground floor space revealed to me that it appeared to have once served as a large kitchen and cafeteria. The presence of several large refrigerators and/or freezers and at least one large commercial gas cooking stove, made my assumption appear logical. All had things piled on top of them, making them less obvious. I queried Dee about this, and he verified the fact that indeed, it once did serve as a kitchen and cafeteria. Upon further inquiry he revealed that the building had originally been erected to house Down's syndrome and mentally and physically challenged individuals in a summer camp environment. Needless to say, I was surprised at this revelation. He then escorted me to the second floor of the building where he showed me the bedrooms and bathroom facilities that were provided for the campers and staff. Not having had any experience with Down's syndrome individuals, the only question I could think of to ask him was had he worked with Down's syndrome individuals during his career? He answered my question with a very modest, "yes," but did not offer any amplifying information. It was not until later that day that I had an opportunity to speak with Arnold about my discovery. Arnold revealed the facts of Dee's long distinguished career working with children with special needs, his years of working as a clinician for Eunice Kennedy Shriver's Special Olympics program, and his twelve years (1968-1980) as Games Director of the New York State Special Olympics program. It was then that I made the connection Dee had with Eunice Kennedy Shriver, Rose Kennedy and Ethel Kennedy, as depicted in the photographs hanging on his living room wall. I had yet to figure out why Rafer Johnson's photo was hanging on the wall of his living room.

The rest of the day went as Dee had planned. We toured the Schoharie Reservoir and Mine Kill State Park, and viewed other local sights of interest. We stopped for lunch at a local convenience store in Grand Gorge, where once again Dee was greeted like a celebrity. We spent a few more hours touring the beautiful countryside, and then returned to his cabin. On the way back, Dee, in passing, pointed out the old Gilboa Central School building. The significance of this casual observation had little meaning to me at that time, but would prove to be a significant detail later on.

About 4:30 on the afternoon of the Fourth of July, the three of us crossed the road to Dee's neighbor's home where the barbeque was taking place. Before announcing our arrival to the host, we strolled by the open barbeque pit to savor the rich aroma of the main entrée, a whole hog being turned on a spit, roasting over the glowing embers of an open pit fire. His party neighbors were from the metropolitan New York City area, and were enjoying the work of refurbishing an old farmhouse as their get-away-home in the mountains. They had invited several dozen of their friends from the city to attend the celebration, along with some of their local area friends and neighbors as well, one of whom was Dee. When we arrived, the party was in full swing. The drinks were flowing, and a long table, with a white paper tablecloth adorning it, was loaded with an array of finger foods, potato salad, and a variety of delicious breads, rolls, pastries and fresh fruit. The host and hostess had obviously gone all out to produce a memorable feast. Dee introduced Arnold and me to the host, and he graciously welcomed us and told us of the fireworks planned for later that evening. Dee, of course, was greeted by his local neighbors, to whom he introduced Arnold and me. It was when I was having a casual conversation with one of his neighbors that I learned more about Dee.

"Are you a longtime friend of Dee's?" he asked.

"No," I replied. "I met him for the first time a few days ago."

"Oh, then you're in for a real treat, because he's quite a character."

"Yes, I am beginning to believe that to be true," I responded. "What I have observed so far is that every time he meets people in this community, he is treated with celebrity-like status. Is that so?" I asked.

"I suppose, in a way, that's true," he responded thoughtfully.

"Perhaps you can enlighten me as to why that so," I queried him once again.

"So, you really don't know much about him, do you?"

"Like I said before, I just met him a few days ago."

"Well, it was about 1980, I believe, he took the job as interim superintendent of our school district, and did a fantastic job. But, even more importantly than that, in 1990 he ran for county supervisor on the Democratic ticket and won. For a Democrat to win in this Republican district was rare," he explained.

"He must have done a good job since so many people seem to like him."

"Yes, he did," he answered. "His personality, his experience as a trustee downstate and his leadership ability seemed to have a way of bringing people together," he added.

Through that enlightened conversation I was better able to understand why Dee was respected by so many people in this small mountain community.

As the party progressed into the early evening hours, I remembered my promise to Dee to remind him of the senior class gathering beginning at 8 o'clock that evening that the three of us had promised to attend. At about 7:30, I located Dee mingling and joking with some of the other party guests, and quietly reminded him of our invitation to the party. At first, he stared at me with a surprised look on his face, and asked me to repeat my statement. I repeated myself, and he acknowledged that he had forgotten and thanked me for reminding him. Together we located Arnold, and the three of us crossed the road to Dee's house, climbed into his red Ford Cobra, and with Dee behind the wheel, we sped off to the party.

It was upon arrival I had one of the rare surprises of my life as an educator. Dee parked his car, and almost before he could disembark, a crowd of teenage kids had surrounded him. Each took their turn embracing him and thanking him for attending the party. They gave him a celebrity escort into the party facility, leaving Arnold and me to fend for ourselves. Upon entering the facility, he was joined by parents and other adoring adults that were in attendance. I was astounded by the reception, and again I repeated to myself, "who the hell is this guy, Dee DaBramo?" In spite of the melee, I managed to quietly ask Arnold what was all this about. Arnold informed me that one of the programs that Dee instituted at the Gilboa Central School was an *alternative school*.

"An alternative school is designed to help kids, who heretofore were academic underachievers, succeed academically and socially," he informed me. "Dee modeled the program after the one he had managed at the Mamaroneck School System where he had been previously employed," Arnold said.

Arnold went on to tell me that the success of the program was measured by the high rate of graduating seniors and the number of these graduates that went on to successfully complete college.

"This is why, tonight, you see this outpouring of affection for the man, by the kids, their parents, and his many friends in attendance," Arnold informed me.

In a very short time, the picture of why so many people in the community had expressed their love and respect for Dee was becoming clearer to me. It was his sense of community, his love of kids-- especially for those with special needs, his sense of fairness, his kind and outgoing personality and his leadership ability that endeared him to all.

On the morning of July 5, 1998, after a good night's sleep and a hearty breakfast at Dee's kitchen table, Arnold and I set out once again on our 1000 mile bicycle tour of New York State. We still had a few hundred miles to go to reach our final goal, the campus of SUNY Cortland, for the 1998 Alumni Reunion Weekend, starting Friday, July 11, 1998. The evening of July 5, Arnold and I stayed at a motel outside of Binghamton, New York. I showered and rested for an hour or so, and then we went to dinner. It was at dinner that Arnold and I had a long discussion about Dee and his career. Arnold spoke, and I listened with great interest and admiration at Dee's accomplishments. Near the end of Arnold's story, he told me something sad about Dee that startled me. Since I was so caught up in the character of the man and the enormity of his accomplishments, it was something that completely escaped my notice.

"Dee," Arnold said sadly, "is losing his memory. His doctors say that he is suffering from a memory loss which is characteristic of aging. The diagnosis is not definitive," he said hopefully.

Arnold proceeded to point out some incidents that occurred that revealed some of the symptoms.

"One of the noticeable symptoms is that Dee was repeating himself, and on occasion he was forgetting what he had said moments earlier."

Arnold reminded me of the night the high school girl came to the door to invite Dee to the senior class party, and what happened after she left. I recalled that he turned to me and asked me to remind him to attend the party the next evening. Then, on July fourth when I reminded him of the occasion, he gave me a blank stare and said, "say again." I repeated my reminder to him, and then he recalled the invitation. My first reaction to the news was it was a terrible injustice of fate for him, a man who had contributed so much to others, and to whom I had become a friend in such a few short days by learning of his deeds and experiencing his infectious personality.

For weeks, after returning to my home in Indiana, the memory of my brief encounter with Emilio "Dee" DaBramo lingered in my mind. I had spoken several times to my wife Mildred of this encounter. She, too, was impressed.

"I'm surprised someone from New York hasn't thought about writing a story about him or perhaps his biography," she remarked to me one evening. Her casual thought was the trigger for the idea that I should write his story. I responded to her remark almost immediately.

"Milly, that's a great idea and I think I would love to take on that task."

Her first reaction was that of surprise, and then her practical mind kicked in. "Do you know what all that entails?" she questioned.

I thought for a moment or two and said, "Since I have never written a biography before, honestly, no." Then I hesitated for a few seconds to gather my thoughts to better answer her question. "A lot of research to start with," I said.

"Yes," she replied, "and a lot of time," she added.

"The most important point here is that if Dee is losing his memory and if someone doesn't write his story, it will be lost forever," I said, with a sense of great urgency. "I can't let that happen, can I?"

"It sounds to me like you have already made up your mind. Am I right?"

"Yes, I suppose you are."

"If that's the case, then you better ask yourself this question. Would Dee be willing to allow you to pry into his private life and that of his family? He does have a family, doesn't he?" she asked.

"I don't know anything about his family, but your question is a valid one that must be considered," I readily admitted.

The idea of writing Dee's biography was enticing, and I made up my mind to do it. Milly and I explored the idea in more depth, and we decided that since Arnold Rist had been Dee's friend for more than fifty years, he was the obvious choice to approach Dee with the idea. A day or two later,

I spoke with Arnold, and he was overwhelmingly in favor of the idea, and he agreed to talk with Dee about it. A week or so later, Arnold called me back and told me that we had Dee's approval. Using Arnold as the liaison, I made the arrangements to visit Dee in February of 1999 to interview him and tape-record his life story.

Dee's Conesville, New York home in winter. (Courtesy Shelly O'Malley)

The Interview.

The 800-mile drive from my home in Nashville, Indiana to Conesville, New York took me two days. As one might expect, the driving conditions in the month of February were not ideal. I encountered ice and snow most of the way. When I arrived at Dee's cabin, it and the entire countryside were covered in twelve inches of snow. As I turned into his driveway I could see white smoke emanating from the chimney of that huge stone fireplace I had admired when I first visited Dee in July. It was a scene that the poet Robert Frost would have done justice to.

Dee was pleased to see me, and immediately made me feel at home by greeting me with a hot cup of coffee to warm my chilled bones. We meandered into the living room where he had a roaring log fire stoked up in that magnificent stone fireplace. Now I had the opportunity to see it in action. I was not disappointed. He had several stacks of split logs piled on the hearth, ready to be thrown on the hot embers when the need arose.

Still chilled to the bone, I sat in one of Dee's old, well-worn overstuffed sofas facing the fireplace, with my hot coffee cup cradled in my hands, soaking up the warmth from the flaming logs. That moment reminded me of the scene in Robert W. Service's poem *The Cremation of Sam McGee*, where near the end of the poem Sam McGee from Tennessee is sitting up in his crematorium, the fire box of the river boat the *Alice May*, telling his cremator who had opened the door to the firebox to check on the condition of his body.

"*Please close that door. It's fine in here, but I greatly fear you'll let in the cold and storm--Since I left Plumtree, down in Tennessee, it's the first time I've been warm.*"

We reminisced about our Fourth of July visit. He asked me how the bike ride ended, and if I had been in contact with his friend Arnold lately. I told him how the bike ride ended and that, indeed, I had spoken with Arnold, and assured him Arnold was fine and working as hard as ever in spite of his age.

Inasmuch as I had been driving since early morning in not-so-ideal conditions, I begged off to bed at about 9 o'clock. The plan for the next day was to start our first interview session right after breakfast.

The next morning I awoke at about 7:30 and well rested. Still in my pajamas, I grabbed my clothes and went downstairs to shower and shave. As I descended the stairs into the living room, I heard Dee's voice and that of a woman emanating from the kitchen.

"Good morning," I shouted to alert them to my presence, and proceeded to the bathroom. After showering, shaving and dressing, I headed for the kitchen. Here I discovered Dee sitting with a young lady, who turned out to be his daughter Shelly. She told me that she had driven to Conesville from her home in Mamaroneck, New York and arrived at about midnight. Shelly was one of four of Dee's children, his youngest of two daughters. I later learned that his older daughter, Debbie, lived in Arizona, and he also had two sons, Michael and Jim. We all had breakfast together, during which time she politely quizzed me on various topics of interest to her, like--who are you, and what's your motivation for interviewing my father? How long will you be visiting? etc., etc. It became clear to me that she was looking out after her father's interests, which I found admirable, especially since she drove half the night in a driving snowstorm from her home in Mamaroneck. I assured her and Dee that I would not be writing an expose', but rather chronicling Dee's life accomplishments as an educator and humanitarian. I assured them that they would have an opportunity to review each chapter of the book. I also told them that I did not have a publisher, and when and if I managed to find one, all the royalties would go for scholarships, in Dee's name, for kids attending SUNY Cortland. Once she felt comfortable with me as a person and of my motives, she spent a few more hours conversing with Dee and me. During this time, I discovered that she, too, was an educator working with kids with disabilities and special needs, following in her father's footsteps.

Around noon that day, she prepared to leave for home. She planted a kiss on her Dad's cheek, shook my hand goodbye, wished me the best, and drove home to Mamaroneck, braving the additional snow that had accumulated during the night hours.

Weeks prior to arriving for the interview sessions, I sent Dee a list of *topics of discussion,* so that he could prepare himself for the interview. As I was setting up the tape recorder, Dee placed the copy I had sent him on the table in front of him. I observed that he had made handwritten notes next to each topic. It pleased me to know that he had done his homework.

To put Dee at ease, I chose for our first topic of discussion a subject which was most familiar and current in his everyday life, his retirement in Conesville. He was quite forthcoming on the topic, and we got off to a great start. In the next few days we traced back his career as an educator, chronicled his Italian immigrant family childhood that was poor in worldly goods, but rich in family love and respect. He spoke of his struggles with learning English in a one-room schoolhouse, his academic problems, and his athletic successes while attending Pawling High School. He lauded over his college days at Cortland State Teachers College (SUNY Cortland). When I broached the subject of his two-plus years in the Army Air Corps during WWII (1943-1945), he was forthcoming in telling the humorous story of the induction process into the Army Air Corps, his boot camp training, his training as a radio operator, his in-flight gunnery training experience, his assignment to a B-24 Bomber combat crew and his combat crew flight training at Tonopah, Nevada and in Florida. He told me of the long flight from Florida to England via Brazil, the Azores and Africa.

The part of his Army Air Corps career he was most reluctant to talk about was his thirty or more combat missions over Europe following

D-Day. On two occasions when I broached the subject of combat, tears welled up in his eyes and he went silent. On one occasion he told me outright, that he didn't want to talk about it. Respecting his feelings, I changed the subject. Later, when he felt more comfortable with me, he loosened up on the subject a little bit. Since he was reluctant to discuss his combat experience, and knowing that it had to have been a defining life experience, I knew that I had a major research challenge ahead of me. As we progressed through the interview it became clear to me that the real story of Emilio "Dee" DaBramo was not all about what he accomplished and the honors that were bestowed upon him, which were no doubt significant, but rather what were the defining events in his life that molded his character and developed his sensitivity for other human beings.

The chapters that follow are, in part, and I stress the words *in part,* the result of my interview with Dee DaBramo in February of 1999. Since time has a way of distorting facts in one's memory, and in some cases the facts were fifty or more years old, a Herculean effort was made by this author to verify every fact and every incident told to me by Dee.

After completing the interview with Dee at his Catskill Mountain home, he and I compiled a list of potential collaborators, which included the names, addresses and telephone numbers of his family members, friends, neighbors, high school and college classmates, former working colleagues and organization committee members. In addition, he assembled the names and last known addresses of his B-24 bomber crew members that he served with in WWII. The list was formidable, but it was just the beginning of the process.

The one person that contributed the most detailed and substantive information regarding Dee's early childhood life and most of his adult life, was his loving sister, Sarah (Sadie) Casey. Without her input, this book could not have been written. Sarah passed away at her home in Pawling, New York on July 29, 2007. I am deeply saddened that she did not get an opportunity to read the published manuscript.

CHAPTER 1

The Immigrants from Compobasso

CHAPTER 1
The Immigrants from Compobasso

Michael DaBramo had sailed back to New York shortly after their wedding day and was not present when his bride of ten months, Marie Josephine Francesshine, gave birth to their first child, Emilio DaBramo, on February 17, 1923, in the mountain village of Compobasso, located on the western approaches to the Apennine Mountains in south central Italy.

Michael was living as a bachelor in an abandoned box car in Stone House, N.Y., a tiny hamlet located on the east side of the Hudson River between the towns of Pawling and Poughquag in Dutchess County about 60 miles north of New York City. He had a steady job working as a *Gandy Dancer* (laborer) for the Newburgh & Dutchess & Connecticut Railroad. This was his first job after arriving in the U. S., at age seventeen, and being processed, with hundreds of other men and boys, at Ellis Island Immigration Center in New York City in 1899. He was part of a group of men and boys imported as laborers to work on the railroads. This was an accepted immigration practice at that time in American History.

By 1921, Michael had 22 years of employment with the railroad, and had fulfilled two of his main ambitions for immigrating to America -- to find a steady job so that he could marry and raise a family with some sense of security, and to become an American Citizen. On March 12, 1921, Michael was sworn in as an American Citizen by the Supreme Court of the State of N.Y., in the City of Poughkeepsie.

Michael DaBramo was now 41 years old and felt secure enough to marry and raise a family. He had diligently saved his money, setting aside fifty cents of every dollar he earned over a period of twenty-three years of hard work. He purchased a round-trip ticket on a ship to Naples, Italy and, with more than three thousand dollars in his pocket, he returned to his birthplace, Campobasso, Italy, to marry Marie Josephine Francesshine who was twenty-five years old. The wedding day was May 14, 1922. The difference in ages apparently did not pose any difficulty in their decision to marry since it was customary for a European man to marry late in his life and to a woman younger than he.

Josephine and Michael DaBramo's wedding picture taken in Compobasso, Italy in 1922. (Courtesy of Julie Czerenda)

When one reads accounts of the Italian village of Compobasso in the travel guides to Italy, one is not impressed, and it is easy to imagine why Michael DaBramo left the village to come to America five years after his father passed away when Michael was twelve years old. The village of Compobasso is located on the eastern slopes of the central Apennine mountain range that splits the Italian boot down the middle of the country. To visit Compobasso from Naples, a traveler must drive northeast for about 100 miles. From Rome, the route leads southeastward about 200 miles. From either of these major cities the roads climb to an elevation of over 6000 feet on the west side of the range and then descends to about 5000 feet at Compobasso on the eastern side of the range. It is the capital of the province of Molise. According to the travel guides, it was once known for its engraved cutlery. Culturally, it is known for its early June religious procession *Sagra dei Misteri di Corpus Domini*, (the Mysteries of Corpus Domini) which dates back to the early 17th century, and two Romanesque churches -- San Georgio (12th century) and San Bartolomeo (13th century). The religious procession is still a practiced tradition, but today Compobasso is better known as the site for the National School for Carabinieri, or, as we would call it, the National Police Academy. Its mountainous terrain lends itself only to marginal farming and the herding of goats, sheep and some cattle. It is truly one of the most impoverished areas of south central Italy.

Dee's mother Josephine, the name she preferred to be called, at first refused to leave Compobasso for life in America, and did not accompany Michael on his return trip to Stone House, New York. Her decision was understandable in light of the fact that she was an unsophisticated, shy peasant girl who had never left her mountain village. She was frightened to leave the security of her family and home for what she perceived as the wilds of America.

And wild it was in the area surrounding Stone House, as described by the Italian immigrant author John Tartaro in his book <u>The Mission</u>, 1966, who had lived in the area for many years.

"The people were illiterate and mostly miners and railroad workers with many robbers and bandits here and there. John Dibble was convicted of killing his wife, and the dynamite house was blown up. It was not uncommon to burn your neighbor's barn filled with animals and no one in his right mind would venture over the mountain at night; for robbers in the "robber rocks" had no fear of holding up anyone that they thought might have money. The drivers returning with full money belts were parted of their money from the sale of cattle that had been driven to nearby cities. The children with no schooling, acted timid and wild, hiding whenever they saw anyone. The roads, mostly impassable except in summer, were narrow with cord wood laid across the wet places."

Josephine really did not want to come to America. Her dream was to build a house near her mother and raise a family in Compobasso. She was a very devout Catholic and attended church every day in her native village. She was schooled by the Nuns in dressmaking.

"My mother had a beautiful pair of hands. She could make anything she laid her eyes on from scratch," said Dee's sister Sadie.

Before returning to New York City, Michael gave Josephine three thousand dollars to support her. She took part of that money and bought some land near her mother's home with hopes of someday building her dream house. One can only imagine Michael's disappointment upon returning to America without his wife, or Josephine's disappointment because he didn't stay. It was a sure bet that he was the butt of many jokes from his fellow laborers when he returned to his job on the railroad in Stone House.

He was not one to give up easily, however, which was one of his enduring traits that he passed on to his children. One can only admire his vision of what America meant to him that he would leave his new bride behind with only the hope of eventually convincing her to come to America. But, now he had a son, and he was more determined than ever.

All through Dee's early life he can remember his father saying to him and his two sisters, Aida and Sarah (Sadie), "you can't pay enough for education." Michael knew that educational opportunities in Compobasso for him had been nil, and he was certain that the same would be true for Emilio if he remained there. He also knew that job opportunities for his son would be non-existent there as well. Being a marginal farmer or a herdsman was not what he had imagined for Emilio's future. He must have reasoned that with the educational opportunities in America, job opportunities would follow as a natural progression of events. He, of course, was right.

Michael was uneducated and could not read or write Italian, in spite of the fact it was his native language. At age 45, three years after the birth of his son Emilio, he made one more of many valiant appeals to Josephine to come to America with his son. His appeal was made in the form of a letter, dictated to a friend who could read and write Italian. The letter was sure to have included some of Michael's innate and sound logic and reasoning that typified his character throughout his life of 93 years. In addition, this time he took a very strong stand in his appeal to Josephine. He wrote, *"If you do not want to come to America then I want you to send my son Emilio to me."* Josephine relented.

The year 1926 was a time in European history when the continent was still reeling from the economic and social disaster brought about by World War I. This fact, certainly, must have had an impact on life in Compobasso, and Michael must have known this. America was booming in the twenties and opportunity abounded. The time was right.

Julie Czerenda, Michael's granddaughter tells of the strange coincidence of Michael's and Josephine's dockside meeting in New York City.

"My grandfather has told me the story at least fifty times of how he happened to meet my grandmother and their three-year old son Emilio dockside in New York City. To him the incident was a miracle, and when one hears the story, it might fall into the category of a miracle.

"In May of 1926 Michael was approached by a fellow railroad worker and an Italian immigrant like him, who asked Michael if he would be willing to accompany him to New York City so he could meet his wife who was arriving by ship from Naples, Italy. Michael agreed and they headed for the city on the appointed day. Now, up to this time, Michael had not received a letter from Josephine in reply to his letter in which he gave her an ultimatum. He and his friend arrived dockside where the Italian liner the *Conte Biancamano* was being moored, to meet his friend's wife. The passengers were lined up along the ship's railing waving to the waiting crowd on the dock below as the ship's crew was engaged in mooring the ship to the pier.

"Michael's friend was scanning the passengers searching for a glimpse of his wife. At the time Michael was doing the same thing, more for the sake of curiosity than anything else. The whole scene was pretty exciting. A few minutes passed and, like a miracle, he spots Josephine with Emilio standing at the railing apparently searching for him dockside. He couldn't believe his eyes and was overcome with joy and happiness. When they finally met after they had disembarked, Josephine told him that she had sent him a letter telling of her decision to come to America and giving him all the details of her itinerary. Michael, of course, had not received her letter and his presence dockside was sheer luck on his part.

Dee, at age three, with his parents soon after he and his mother arrived in the U.S. in 1926. (Courtesy of Julie Czerenda)

"Since my grandfather was a naturalized citizen, Josephine and Emilio had a U.S. Passport she did not have to go through all of the immigration process at Ellis Island. The irony of the day turned out to be that his friend's wife had to be processed through Ellis Island before he could take her home. It was Michael that brought his wife and son home, and not his friend. In later years Josephine described the Atlantic crossing with a three-year child as the most dreadful experience of her life. She made a solemn promise to herself to never make the return trip as long as she lived."

Michael transported his family home to Stone House. Together at last, after a four-year wait, the delighted Michael DaBramo, his wife and their three-year-old son Emilio, set up housekeeping in a small basement apartment in a house owned by a Mr. John David Whittick. John Whittick was the Postmaster of Stone House and operated a small general store in the large stone house for which the hamlet was named. The apartment was small with a kitchen and living room area and one bedroom. It had no running water, no electricity and an outdoor privy. Josephine didn't miss any of these creature comforts because she didn't have them in Compobasso either. At last Michael could proudly show off his wife and son to his friends, fellow workers and neighbors.

In December of 1941, at the beginning of World War II, the Italian ship *SS Conte Biancamano* was seized by the U.S. Navy at the Panama Canal Port of Cristobal where she was moored. The U.S. Navy converted her into a Troop Transport and gave her the name *USS Hermitage AP-54*. Her first action in the war was on November 10, 1942 in the invasion of North Africa. Later, in 1943, she served in the Pacific theater of operation.

CHAPTER 2

Life in Stone House

CHAPTER 2
Life in Stone House

The information for this Chapter was provided by Dee and his sister Sarah (Sadie) DaBramo Casey.

Life for Josephine during the first year at Stone House was very difficult. The remoteness of the hamlet gave her a deep sense of isolation. Her worst fears of living in rural America were realized. The family had no car and never owned one. Nearby, housed in the stone house for which the town was named, were a small general store, a U.S. Post Office and a resident apartment. Neighbors were few and far between, and none spoke Italian. Michael walked to work every day, regardless of the distance or the state of the weather. Without a car, it was impossible for Josephine to attend daily Mass at the Catholic Church in Pawling, New York, which was about five miles distance. The fact of the matter was, she couldn't attend Mass at all.

Shopping was a major problem for Josephine as well. For many years she could not speak English, and was relegated to pointing to items she wanted to buy. She shopped for groceries at the Stone House General Store, and from Tony Trobasso's grocery store on wheels that traveled from Poughkeepsie, New York twice weekly. Tony sold groceries and fresh produce, and Josephine could order special food items for delivery on his next round. In addition, a Mr. Eikner, also from Poughkeepsie, made weekly visits in his car to the rural folks in the area selling wearing apparel. Because of her English language deficiency, Josephine feared traveling by bus to shop in larger towns, and this chore fell onto the shoulders of Michael. He would accompany her on the bus or go alone.

In the traditional Italian families of those days, there was a strict division of responsibilities between the wife and the husband. The wife took care of the home and children and the husband went to work and earned the family's living. Michael was sensitive to the handicap under which Josephine was living, and often crossed the traditional lines of demarcation to make life easier for her.

The DaBramo family grows.

To make life more complicated, it was but a few months after the DaBramo family had been united in Stone House that Josephine disclosed the fact to Michael that she was in the early stages of pregnancy. On February 7, 1927 their first daughter Aida was born. She was named for the lead character in Giuseppe Verde's opera *Aida*. Dee now had to share the love and attention of his parents with his baby sister, and a new chapter in his life began. Michael and Josephine must have done a good job in making Dee feel comfortable about his new situation because he did not remember experiencing sibling rivalry between him and Aida.

"Quite to the contrary," said Dee, "I was always very close to my sisters. Love and respect for each other was the hallmark value taught in our home. I can never remember my parents fighting, verbally or physically. This, of course, set the example for us kids. We kids had nothing but love and devotion for our parents. Somehow they transmitted their love of us through their hard work, the discipline that they imposed upon us, and the responsibilities they gave us at home, their insistence that we get the best education we could get, and the love they had for each other gave us the feeling of being a part of it all."

"Our father was a grass roots philosopher of sorts," said Sadie. "He would say to us, in an instructive way, things like, 'Do good and God will bless you. Always throw a slice of bread and never a stone. There is no price too great to pay for an education.'

"Best of all," Dee remarked, with a look of admiration on his face, "he lived his philosophy. A good example of this occurred during the *hobo* times when the depression was in full swing. I can remember sharing our table with one, two or three hobos every Sunday. Sunday was the day our mother would make a special family meal of macaroni, meat balls, sausage, oven-baked bread and a special dessert, served with my father's homemade Italian wine. Since we lived near the tracks, the hobos would jump off the train and make a beeline for our house. Somehow they knew where the compassionate people lived. My parents never turned one away."

With a new mouth to feed and the prospects of more to come in his Catholic family, Michael took on as many part-time jobs as he could find. In the spring and summer he worked as a part-time groundskeeper at George Scheele's Estate at nearby Whaley Lake. This was a summer resort for the wealthy. One of his prized jobs, however, was working as a part-time groundskeeper for Henry C. Enders, Professor of Chemistry at Cooper Union College in Manhattan. He paid my father a living wage of eight dollars a day, which was nearly the equivalent to his weekly salary as a *Gandy Dancer* with the railroad," Dee remarked.

Seventeen months after the birth of Aida, Josephine was pregnant again. With the new baby due in early March 1929, Michael set out to find a more habitable home for his expanding family. As it turned out, his landlord, John Whittick, offered to rent Michael the residence space at Stone House. The rent was ten dollars per month. The house was located at the intersection of County Roads 216 (today 292) and 55.

*Early photograph of the old Stone House
(John Tartaro's Book* The Mission, *1966.)*

The house was built before 1775, and some say that General George Washington was quartered there during one of his Revolutionary War campaigns against the British. In the 20th Century it would house the poor Italian immigrant family of a railroad worker. Surely George Washington would have approved.

"The best things that could be said about the place, at the time," said Dee's sister Sadie, "was that it was sturdy and could hold off the wind and weather in winter, and it was conveniently close to the general store and the U.S. Post Office which were housed under the same roof," she added. "Its interior provided more space, and it had a yard that could be transformed into a seed and vegetable garden. We had no indoor bathroom or running water and no electricity. It did have wooden floors though. Fresh water was retrieved from a hand-dug well, and an outdoor privy housed the toilet. My mother used a cast iron wood and coal burning stove to work her magic as a master cook and baker, especially her lemon meringue pie that our father liked so well. Along with the large fireplace in the living room, the kitchen stove also served as the central heating system in winter. Heat from the stove and fireplace helped to warm the two bedrooms upstairs. In summer my mother prepared the family meals on a two-burner kerosene stove that had an attached baking oven. In the spring and summer the house was very damp due to the stone construction. The basement was damp and cool, and it was here where my father processed and stored his homemade Italian red wine. Our mother took advantage of the same space to store food stuffs, such as smoked meats and salt pork preserved in large crocks."

*Stone House in 1929 when Michael DaBromo
rented the residential part of the building.
(Courtesy of Sarah DaBramo Casey)*

Earn, save and become self-sufficient.

"In the early days, life at Stone House was preoccupied with three goals -- earn enough money to buy the necessities of life, save for the future, and produce enough food to be self-sufficient," Dee remarked.

"The yard outside the house provided space for a large vegetable garden, and there was a shed to house domesticated animals," Dee said. "It didn't take our parents long to convert the shed and the garden into a subsistence farm like those they were familiar with in their home village in Italy. They soon had a Jersey cow for milk and cream," he added. "All excess milk was sold to our neighbors for five cents a quart. They also raised geese for meat, chickens -- mainly for their eggs, and they fattened one or two hogs a year for meat. They were experienced in slaughtering hogs and converting every scrap of flesh into edible meat and sausage, and rendering pork fat into cooking lard. One of my mom's favorite meat specialties was making dry sausage, better known today as pepperoni. These skills were learned during their childhood years in Italy and served our family well in America," Dee remembered with great pride.

"In the spring, my Dad set out hot bed flats of seed, using the warmth of decaying fresh cow manure to germinate the seeds," Sadie remembered. "He raised seedlings of tomatoes, peppers, broccoli, cauliflower and cabbage for spring planting in their garden, and to earn extra cash selling them at a roadside stand in front of our house. After a few years, his seedlings became a popular commodity, and people came from miles around to purchase them. The garden produced a large array of fresh vegetables and staples that were preserved or stored by our mom for year-around use. Our father built an earthen root cellar to store hardy fruits, root type vegetables and potatoes to be eaten during the winter months. With his clever hand work he split the local stone to make storage bins in the root cellar."

"When I was about six years old, I sold our surplus produce from a roadside stand in front of our house for cash," Dee remembered. "I also delivered fresh milk to our neighbors for five cents a quart. This all contributed to my learning to accept responsibility, sharing with others and the importance of living a disciplined life."

Born Survivors.

On the fifth of March, 1929, the year of the October stock market crash, Josephine gave birth to Sarah (Sadie), their second daughter.

Dee had just turned six years old a few days earlier on February 17. The DaBramos were now faced with the prospect of raising three small children in the midst of a world-wide depression.

"My folks were survivors from birth," Dee remarked with a determined look on his face. "It was a trait which served our family well during the *Great Depression*. We survived better than most because my parents knew nothing but subsistence living in Italy and were already set up to deal with it, beginning in 1929, before it enveloped us all. Lady luck helped too. My father was able to keep his job with the railroad throughout these terrible years, earning one or two dollars a day, and maintained his part-time jobs at Whaley Lake and with Professor Enders in the spring, summer and fall seasons. He worked for Professor Enders for sixty years of his life. We lived a very Spartan existence. Thank God we never went without food. My mother made most of our clothing. But, most fortunately of all, when I look back at it now, I, the oldest of us three kids did not have to quit school to help support the family. I commend my parents for this. They knew, in spite of their lack of education, that education was the key to success, and they weren't about to deprive their kids of this opportunity."

Responsibility, Discipline and Respect.

As Dee and his sisters grew older, they were given more responsibilities at home. Sadie recalled that at age ten she and Aida, who was twelve at the time, were responsible for filling a fifty-gallon drum with water which was used as a gravity feed reservoir for watering the garden in the summer.

"We would carry five-gallon buckets of water from an open well and dump it into the fifty-gallon drum. I think I got more water in my shoes than I did in the drum," quipped Sadie. "A spigot and hose were attached to the bottom of the drum to irrigate the garden plants. We also carried water to the house for daily washing of dishes, clothes and taking baths year around," she added.

"In the summer we took a bath once a week in a metal tub, usually outside," Dee recalled. "In winter we took our baths indoors, but I can also remember taking some baths in the woodshed. Man, it was cold. But once I got to high school, I took a shower every day in the locker room. That was like dying and going to heaven."

From an early age Dee remembered helping his mother and father with the chores in the house and in the garden. As he got older and stronger he took on greater responsibilities. In the early spring, as soon as the ground thawed, it was Dee's responsibility to clean out the barn of the winter accumulation of cow and pig manure and spread it over the garden plot, using a wheelbarrow and a pitchfork. He, together with his father, turned the garden over with hand shovels and pitchforks. All the cultivating was done with a shovel and hand-held hoe. The weeds were plucked from the ground in the traditional way using their thumbs and forefingers.

One of his daily chores, from the time he was about ten or eleven, was to cut and split wood for Josephine's cast iron cook stove.

Dee tells the story of an incident in which he was negligent in carrying out this task one day and how his father handled the situation.

"One day I was late getting home from basketball practice and was a bit tired. I took it upon myself to make the decision not to cut the wood that evening. When my father got home from work he questioned me about it, and I gave him some veiled excuse. He listened patiently to my ramblings and said nothing. After he figured I was through with my useless rhetoric, he calmly walked over to a cupboard in the kitchen and retrieved a kerosene lantern. He lit it and motioned to me to follow him outside. I followed him not knowing what punishment he had in mind. I envisioned that a whipping with a hickory stick was not beyond the realm of possibility. He set the lantern on the ground next to the wood pile, handed me the buck saw and ax, turned and slowly ambled back into the house without uttering a word. At the moment, a feeling of relief swept over me. It was about ten o'clock that evening before he came out to inspect my work and give his approval to quit for the night. I learned from this and other similar experiences with my father that I couldn't beat him, and, if I thought I could, I was sure to be the loser. No one shunned responsibility in our home."

Contributing to the Family Welfare.

Dee began working outside the home in the summers when he was about the age of 12 or 13. He would help his father at the George Scheele's estate at Whaley Lake, earning two dollars a week. Later he worked at Professor Ender's house too. There were some summers when he worked for the railroad. He would take any job that paid money.

One summer, when Dee was 14 years old, he worked as a water boy on a construction project where the Green Haven Correctional Center was being built in the nearby town of Beekman. It was at this job that he came up with an interesting idea to earn extra money. One Friday he prepared cold lemonade for the construction crew, which became an instant hit with the men. The payoff was enormous for those days -- forty dollars in one day. He served lemonade every Friday after that. All the money he earned he gave to his mother to help run the house.

"Giving my mother the money I earned, without feeling as though I was being taken advantage of, was as natural as breathing," said Dee. "In fact, it gave me a strong sense of worth knowing that I was contributing to the maintenance of our family. We kids just never gave it a second thought. When I needed money to go to the movies or take out a date, my mom was always forthcoming. When my sisters were old enough to earn money, they contributed to the family welfare as well and felt the same way as I did."

There was Time for Play too.

Life at Stone House was not all work. There was time for play as well. During Dee's elementary and high school days he played baseball in the summer and soccer and basketball in the fall and winter. One of the perks of working at the Scheele Estate at Whaley Lake was access to the recreational facilities. This included boating, swimming and even tennis.

Dee at age 10, with his Sisters Sarah and Aida at Whaley Lake, N.Y. in 1933. (Courtesy of Julie Czerenda)

As a teenager, Dee became a very good tennis player which he learned from the estate guests. The guests would often invite Dee to play, and before long he was winning most of his matches. In the closing days of summer at Whaley Lake, there was a summer swim competition which he often won.

When Aida and Sadie reached their teens, they also worked at the lake with Dee and their father and enjoyed the privileges of the recreational facilities. In winter they enjoyed fishing and skating on the ice-covered lake.

Heeding the Doctor's Advice.

Living in the damp environment of Stone House was taking a heavy toll on the health of Josephine and the other members of the family. In 1938 Aida came down with rheumatic fever, and by 1939 Josephine was diagnosed with a serious case of rheumatoid arthritis. Their family doctor predicted that her condition would become progressively worse if she was not removed from the persistently damp environment. Michael took the doctor's words seriously, and from his cash savings purchased a house across the street from Stone House. The house was a plain two-story bungalow, built of wood construction with a wood shingle roof and siding, that sat on a native stone cellar foundation. Across the front of

The Bungalow purchased by Michael DaBramo in 1939.
(Courtesy David E. Hennessy)

the house, facing the road was a roofed-in porch with four sturdy pillars holding it up. It sat back from the road about fifty feet, with a green lawn and flanked by several large Norway spruces shading it in the front. The interior housed three bedrooms, a kitchen with running water, an indoor bathroom, and best of all, it was equipped with electricity. Dee was sixteen years old, Aida twelve and Sadie ten.

Special Friend.

One of Dee's best friends through elementary school and most of high school was Ed Reed. The fact that Ed was African American and Dee was Caucasian was irrelevant to their lives. Ed lived in one of the four houses in Stone House, a short walk from the DaBramo's place. The two were inseparable. Every day they walked to and from elementary school together, and played together during recess at school and during their free time from home chores. When they went to high school they rode the school bus together to Pawling. They often visited each other's home and ate lunch or supper together.

"Ed's mother was a very good cook," Dee remembered. "The first time I ever ate a wild woodchuck was at Ed's house and, surprisingly enough, I liked it very much. Ed's father worked for the railroad with my father for many years," said Dee. "They, too, were good friends. I can remember when the Joe Louis championship fights were broadcast on the radio, Ed's dad would visit my father at our house and the two of them would cheer for Joe Louis. Growing up, we knew nothing of racial prejudice in our home. We were all in the same boat, struggling to survive and make the best of our lives."

The Mischief Makers.

Ed and Dee were a mischievous pair at times. As elementary students they took up the habit of jumping a slow freight train for a quick ride home after school. It would save them a two-mile walk.

"Besides being a bit dangerous, we had to keep an eye out for the railroad detectives who were hired to keep the hobos from riding the rails," Dee explained. "We were quite successful for a long time until my father found out about it. That's when you know what hit the fan," Dee said laughingly. "I don't remember how Ed's father handled the situation, but I do remember that my punishment from my dad was hard and swift with a newly cut switch. Unlike us kids, who thought only of the pleasures of the events of the moment, I suspect my dad was thinking ahead of the consequences of me getting caught by the railroad detectives and connecting my name with his, and the possibility of him losing his job. From that time on, we never again rode freight cars home from school."

Another favorite mischievous activity of the pair was to steal coal from railroad cars parked along the tracks. Dee described the operation.

"When the coast was clear we would climb onto the parked coal cars and throw the coal down onto the siding. At night we would return to the site and gather the coal up in potato bags and bring them home for use in the kitchen stove. It was our way of helping out our families. Our parents never caught on, mainly because we never got caught. We would tell them a half truth that we picked up the coal that had fallen out of the railroad cars onto the sidings. This explanation apparently was plausible enough and they never pursued it further."

As they became teenagers, their adventures became more daring. On occasion they committed petty theft. "It wasn't much, but it was still petty theft," Dee admitted sheepishly. "We would steal candy and soda pop from the local grocery store, and once in Danbury, Connecticut," Dee admitted rather embarrassingly, "I stole a pair of shoes and some socks by hiding them inside my shirt. Luckily we never got caught. If we had, I know that the punishment I would have suffered from witnessing the embarrassment, humiliation and disappointment in the faces of my parents would have been devastating, especially to my mother, who worshipped her only son," Dee explained remorsefully.

"Ed left school before his junior year and went to work, and in the ensuing years we lost contact with each other, especially during the WWII years," Dee said sadly. "It was subsequently reported that in later years, Ed had pursued his education and became a registered nurse. I was very happy to hear that news."

Getting Religion.

Josephine and Michael were deeply concerned over the fact that Dee was not able to attend a Catholic Church and receive religious training in the isolated village of Stone House.

The nearest Catholic Church was five miles away in Pawling. Within walking distance from their home, however, was a small missionary church known as the West Mountain Mission. Michael made arrangements for Dee to enroll in Sunday School. Their rationale was that Christian training at a young age was important, regardless of whether it was Catholicism or not. Enrolling Dee in this church may have had special meaning for Michael. When he arrived in Stone House in 1899 as a seventeen-year-old boy, the West Mountain Mission Church had been in operation for about six years. It was established by the Episcopal Church in 1892 with the encouragement of the wealthy ladies of the Quaker Hill neighborhood in Pawling, located on the east side of the mountains. One of these ladies was Sarah Delano Roosevelt, mother of the President-to-be, Franklin Delano Roosevelt. In those days there was a distinct difference in the socio-economic conditions of those who lived on the east side of the mountains in Quaker Hill, and those that lived on the west side of the mountains in Stone House and thereabouts. The mission of the church, as laid out in 1892, was to help educate the 200 or so subsistence living inhabitants of the Dutchess County west mountain area. To educate them meant teaching them the basics of living -- like sewing, hygienic living, child care, cooking and other homemaking skills and, of course, some Christian training as well. The job fell to a young man of means, named Albert Charles Burdick. He was from the northern town of Gouverneur, N.Y. located in the western foothills of the Adirondack Mountains and just south of the St. Lawrence River in Lawrence County. Albert was a well-educated young man with good social and organizational skills. Within a few years he had established a school for the children and adults, mostly girls and young women. He had also managed to engage many of the railroad workers to help in building the mission facility. During the twenty-one years of Michael's bachelorhood in Stone House, the West Mountain Mission was the social center of Stone House and the immediate surrounding area.

"The railroad men were very helpful, and they enjoyed playing games and talking over the state of affairs in the evenings. The neighbors would also drop in to stay a few hours," wrote John Tartaro in his book The Mission, 1966.

It has been said, but not confirmed, that Albert was responsible for teaching English and American history to many of the Italian immigrant railroad workers, so that they could pass their literacy and American history exams in order to fulfill the requirements to become naturalized citizens. Since Albert operated the only educational facility in the area, prior to Michael becoming a naturalized citizen, lends credibility to the story. Michael, then, was no stranger to the West Mountain Mission

Church when he and Josephine decided to enroll Dee in the Sunday School. Another reason which may have influenced their decision to enroll Dee in the Sunday School was Dee's best friend, Ed Reed, was also in attendance.

The Old Mission (Photo from John Tartaro's Book, The Mission, 1966)

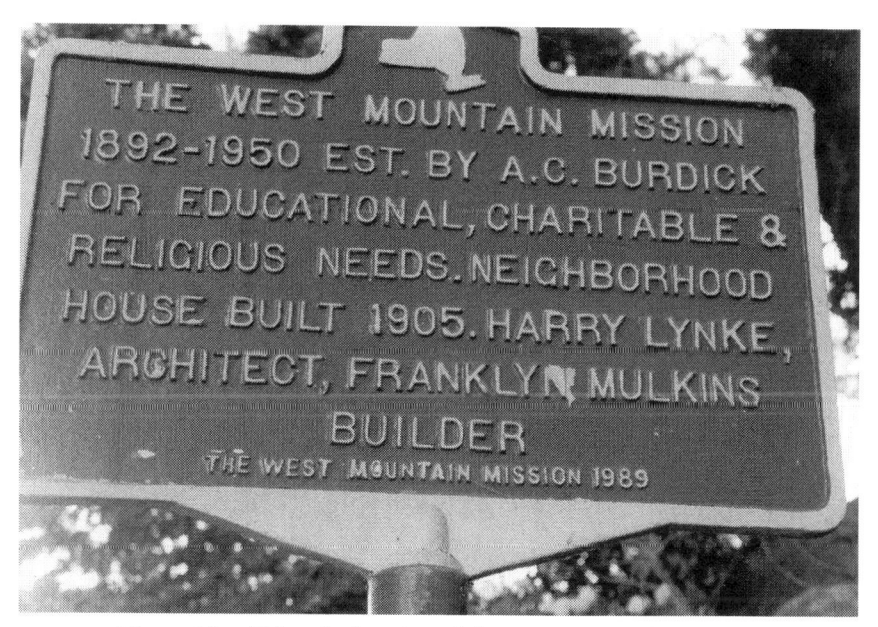

Plaque identifying the location of the West Mountain Mission. (Courtesy of David E. Hennessy)

A few years later, a Baptist minister from the Pawling First Baptist Church at Whaley Lake happened by the DaBramo's house one evening and convinced Dee's parents that he should attend his church. The church had a private car that would stop by on Sunday morning to pick up Dee and take him to church a few miles down the road. Dee was delighted, not so much that he favored the Baptist Church any better than the West Mountain Mission Church he was presently attending, but that he was given the opportunity to ride to church in a private car every Sunday, a rare treat in those days. In addition, the church was at Whaley Lake which he enjoyed visiting.

When Dee was sixteen years old he was attending high school in Pawling, which was a five-mile school bus ride from Stone House. He had a lot of friends in Pawling, and when he had time off he would hitchhike to town to be with his friends. One Saturday afternoon he was picked up by a gentleman driving a 1937 Buick, which was a very nice car for those days. The gentleman turned out to be a Catholic priest.

"What's your name, son," the priest asked.

"Emilio DaBramo," answered Dee.

"That sounds like a good Italian-Catholic name to me. Am I right?" he asked.

"Yes," Dee replied.

The priest smiled and looked directly at Dee and said, "Why is it that we haven't met before? Do you not attend church?"

"Oh yes, Father, I do," said Dee without hesitation. "I go to the Baptist Church."

"Why do you go there?" he asked, surprised at Dee's reply.

"My family doesn't have a car and they don't care where I go to church as long as I go," he said unabashedly.

Before dropping Dee off at the Pawling Theater, Dee revealed to him that he was a student at Pawling High School. The following Monday at school, Dee was summoned to the principal's office.

"My heart skipped a beat," he remembered vividly, "and I said to himself, 'what did I do now?'"

Father Dyer had spoken to his principal, Mr. Earl Norton, whom he knew, and asked him about Dee. After a brief conversation, the two men agreed that Dee could visit with Father Dyer on Monday afternoon at the Rectory and talk about taking religious training at the Catholic Church. Now, Dee was not one of Mr. Norton's dedicated students, but he liked

Dee in spite of his mischievous antics. Dee was somewhat of a disciplinary problem. Mr. Norton must have been delighted with Father Dyer's idea, thinking that he would provide a favorable outside influence on Dee. Anything would help and certainly it couldn't possibly do any harm.

The First Baptist Church where Dee attended as a young boy.
(Courtesy of David E. Hennessy)

Mr. Norton told Dee of the call and said, "I am going to give you permission to visit Father Dyer at the rectory today at two o'clock this afternoon." Dee was delighted with this idea. Any excuse to get out of schoolwork was okay with him. He was a bit confused, however, because he did not know what the word *rectory* meant. Mr. Norton explained that it was the home of the priest. Upon Dee's arrival at the rectory, Father Dyer invited him into his office and they both sat down. Father Dyer's approach was to try and win Dee over using flattery.

"Well, Dee, you seem like a nice kid, etc., etc."

Dee was street-smart and wasn't fooled by the flattery. He knew that if Father Dyer had talked to Mr. Norton, then the good Father knew he was a disciplinary problem at school and not the so-called nice kid he tried to make him out to be. Dee listened intently and put on the appearance of being receptive. When Father Dyer felt that he had won Dee's confidence, he handed him a *catechism* book.

"A catechism, what's that?" he thought.

The word catechism, to him, was just another big word he had never heard of before. Father Dyer explained what the catechism was and gave him a reading assignment.

"Dee," he said, "I want you to read and memorize three prayers --Our Father, Hail Mary and the Act of Contrition, and come back next week and recite them to me from memory."

"But, Father, I have school," Dee told him, trying to portray himself as a caring student.

"That's okay," he said. "I'll get you out of school."

"What a deal this is," Dee thought.

He learned the three prayers in two days and returned to the rectory to recite them to Father Dyer. Needless to say, Father Dyer was pleased with Dee and with himself. To reward Dee, he doled out one catechism assignment each week, and Dee's religious training as a Catholic was in full swing, much to the delight of his parents, and especially his mother. And Dee, well, he was getting out of his classes which certainly made it a win-win situation for him.

CHAPTER 3

School Begins

CHAPTER 3
School Begins

By the fall of 1929, Dee was of school age and unaware of the hardships he was to face upon entering school. His father spoke some English, but his mother spoke only Italian. For his father to communicate with Josephine and Dee, the common language in the home was Italian. At this time Dee knew only the very rudiments of English. With English not spoken in the home, he was sure to be at a distinct disadvantage when he entered first grade. To describe this dilemma in the baseball vernacular, Dee had a count of two strikes and a foul ball on him from the beginning.

The wonderful Pansy Baker.

There were more than thirty kids in Pansy Baker's one-room schoolhouse. Miss Baker, as she was known to all her students, was middle-aged with an imposing figure. She was about five feet six or seven inches tall and portly, as one of her ex-students described her, with brown hair and brown eyes. Her stature and lack of beauty were perfect for the job in the West Mountain area of Dutchess County, where young women of beauty and education were looked upon with suspicion and jealousy by the West Mountain folk, as described by John Tartaro in his book <u>The Mission</u>, 1966. He describes the fate of one young woman sent to work at the Mission as a teacher.

"Her downfall was the evil minds and jealousy of the people. When they saw that she was young, innocent, and good-looking, which in those days was not popular in a woman teacher, she lasted a short time."

"Apparently Pansy Baker was politically correct for the times," Dee remarked. "She was also an excellent teacher. Myself having had a forty-five year career as a teacher and administrator, I often think back at the job Pansy Baker did in that one-room school house in Poughquag, and feel only great admiration for the woman," said Dee with deep sincerity in his voice. "Her classroom management system was superb. She was given an almost impossible task, with thirty-five kids in eight grade levels with differing learning abilities at each level, and me, who couldn't speak English very well. How she managed the situation was to get every student involved in the teaching and learning process. Teamwork was the *watchword*. Kids with good reading skills, math skills, etc. were teamed up with those with lesser skills. Pansy was the conductor and her students the players and the learners. To get me off on the right foot, Pansy assigned a seventh grade classmate, Dick Wooden, to be my English tutor."

The one-room elementary school house that Dee attended in Poughquag, N.Y. (1929-1937) The girls and boys privies are show to the far right behind the school building. (Courtesy of Dee DaBramo).

"When Pansy Baker gave me the assignment to help Emilio with his English, I accepted the assignment without fanfare," Dick Wooden remarked, with a tone of pride that could still be heard in his strong but aging voice of eighty-three years. "In a one-room schoolhouse it was expected of each and every one of us to help each other out. This was the prevailing attitude fostered by the leadership of Pansy Baker. We learned from the other kids, as well as from her. When Pansy asked one of us to take on an assignment, we felt that we were looked up to as someone who was capable of helping someone else, and we were proud of that. Pansy made us feel proud of our accomplishments and rewarded us for our abilities by making us teachers. I tutored Emilio during my seventh and eighth grade grammar school years, and then I went off to Pawling High School. He was an intelligent and very active kid for sure. He picked up spoken English and math quite well during that time. Most of what I taught him in English was by word association --words with objects. We used math a lot to teach English. Math terms like add, subtract, multiply and divide gave us a starting point. Along the way he learned how to perform these math functions as well. My experience with Emilio was a rewarding one. After I went off to high school I didn't see much of him, and besides, there was an age difference of some seven years."

Front row: (L to R) Kenny McIntosh, Don Wooden, Richard Wooden, Emil Johnson, Sevenus Van Anden, Back row: (L to R, identity not certain) Milton Jeffords, Louis Bierce, Paul Farrington, Frank "Red" Davis, Wilbur Knapp, Bluford Jackson Jr., Henry Lee, Donald Aiken, Eddie Lieseski and Jim Belcher.

Dick Wooden, Dee's first English tutor, is seated in the front row center with the baseball bats. He is shown here as a member of the Pawling High School, Dutchess County Baseball Championship Team of 1934. (Courtesy of Dee DaBramo)

"Learning English as a spoken language for everyday communications is relatively easy for a young kid with a second language. Learning English grammar is another story," remarked Dee. "I had a lot of difficulty with that part of English in my public school days. As a result, it affected my reading comprehension and writing, which in turn adversely affected most of my other academic subjects, except math."

Two Pees in a Bucket.

"Yes, I was an active kid in grammar school," said Dee. "I was always pulling off pranks on the other kids, and sometimes on Pansy Baker, but she handled it well. On one occasion she turned a trick around on me in grand style.

"Jake Morton, a classmate of mine in 7th grade, and I were assigned to fetch water to fill the drinking jug in the classroom from the well at Knapp's grocery store that was located about a quarter of a mile from the school. This assignment was usually carried out near the end of the school day and passed around to the older boys in the room. This time it was Jake's and my turn. On the way to the well Jake announced that he had to take a pee.

"A devilish idea came to me in a flash, and I said to him, 'Jake, here pee in the bucket. It'll be the biggest joke of the year.'

"That's awful," said Jake, with a tone of disgust in his voice and a scowl on his face.

"Okay then, if you won't pee in the bucket, then pee in this cup and

Pansy Baker's class of 1933 with thirty-five students. Dee at age ten, is shown in the second row, fourth from left. Ed Reed, Dee's African American friend is shown in the back row to the far right. Dee's sister Aida DaBramo appears in the second row, sixth from the left. Conspicuously absent from the picture is Miss Pansy Baker. (Courtesy of Dee DaBramo)

I'll dump it into the bucket. My suggestion took Jake off the hook, and he relented. We filled the bucket with water and I dumped the cup of Jake's pee in the bucket. Since this was the end of the day the chances of anyone drinking from the jug in the classroom before the next morning were slim.

"During our two-mile walk home from school that afternoon, we couldn't help from bragging about what we had done to the other kids walking home with us. They didn't believe us, but they were afraid we might be telling the truth. The next morning one of the girls we had bragged to, told Pansy Baker. Pansy listened patiently to the story without giving any signs as to whether she believed it or not. She thought for a moment or two, and then said, 'Well then, if it's true, then I think that Emilio and Jake should drink the first cup of water, don't you?' she asked the class to which they all agreed with great amusement.

"The jig was up, so to speak. Pansy Baker won big time," said Dee.

Pansy Baker the Master Teacher.

"Pansy Baker's talents did not end with the classroom academics," Dee said. "She organized and ran the Christmas program that involved every student in the room. There were plays, dances and carol singing. In the spring she organized the annual field events day in which our school competed in various track and field events, vying against several other area schools. This is where my talent as an athlete began to show up. I won almost every event in which I was entered. It was at these spring events that the Pawling High School coaches began to take notice of me. Today, in my estimation, Pansy Baker would be classified as a master teacher. She knew her subject matter well, and taught thirty-five kids at eight grade levels in a dingy, one-room wooden building with a single pot belly stove for heat in the winter and an outdoor privy, one for the girls and one for the boys. In addition, she was a master psychologist."

A Chip on his Shoulder.

"In 1937, I finished eighth grade with Pansy Baker, but was still deficient in reading comprehension and writing skills, in spite of the Herculean efforts of Pansy Baker and my classmates," Dee said disappointingly. "Arrangements were made for me to repeat eighth grade at Pawling High School before taking a full load of high school courses. The lack of reading comprehension and writing skills plagued me all through high school. As a result, I often had to double up on courses to make up for previous failures. The psychological impact on me was that I didn't like the academic side of high school very well, and it often showed up in my behavior and attitude. Because of this, I had a chip on my shoulder most of the time.

"After having a career as a teacher and administrator, I am convinced that kindergarten through the fourth grade are the most important grades for learning to read. It has been my recommendation, as impractical as it may sound to some, that there should not be more than twelve students in each of these grades, and all efforts should be concentrated on READING," Dee said emphatically.

"The other condition that made me feel insecure in high school was my socio-economic status. When I was attending school with Pansy Baker, every one of us in the school were poor West Mountain folks. Now that I was attending eighth grade at Pawling High School, I was mixed up with kids from middle class and up on the social scale, in classrooms with thirty or more eighth graders, not just three or four eighth graders as there were in Pansy Baker's room.

"The system for handling disciplinary problems was well-established at Pawling High School. The architect of the system was the Principal, Mr. Earle W. Norton. He was an extraordinary man and deserves praise for keeping me on the straight and narrow during my high school years. When I arrived on the scene at Pawling High School, Earle W. Norton had been Principal of the elementary and the high school for seven years. He later became Superintendent of Schools and served three generation of kids in the community from 1930 through 1963 when he retired. He believed in strict discipline and it produced results. For example, when you were caught chewing gum, the punishment was to stick the gum on the bridge of your nose and then you were paraded from classroom to classroom for all to see and ridicule. Being late to class was not tolerated either and the punishment was swift. First, you were sent to Mr. Norton's office, who in turn, escorted you to the boiler room where he applied one or more swats on your behind with a rubber hose. Mrs. Summers, our homeroom teacher, God bless her soul, had her own punishment specialty. If you misbehaved in her class, she gave you a wooden ruler to rap yourself across your knuckles. If she thought your efforts were meager, then she would perform the act herself. Oh, how I longed for Pansy Baker."

"I can remember how uncomfortable Dee appeared when he first entered our eighth grade classroom at Pawling," commented Teresa Swalagin, one of Dee's former classmates. "He looked very shy, probably because he came from a small rural school and now found himself in a large high school. All the girls liked him almost immediately. He wasn't very tall, but was well-built and handsome. He became even more popular after he had a chance to show off his athletic ability, which helped him win over the boys as well. No one made fun of him or intentionally made him feel insecure. If he had feelings of insecurity at the time, it was of his own making. He was poor, as I was, but as an outstanding athlete he easily overcame the stigma of being poor in the eyes of his classmates. As a young girl like myself, from a poor family, it was more difficult in those days to overcome your social status. I remember not being accepted in the campfire girls and later not being picked as a cheerleader. As poor kids in those days, we were conditioned to accepting these inequities. Coming from a poor family was not a good thing."

Dee recalled a social experience that vividly illustrated his awareness of his social status at Pawling High.

"In 1940, when I was a junior in high school I met my first girlfriend. She was the daughter of a socially prominent member of the Pawling community. She was what I would have described in those days as being *well off,* both materially and socially. This fact bothered me a lot, in spite of the fact that I did like her very much. She always wanted to visit me at my home in Stone House, and I always managed to put her off because I was embarrassed with the way we lived compared to how she lived. One day she rode her bicycle over the mountain from Pawling and ended up on my front porch. When I opened the door, I was shocked to see her and felt very uncomfortable that she had come. I would not let her in the house. She didn't understand it at the time, but many years later we talked about it. I told her how I felt so insecure with her because my family had nothing materially, and her family seemed to have it all. I actually had everything in terms of family and love, but that was not how you compared your life with other kids' lives at that age and in those times.

"Another incident involved Mrs. Fenwich, the Pawling High School music teacher. I was interested in playing a musical instrument and approached Mrs. Fenwich. She gave me one lesson on the clarinet and she quickly found out that I had no experience playing a musical instrument and could not read music. Then, when she told me that I had to bring five cents for a reed, I knew I couldn't afford a musical career. Besides that, at the time I had no idea what a reed was. I was beginning to realize how intellectually deprived I really was.

"The one thing that saved me from quitting high school was my athletic ability and, of course, my father who I knew would not have allowed it. I broached the subject with him only once and he won out."

Playful Antics.

It is impossible to change a leopard's spots, and Dee was no exception. Dee's penchant for practical jokes carried over to his high school days, and did not endear him to some of his teachers.

"I remember one afternoon I dismantled the door knob to the Latin/French classroom as a practical joke," Dee said, with a chuckle, as he reflected back on the incident. "The Latin teacher was locked in the room, and I stood in the hallway with the knob in my hand. When she threatened to tell Principal Norton, I finally inserted the door knob and opened the door. She was furious about it and gave me a good tongue-lashing. Years later we had a good laugh reminiscing over it."

A Knockout Blow.

On one occasion, one teacher took some stiff measures in reacting to one of Dee's practical jokes. Dee explained what happened.

"When I was a junior I was enrolled in Mr. Wagner's geometry class. I was having difficulty and wanted to quit the course to spare me the embarrassment of failure. Mr. Wagner insisted I stay in the course and get down to work and apply myself. To get even with him for his persistence, one day I placed a handful of tacks on his chair. When he sat down he jumped up quickly with a shout and grimace of pain on his face. The whole class momentarily went into a fit of laughter, which I'm sure hurt his ego as much as the tacks hurt his backside. I had gotten what I wanted out of the prank-- his humiliation in front of the class. He quickly got the class back under control and accused no one of the incident at the time. It was almost as though he knew who had done it, and, of course, he did. After the bell rang to dismiss the class, he refused to let me leave."

"DaBramo, come back here and sit down," he shouted as he faced me nose to nose.

"Why did you put those tacks on my chair?" he shouted.

"What tacks?" I responded quickly with as much conviction as I could muster up, with my voice cracking slightly.

"You know what tacks," was his angry retort.

"You're always blaming me for everything," I snarled back at him. "I'm leaving for basketball practice."

"Oh, no you're not!" he snarled back in a loud whispering tone to his voice. "Stay right where you are!" he demanded emphatically.

"In defiance, I lifted myself out of my chair to leave and that's when he cold-cocked me with his fist, knocking me to the floor, and without another word, he walked out of the room leaving me there. I recovered after a few minutes with a swollen jaw and a black eye, and went to the gym for basketball practice. Mr. Wynkoop, my coach, looked at me in astonishment and said, "What happened to you, DaBramo?"

"Mr. Wagner knocked me out," I told him. His reaction was not to say a word in response. He knew I probably deserved it. When I think of that incident today, I often wonder how a parent would react under the present day social environment. I know that in those days if you went home and complained to your parents about your teacher, they would have believed the teacher's version of the story, and you would have received an equal or more severe punishment from them. The teacher was always right in their eyes, and 99% of the time that was the case. I know it was true in my case.

"The bottom line result of the incident was that I stayed in Mr. Wagner's geometry class and garnered a score of 86% on the State Regents Exam. That turned out to be one of my best grades in high school.

"Academically, I graduated from high school with regents' course credits, most of which were minimum passing grades of 65 percent. The day of the graduation ceremony had to have been the finest day in the life of some of my teachers."

"The quote inscribed over the entrance of the field house at West Point best expressed my philosophy of the meaning of sports that I carried throughout my professional career as a coach," said Cliff Wynkoop, Dee's former High School coach.

On the fields of friendly strife
are sown the seeds
Which on other fields in other years
will bear the fruits of victory

"Dee was a three-sport athlete at Pawling High School that included soccer, basketball and baseball -- and he was outstanding in all three," reminisced 86-year-old Cliff Wynkoop whom I caught up with at his retirement home in Brookings, Oregon.

"When Dee came to Pawling High School as a freshman," said Coach Wynkoop, "we offered cross country to the boys who had to ride the bus home after school. Dee participated but always came in last. He was not built for cross country. What caught my eye about Dee, however, was his determination and grit. He was no quitter. In his sophomore year Dee came out for soccer. He did this in spite of the fact that he had to hitch a ride or walk the four or five miles home each night after practice. He played soccer three years, and during that time our team was a winner because Dee was the soul of the team.

"Pound for pound, Dee, or *Pizon*, as his teammates called him with great respect, was the best basketball player I had ever seen," said Wynkoop. "He could dribble the ball behind his back when it was necessary. This was unheard of in the 1940s, but commonplace today. During practice I have witnessed him making 8 out of 10 shots from the free-throw line with his eyes shut. The year we won the county championship, Dee scored 20 of the 26 points in the championship game. One day after a victory, he came to me and asked if I could give some of the points to his teammates for the box scores that went to the newspapers. He was no glory hound. There was only one time, which I can remember, that Dee wanted to quit the basketball team and leave school. The incident occurred when he was a sophomore, and took offense to being called the "W" word, *Wop*, by the brother of one of the high school teachers. A vicious fight ensued. To an Italian, in those days, making reference to him using the "W" word is like an insult to an African American being referred to using the "N", word. Mr. Norton, the principal, came down on Dee pretty hard for the beating he inflicted on his opponent. The punishment was so hard, that Dee quit the basketball team and wanted to leave school for good. I spent a few evenings at supper with his father Michael, devouring Josephine's delicious spaghetti and meatballs and drinking Michael's homemade red wine, trying to convince Dee not to quit school. We finally prevailed and Dee returned to school and the team. Soon all was forgotten.

"As a sophomore, Dee also began his baseball career," Coach Wynkoop continued. "He played second base that year and did well. His arm was stronger in his junior year, and I moved him to third base where he excelled. When he was a senior we needed a catcher, and Dee went behind the plate. I am convinced that if Dee had chosen baseball as a career, there is no doubt in my mind that he would have played second base for the New York Yankees, and later would have become their manager. He had the spirit and leadership that always produced a winning team."

"Cliff Wynkoop literally saved my life as a teenager in high school," Dee confessed, with signs of tears in the corner of his eyes. "If it wasn't for him, I would never have made it. He was a great athlete in his own right and a great coach. He graduated from the University of Illinois and once played baseball with Lou Boudreau, the legendary player/coach of the Cleveland Indians during the Bob Feller days in the 1940s and 1950s. He saw something in me as a human being that few others did. He would sit me down and counsel me about my studies and give me straight talk, man-to-man, about life, and no bull. He and his wife Marge would have me over to their house for dinner on occasion, under the guise of talking strategy for the next game. But what they were really doing, which I didn't realize at the time, was keeping me on the path to success. They made me feel very important, which helped tremendously to raise my self-esteem and confidence. I was the leader of the team, and once he harnessed me, the rest of the team followed my lead. My high school sports days were a very important part of my young life. Through sports I learned how to do the right thing, how to win, how to accept losses, and how to play fair. This I attribute to Cliff Wynkoop and his wife Marge."

Dee summed up his school days in Pansy Baker's one-room school house and at Pawling High School in an article he wrote for the Pawling High School Alumni Association Newsletter <u>Focus</u>. The occasion was the forty-fourth class reunion of the graduating class of 1941.

Pawling H.S. Alumni Assoc. Newsletter, <u>Focus</u>, Feb. 1985.

Looking Back At Pawling High School

"What a privilege to be asked to write an article on the P.H.S. reunion of last year! As I look back on that occasion, my general thoughts and feelings are that it was a first-class affair. Congratulations from all of us to the committee for a job well done! You all truly made it a pleasure to come "back

home" again. Seeing us all together after so many years, I couldn't help but think back to how it all began years ago. We came together at Pawling High School from Towners, Holmes, Patterson, Stormville, Green Haven, Wingdale, Poughquag, Gardner Hollow and Stone House -- many of us having attended only multi-grade, one-room school houses. For example, Miss Pansy Baker taught grades 1-8 in my one-room school in Poughquag. We had two outside toilets, a wood stove for heating and our water had to be carried from Knapp's store, which was a quarter-of-a-mile away! Things were so different then. Although times were rough, and some of us had difficulties, we all seemed to be helping each other and working together. Another Example: When I came here from Italy, I couldn't speak a word of English. Miss Baker assigned Dick Wooden (class of 1934) to help teach the language. I'm so thankful to him for that, because it was the beginning I sorely needed. Today, schools have all the modern conveniences, special programs for individual needs, and bilingual teachers. It's a changed world from the one in which we were educated, but I, personally, wouldn't have traded the experience for anything!

"As I think of the alumni, I think of all that has been accomplished in our lifetimes and how much credit belongs to those who taught us. It's really amazing to think about the impact that just one teacher can have. From them we learned the value of hard work and meaning of trust, friendship and love. Perhaps, most importantly, they taught us to respect ourselves, our neighbors and our country. They worked tirelessly and with dedication. No reunion remembrances would be complete without mention of such important people as Mr. and Mrs. Earle W. Norton, John Wagner and his fine wife, Christine, Jim Belcher and Monica, Cliff Wynkoop and his wife Marge, Mr. and Mrs. Jeffords, Joe Kowal and many others, who helped us along the way. They will not soon be forgotten.

"On a more personal note, I can remember how close I came to dropping out of P.H.S. Two really great programs changed the course of my life at about that time. They were *school sports and scouting. It took me a long time to admit to myself that some of my early problems in school were the result of my feelings of insecurity. But sports and scouting gave me, and many others, the opportunity for success, and I thank God it was there for us. Perhaps the greatest shock I had at the reunion was hearing that P.H.S. did not have a sports program last year. I was saddened to think of the loss to the students by the failure to provide such valuable school options as a sports program, performing arts, library services, etc. At our reunion we spoke of academic successes, to be sure, but our hearts and minds were focused on memories that came from participating in the very same programs that were cut from the P.H.S. last year.*

"To summarize, it was a pleasure to see such a happy and productive group. What we gained through our attendance at P.H.S. and in our daily contacts with the fine teachers of our past, was a sense of responsibility that helped us all through our lives. Their guidance and support sustained us through World War II, for some of us through college, and for me graduate school and a career in education. We are grateful to them and hope they are proud of us. I am sure we are all looking forward to an evening of sharing more experiences at the next reunion. Let's do it again next year! Have a happy, healthy and productive 1985!"

Emilio DaBramo, Class of '41.

"In addition to being my coach, Cliff was my Scoutmaster for a short time until Mr. McGregor, one of the science teachers, took over Troop 34. The responsibility for scouting in those days was also borne by the high school administrators and teachers. Our meetings were held after regular school hours in the high school building. I was an enthusiastic scout and loved working on obtaining the required badges. I came within two badges of making Eagle Scout before my scouting career was over. It was in scouting that I had the opportunity to take overnight camping trips and attend the county jamborees."

"During one of those jamborees a very funny incident took place involving Dee," said Earnest Mott, one of Dee's childhood friends and brother scout. "It happened one evening during a horrendous lightning and thunderstorm. We were all in our cabin just hanging around and the lightning caused the electric power to fail. Well, resourceful Dee reached up on a shelf in the cabin and pulled down a kerosene lantern. Since it was pitch black Dee unscrewed the cap from the kerosene reservoir and stuck his finger in the opening to check for the presence or absence of kerosene. This is when the fun began. He got his finger in so far that it got stuck. Working in the dark, we tried everything we could think of to get his finger out, short of cutting it off, but we couldn't free his finger. Finally, one of the other boys fetched the doctor. The best the doctor could do was to separate the reservoir from the lantern and bandage his finger, which had managed to get cut a bit. That left Dee walking around with the reservoir attached to his finger for a day or so until the doctor could find someone to cut the metal reservoir and free his finger."

"During my Boy Scout days I learned one of life's most important lessons," said Dee, "and that was humility through service to others. In a small log cabin right next to Ernie Mott's house lived a 75-year-old man who had no legs. I still have a vivid image of this man propelling himself around his house on the heels of his hands and the rudiments of his legs that extended just below his waist. One of Troop 34's civic projects was to keep him from freezing during the winter months. Our daily job was to cut and stack wood for his stove and maintain the oil level in his kerosene lanterns.

"It was also during my scouting days that I learned the rudiments of sending and receiving Morse code which, unbeknown to me at the time, would have a major impact on my early adult life."

"Ironically during the summer after Dee graduated in 1941," said Cliff Wynkoop, "Dee and I had a summer job together in Torrington, Connecticut at the Warren McArthur Plant. The plant manufactured aircraft seats and chairs for Army Air Corps combat planes. The bombing of Pearl Harbor had not yet occurred, and little did I or Dee know at the time, that he would soon be flying in combat, strapped in one of those seats."

CHAPTER 4

The War Years

CHAPTER 4
The War Years

"After graduating from High School in June of 1941, I set out to find a full-time job and earn as much money as I could," said Dee. "One of my primary goals was to save enough money to buy a car that I could afford. For a short time I worked as a laborer with the railroad until my high school coach, Cliff Wynkoop, got me a job with the Warren McArthur Company in Torrington, Connecticut, a 35-mile commute from Stone House. The company made seats for Army Air Corps combat planes. After a few months I had saved enough money to buy a 1931 DeSoto Coupe for sixty bucks. It was not only my first car, but also the first car in the DaBramo family. I was really proud. Now I could take my mom and dad shopping, and, of course, pick up my buddies and my girlfriends.

"Almost immediately after the bombing of Pearl Harbor, on December 7, 1941, initiating the beginning of WWII for the United States, I found employment at an ammunition manufacturing plant near Bridgeport, Connecticut, as an operator of an automatic screw machine. My job was part of the process in the manufacture of 50-caliber and other machine gun ammunition. I lived in a small cabin near Bridgeport. Whenever I had enough fuel ration stamps to fill the tank of my car, I would commute home to Stone House on my days off.

"By December of 1942, several of my friends were already serving in the Armed Forces. John Holiday, a teammate of mine on the baseball team, was killed in action on February 28, 1942, when the U.S. Navy Destroyer he was serving on, the *USS Jacob Jones, DD-393*, was sunk by the German Submarine *U-578* off the coast of Cape May, New Jersey. He would not be the last to fall.

On February 28, 1942, John Holiday, Dee's team mate at Pawling High School, was killed in action aboard the U.S. Navy Destroyer USS Jacob Jones DD-393 when it was torpedoed and sunk by the German submarine U- 578 off the coast of Cape May, N.J. (Courtesy of Dee DaBramo)

"In December 1942, I was ordered by Local Draft Board 322 of Dutchess County, N.Y. to report for my pre-induction physical examination on the eighth of the month. After the examination I was given the draft status of 1-A. It was only a matter of time before I would be in uniform.

"A few days after the first of January 1943, I received my draft notice in the mail, and on the eighth of January I attended the induction ceremony in Albany, New York with a large group of other draftees. On January fifteenth, I bid my family and my girlfriend Helen goodbye with the promise to send my mailing address to them as soon as I knew what it was. Helen was one of my special girlfriends, but we were not committed to each other at the time, although later I wished we had been. That is another story for another time.

"My first duty station was Camp Upton Reception Center near Yaphank, Long Island, New York. This was my first trip to Long Island. I took the train from Pawling to Penn Station in downtown Manhattan. From there I caught the Long Island Railroad to Yaphank, which was about eighty miles east of Manhattan. The journey took several hours. I shared the train with other inductees and volunteers from New York, Connecticut and some of the other New England states. The railroad station at Yaphank was a simple wooden structure, much like the station in Pawling."

In 1943, Camp Upton was a sprawling camp with a mixture of old barracks built during World War I, newly constructed barracks and a sea of pyramid tents spread out over 10,000 acres of yellow sand and scrub pines. It was originally built as an induction center and basic training facility for WWI troops. The famous composer Irving Berlin, was once a resident of Camp Upton as a soldier in the First World War, which inspired him to write the Broadway Musical, *Yip, Yip, Yaphank* and the famous wartime song, *Oh! How I Hate to Get Up in the Morning.*

"When I arrived, with hundreds of others, we were transported to the camp and were immersed in a sea of khaki uniforms. I had never seen so many soldiers in my life. It didn't take long for the induction process to begin. The first step in the process was a medical check of our genitals for venereal disease. We were ordered, not asked, to drop our trousers for what was commonly referred to as a short arm inspection. If you were at all embarrassed about undressing in front of others, this was a sure cure. Then, an Army doctor gave us a lecture on sexual morality. All this before we were issued our clothes. Certainly they were not going to issue clothes to a guy that had a venereal disease.

"Next on the agenda was a lecture on the Code of Military Justice and military courtesy. We were instructed on the rudiments of when and how to salute an officer and the use of the words *Sir, Yes Sir and No Sir*. This was followed by the administration of smallpox and typhoid shots by the Medical Corp personnel who seemed to enjoy sticking a needle into your body.

"We were finally issued our G.I. clothes and shoes and given our barracks assignment. My assignment just happened to be a large pyramid tent that I shared with about a half dozen or more inductees like myself. In the center of the tent was our only source of heat, a coal-fired cast iron pot-bellied stove that reminded me of the one we had in Pansy Baker's one-room schoolhouse in Poughquag. In the few days I was at Upton, the temperature in that tent never got more than slightly above freezing. It seemed like the wind blew constantly and the scrub pines offered little or no barrier from the cold wind and the blowing sand. The winter of 1942/1943 was recorded as being unusually cold and windy.

"The testing process came next, followed by a personal interview. This process was designed to inventory your education, work history, hobbies and sports and any other special skills you might have acquired during your lifetime. First, we all took the Army General Classification Test (AGCT). After that, an officer interviewed each of us. It was during this interview that I revealed the fact that I had learned how to send and receive Morse code at the rate of twelve words a minute, a skill I had acquired during my Boy Scout training with Troop 34 in Pawling. The interviewing officer made a note of it, and I was later given a special aptitude test. Apparently I did well enough on this test to qualify for the Army Air Corps Radio School in Sioux Falls, South Dakota where I would go after I completed my basic training. My future in the Army was in flying, and I had never flown in a plane in my life. I was in and out of Camp Upton in about four or five days.

"In the next sixteen months, my life would change dramatically. I would undergo training at a hectic wartime pace at five different training facilities. First, was six weeks of basic training in Miami Beach, Florida. Can you imagine my good fortune of leaving the freezing wind-swept tent camp at Camp Upton to America's tropical paradise--Miami Beach? The recruiting posters were right, *Join the Service and See the World.* Growing up in Stone House I had only dreamed of going to Miami Beach. After all, only the rich and famous frequented Miami Beach--like those in the film, *Moon Over Miami* with Betty Grable, Don Ameche, Carol Landis and Robert Cummings.

"The U. S. Army had literally commandeered most of the Art Deco resort hotels and turned them into barracks. Miami Beach was one big boot camp. Aside from the tough physical regime of boot camp, the occasional nightlife on the beach was nothing short of great."

In a letter to his family on January 22, 1943, Dee describes his impression of Miami Beach.

January 22, 1943

Florida is swell. I am living in a hotel and it is two stories up and I can see Miami Beach which is about 200 feet from our hotel. It is beautiful here. People used to pay up to thirty dollars a day to live in this hotel, but we get it for nothing. I am in the Air Corps but I don't know what branch yet. Our room has a large rug, 4 beds just like at home. Palm trees just outside our window and right now the temperature is about 85 or more. I can see people swimming from my room. We have two large bureaus and one writing table. I just can't explain how nice it is here. (Letter Courtesy of Julia Czerenda)

Dee at basic training in Miami Beach, Florida. The Art Deco Hotels, shown in the background, served as barracks for the Airmen. (Courtesy of Dee DaBramo)

"Upon completion of basic training at the end of February or early March of 1943, I was issued orders to report to radio school at the Army Training Facility in Sioux Falls, South Dakota. I caught a train from Miami and headed northwest to Sioux Falls. In the scope of about two months I had traveled the farthest I had ever traveled south and west in my life, almost three thousand miles. Again, I found myself in one of the coldest climates I had ever experienced. It was worse than what I endured at Camp Upton. Although the barrack accommodations at Sioux Falls were better than the tent at Camp Upton, the walk to the mess hall was far enough away that you froze your butt off getting there. I wondered if this was the Army's way of punishing me for my wonderful days in the sun at Miami Beach.

In a letter to his family Dee describes the trip from Miami to Sioux Falls, South Dakota. (Letter courtesy of Julia Czerenda)

> *Dear Mom, Dad, Aida and Sadie,*
> *Here are the states we went through to get here. Fla., Ga., Ala., Tenn., Ark., Mo., Iowa, Minn., and then So. Dakota. I have seen more of the U.S. in the last 3 months than I have all my life. I have seen nearly half of the states so far. I expect to be here for 5 or 6 months so I will have to study while I am here. This is a tough course on Radio and Radio Mechanics. After I finish here, I expect to go to aerial gunner's school. I am glad I was in the scouts now because that code I learned there is the same one we have to learn here and I already know how to send and receive a little. It's snowing hard now.*
>
> *Your son,*
> *Emilio*

"When I arrived at the radio school in Sioux Falls, I was given a proficiency test. The results of this test determined the length of training that would be required for me to reach the level of competency required of a combat Radio Operator/Mechanic. The course was intense, to say the least. We were in the classroom or at the workbench eight or more hours a day, five days a week. Extra hours were made available for one-on-one training to all trainees who needed additional help. Looking back at that experience, from the prospective of an educator, I can only marvel at the teaching process that took place. The instructors took mostly raw recruits, with no experience in radio operation and maintenance, and turned them, myself included, into very competent operators and mechanics that would be responsible for the safety of a bomber crew in combat. One of the very interesting things about the course was that much of the credit for its success could be attributed to the many civilian women instructors that we had. We learned how to operate and maintain several types of radio equipment that we would be required to use in a combat aircraft."

In a letter to a friend at home Dee describes his observations about attending Radio School. (Letter courtesy of Julia Czerenda)

> *April 28, 1943*
>
> *I am now going to a Radio Operator and Mechanic's school and I expect it to take me seven months to graduate. We have a lot of ladies for instructors and books, so it feels as if I was back to High School. This place is not as nice as Miami but here we don't have K.P. or guard duty, all we do is go to school. We get a 36 hour pass from camp every week so I guess it won't be too bad. The only bad part is I go to school at night. I just wasn't lucky enough to get that day shift.*

"Included in our daily routine was physical training, which consisted of running and jogging to help us maintain the conditioning we had attained in basic training. For recreation we were allowed to go to the base gym in the evenings to shoot baskets or play a half-court basketball game. We were allowed off the base to visit Sioux Falls once a week after Saturday inspection, from Saturday noon until Sunday at noon. If you were late getting back to the base, the MPs took you right to the guard house. There was no fooling around with disciplinary problems.

As best as I can remember, Sioux Falls, at that time, was the largest city in South Dakota. I would estimate that it had about 50 or 60 thousand population. The main occupation in those days was farming and cattle raising. It was a cowboy town with several bars or saloons, as the locals referred to them, and dance halls. Many of the soldiers dated the local girls, including myself, and this is where I began my education about women.

Radio School

Civilian women made up most of the instructors at the Army Air Corps Radio School at Sioux Falls, SD. (Courtesy of Dee DaBramo).

"The course lasted about eight months, and I graduated in October of 1943 and obtained the rank of buck sergeant, a three-striper. Needless to say, I was very proud of myself. After all, it was the first school success of my life, and I had done well.

"To be part of a combat flying crew you not only had to be competent in your specialty, but you also had to be proficient in gunnery. Even as a radio operator I had to be counted upon to man a fifty-caliber machine gun during a combat mission when necessary. To acquire this skill, I was transferred to the Army Air Corps Flexible Aerial Gunnery School at Laredo, Texas. This was where the fun began. Up to this time in my Air Corps career, I had not yet flown in an airplane. All the traveling I had done had been by car, bus or by train.

"Phase I of the gunnery training was skeet-shooting. Now, I had had some experience shooting a shotgun, hunting small game around home. We were each issued a 12-gauge shotgun at the skeet range and the training began. The purpose for us learning to skeet-shoot was to teach us how to lead a target. Once we mastered the skeet-shooting phase of the program we moved to Phase II at the 50-caliber machine gun range. Believe me, the 50-caliber machine gun was an intimidating weapon. First, we learned how it operated and how to strip it down and put it back together while blindfolded. Then, we learned how to troubleshoot operating problems and clear breech jams. Our first experience with firing the gun was at a ground firing range. Targets were fixed on trailers mounted on tracks and set up behind an earthen mound. The trailers were made to move in a straight line behind the earthen mounds at various speeds. We were given the opportunity to fire off a few rounds to get a feel for the gun before firing at the moving targets. That was an experience in itself. You had all you could do to keep from blinking your eyes with each firing. What made it worse was other gunners were firing at the same time. Firing at the moving targets with the machine gun was an extension of our skeet-shooting experience. The training followed a logical progression of steps. But this was not the last step in the progression.

"Phase III was to practice shooting the 50-caliber machine gun from a moving airplane at a moving target. For me, this was the most intimidating of all the training I had had up to this point in time. The plane being used for this phase of the training was an AT-6. It was a single engine, tandem seat trainer used by the Air Corps to train their cadet pilots. The pilot flew from the front seat and I, as the aerial gunner, was stationed in the rear seat with the 50-caliber machine gun mounted on a tripod-like device. To make things worse, the cockpit was open. I was instructed on the features of the plane and shown how to get in and out of the rear cockpit. I was also instructed in how to use my parachute for bailing out if indeed the occasion arose. That part of the instruction was not very encouraging to me since, to start with, I had never been in a plane, let alone having a desire to jump out of one. At this point in the training, I was quite nervous and apprehensive. The objective of the exercise was to fire rounds at a moving target in the air from a moving airplane. The target was a large sleeve-like device towed behind another AT-6 airplane. Prior to leaving the ground we were given 250 rounds of ammunition and the job of dipping each bullet head in colored paint. Each trainee was given a different color paint for his 250 rounds of ammunition. The purpose, of course, was to be able to identify the hits we made on the sleeve after we landed. The pilot gave me last minute instructions."

"Now, DaBramo, when it is your turn to shoot I will bank over into a position parallel with the target," which he demonstrated using his hands as the two planes. "When I am ready for you to start shooting, I will wag my wings. Do you understand?"

"Yes Sir," I acknowledged nodding my head in the affirmative. He ordered me to climb into the back seat, and I was scared stiff as I secured myself in my seat with my seat belt. The sensation of flying was like nothing else I had ever experienced. At first, it was scary, and then it was exhilarating and scary. Like most beginners, I became mesmerized with looking down at the ground where everything appeared so very small and insignificant. The roar of the engine and the wind racing by my ears in the open cockpit was deafening. My stomach turned over with each new maneuver the pilot made.

"Finally it was our turn to approach the target sleeve. The pilot made a sharp banking maneuver to position our plane parallel to the target, as he told me he would. The move was so sudden and sharp that I felt faint from vertigo. Then he wagged his wings, indicating for me to start firing. I was so frightened I became almost paralyzed and did not respond. He wagged his wings again, and I still did not respond. Finally he turned in his seat, and shouted above the roar of the engine and the wind, and yelled as loud as he could to START SHOOTING. That was my wake-up call and I started firing. I couldn't wait to expend every one of the 250 rounds in my arsenal. When we landed and counted the hits, much to my surprise, I had done a fair job. How that happened, I'm not sure. With each flight I became less scared and more proficient. I graduated from Aerial Gunnery School in December of 1943 and was presented with my silver Aerial Gunner's wings. I had now completed the requirements to be selected as a member of a combat air crew and was promoted to Staff Sergeant. How proud I was of my accomplishments.

"Upon graduating I was granted a furlough and traveled home to Stone House to spend Christmas 1943 with my family and friends. I remember the pride I felt in wearing my uniform trimmed with my silver Aerial Gunners Wings and those sergeant stripes. My parents and sisters, Aida and Sadie, and friends were proud of me too.

Dee on his first Christmas furlough with his family in December 1943. L. to R. Dee's mother Josephine, Dee, sisters Aida and Sarah and his father Michael. (Courtesy Julie Czerenda)

"After a wonderful Christmas furlough, my orders directed me to an Air Corps facility near Fresno, California, for combat crew selection. I realized now that I was in the final phase of training before heading into combat. It was here that the permanent six-man crew was selected for the heavy B-24 Liberator bombers that we were to fly. The six-man crew was comprised of four officers and two non-commissioned officers. The officers were the pilot, co-pilot, bombardier and navigator. The non-commissioned officers were the Flight Engineer/Crew Chief and the Radio Operator. The full combat crew included four aerial gunners, which were subject to change, depending on the circumstances and availability of gunners."

The events that follow have been abstracted from the memories and documents provided by Dee and four of the other men that made up the permanent crew of the original B-24 Bomber designated No. 40288-S and given the name *Bad Girl*. They are, Pilot, retired Lt. Colonel Frank C. Fuson, Jr. of Norman, Oklahoma, Co-pilot, 1st Lt. William Kotowitz of Houston, Texas, Bombardier, retired Lt. Colonel Fielding Washington, of Denton, Texas, and Flight Engineer/Crew Chief, Staff Sergeant U.B.

Simoneaux of Bella Rose, Louisiana. I located the family of Navigator, First Lieutenant William Jamerson, only to find out that he was deceased. I was unable to locate the four gunners that made up the remainder of the original crew assigned to the *Bad Girl*.

"Our pilot, 2nd Lt. Frank C. Fuson, was a tall, slender, soft-spoken twenty-two year old from Wellington, Texas. He was born on a farm in Wellington, Texas, on January 26, 1920. After graduating from High School in 1938 he attended Bethany Peniel College in Bethany, Oklahoma for two years. This college is now known as Southern Nazarene University. On June 18, 1942, he volunteered for and was inducted into the Army Air Corps as an Aviation Cadet, designated to attend flight training school. He began his Cadet training on December 2, 1942. A year later in December 1943, he graduated from flight school and received his pilot's wings and his commission as a 2nd Lieutenant. He was 22-years old.

"Our co-pilot was 2nd Lieutenant William J. Kotowitz. He was born on June 24, 1923, in Syracuse, New York. He attended Syracuse Central High School and joined the Army Air Corps shortly after the bombing of Pearl Harbor. He was accepted for Aviation Cadet Flight Training in January 1942, and graduated from flight school in December 1943, receiving his pilot wings and was commissioned a 2nd Lieutenant in December of 1943. He was 20-years old.

"Our bombardier was a tall, quiet Virginian, 2nd Lt. Fielding Washington. He was born on January 23, 1924, in Alexandria, Virginia, where he grew up and graduated from high school in June 1942. From June 1942, up to the time he enlisted in the Army Air Corps on November 9, 1942, he worked as an apprentice machinist at the U.S. Navy Shipyard in Washington, D.C. He was selected to attend the Army Air Corps Bombardier School. Upon graduation on December 4, 1943, he received his Bombardier Wings and was commissioned a 2nd Lieutenant. He was 20-years old.

"2nd Lt. William Jamerson was our navigator. He was born on March 27, 1919 in Sherman, Texas. He graduated from Austin High School in 1935 at age 16. He attended the Texas College of Mines in El Paso Texas (now UTEP) for two years and studied pre-law from 1939 through 1941. He enlisted in the Army Air Corps in 1941 and was selected to attend Basic Aviation Mechanics School in Champaign, Illinois. He later was assigned as a Link Trainer Instructor for Army Air Corps Cadets stationed at Shaw Field in Bennettsville, South Carolina. He then volunteered for

Navigator School and earned his Navigator wings in December 1943, and was commissioned a 2nd Lieutenant. He was 25-years of age and the oldest member of the permanent crew.

"Staff Sergeant Ulgere B. Simoneaux (known to his friends as "UB") was our Flight Engineer/Crew Chief and Top Turret Gunner. He was born on October 31, 1921, in Plattenville, Louisiana, and was brought up on a sugar cane plantation that his parents owned and operated. He graduated from Plattenville High School in 1939. After high school he attended Business College for one year and then spent a semester at Louisiana State University studying sugar chemistry. When he wasn't going to school he worked for his father on their sugar plantation. U.B. volunteered for the Army Air Corps in January 1942. After completing basic training he was selected for aircraft mechanics school. He was 22-years old.

"I was selected as the Radio Operator/Mechanic, rounding out the crew. Four gunners were also selected for our crew. They were Sgt. C. Bedard, Sgt. F. Underdahl, Sgt. F. Coppa and Pfc. W. Parr. The average age of the crew was 21 years old.

"After the selection process was completed, we were transported by bus from Fresno to the Combat Flight Training facility near Tonopah, Nevada, a trip of about 250 miles. Tonopah is located in the Nevada desert at the junction of Routes 95 and 6. The area's desert isolation, its sparse population and varying terrain made it an ideal place for a bombing range. The town of Tonopah, situated between Mounts Oddie and Brorgher, was a shabby old gold and silver mining town that had seen its best days just before the First World War. In 1943, ranching and the passing highway trade from Routes 6 and 95 were its main sources of income. The closest city of any significance was Reno, a 240-mile ride to the northwest on Highway 95.

"At Tonopah we were issued our fleece-lined flight suits, helmets and other flight gear and given our living quarters assignments. The officers were housed at the BOQ and the enlisted men of the crew were assigned to comfortable barracks facilities.

Our pilot, Frank Fuson, and co-pilot, Bill Kotowitz, were the only members of the crew that had experience flying a B-24 Bomber. It was up to them to orient us to the plane and its equipment and mold us into a cohesive combat flight crew. They had from early January 1943 to about the end of March 1943 to get the job done. The training at Tonopah was three-fold --navigation, bombing run practice and gunnery practice. During the three-month period at Tonopah our bombardier, 2nd Lt. Fielding Washington, recorded 250 bomb drops, using 100 pound bombs filled with sand, dropping then on a variety of targets in the desert. In addition, we made numerous camera-bombing missions over several cities in Nevada and California. All of these missions were designed to sharpen the navigation skills of our navigator and our pilots. The crew's gunners and I were given gunnery practice. We would fly low to the ground and fire our 50-caliber guns at fixed targets on the ground to hone our gunnery skills.

Training crew at Tonopah, Nevada. Front row left to right: Sgt. C. Bedard, Asst. Flight Engineer,(not a permanent crew member), E. DaBramo, Radio Operator, Sgt. F. Underdahl, Nose Gunner, Sgt. U.B. Simoneaux Flight Engineer and Crew Chief, Sgt. F. Coppa, Upper Turret Gunner, Pfc. W. Parr, Tail Gunner. Back row left to right: 2nd Lt. W. Jamerson, Navigator, 2nd Lt. M.J. Kotowitz, Co-pilot, 2nd Lt. F. Fuson, Pilot and 2nd Lt. F. Washington, Bombardier. (Courtesy of Dee DaBramo)

"All our time at Tonopah was not confined to training. We did find time to take in the sights and saloons in Tonopah. In 1943, the city was not what one would call a thriving community. The troops frequented the saloons and other recreation spots, but for real fun we had to drive the 240 miles to Reno."

"I remember once," said Fielding Washington, "I rented a car and took all the enlisted crew members to Reno for a weekend of fun. Reno, in 1943, was one of the well-known gambling spots in the country. We were in one of the hotel gambling casinos and were playing black jack and Dee was participating in the game, and this is where the fun began."

"Ma'am," Dee called out to the woman dealer, "I don't have much money and I have to buy my mother a gift for her birthday."

"We all knew Dee was kidding her," Fielding pointed out, "and we were quite sure that the dealer knew it too."

"Well," she replied, "do you think you should be gambling then?"

"No," Dee replied with as straight a face as he could muster up. "But I need more money for the gift," he said somewhat pleadingly.

"Well, then, if you win, will you quit?" she asked with a cute smile.

"Oh yes," Dee solemnly promised, "You bet I will," he said smiling back at her.

"The dealer proceeded to deal Dee a black jack and he won," said Fielding. "I don't think Dee knew what had gone on, but I'm sure the dealer did. He left the table with his winnings as he had promised," Fielding concluded the story with a chuckle and a smile.

"By the end of March our crew had been molded into a smooth-operating machine under the leadership of our very competent pilot, Frank Fuson and Co-pilot, Bill Kotowitz," said Dee. "Not only did we feel confident, we were also one happy family. We had established an unbreakable bond between the officers and enlisted men. We were indeed a team."

Fielding Washington summed up Frank Fuson's character best. "Frank Fuson was a dammed good pilot. He was a Texan and looked like a Texan. He got along well with everyone. He was sharp, but disguised it with a disarming country-boy approach."

"After completing our combat readiness training at Tonopah," said Frank Fuson, "we were transported to Hamilton Field, California. Hamilton Field was located north of San Rafael, about fifty miles north of San Francisco via the Golden Gate Bridge and route 101.

"The base was a staging area for combat flight crews who were designated for overseas assignments. It does not exist as a military or civilian airport today. Shortly after our arrival we were issued our combat flight gear. The gear consisted of watches, clothing, a Colt-45 automatic pistol with holster, and electric-heated suits to replace the fleece-lined suits we wore at Tonopah," Fuson recalled.

Dee with Friends in Reno, Nevada on a weekend pass from their base at Tonopah, Nevada. (Courtesy of Dee DaBramo)

"The reality of going into combat began to sink in a little deeper now," Dee confessed. "This time we were to travel by air transport from Hamilton Field to Morrison Field in Orlando, Florida. Morrison Field was also known as Orlando Army Air Corps Base. Today it is a civilian field named Orlando Executive.

"About two days prior to our departure, a few of my buddies and I decided to go into town for one last fling," Dee remembered. "As per usual, we drank more then we should have. When returning to the base on a bus, I got into a confrontation with a rookie 2nd Lieutenant and he put me on report. The only thing I can recall about the incident is the outcome. Justice was swift the next day and I ended up in the brig. I was busted from Sergeant to Private First Class. This meant a loss of some $140 a month. My pay was now about $75 a month. I was very angry at the outcome. On the morning that we were to leave for Orlando, I refused to get out of bed and made the bold statement that if I wasn't getting sergeant's pay and flight pay, then I wasn't going to fly. When the rest of the crew reported to the flight line, I wasn't there."

"Where's DaBramo?" Fuson asked commandingly.

"Someone told him that I was in the barracks and wasn't going to fly. Fuson left the flight line and got an MP to drive him to my barracks. He came into the barracks with the MP and I was still in bed."

"Let's go, DaBramo," he told me in a very commanding voice.

"I'm not going," I replied, and pulled my blanket over my head. Obviously I was acting like a petulant child. And, as I look back at the situation I can recall an incident in my sophomore year in high school when I quit the basketball team after being disciplined by my high school principal for fighting. It took a good tongue-lashing from my father and a threat of a good whipping to convince me otherwise.

"It was either Lt. Fuson or the MP, I don't remember which one, said Dee, "who grabbed me by my tee shirt and literally lifted me out of bed and onto the floor, threatening to whip the daylights out of me if I didn't get up."

"Get up," Fuson shouted. "Get dressed and get out to the plane NOW!"

"How stupid I was. I could have been court marshaled, thrown in the brig for the duration of the war, or perhaps longer, for a variety of violations of the Military Code of Justice. I was thankful later for the discretion Lt. Fuson exercised in his decision. When I arrived at the plane, none of the crew said a word about the incident. Fuson's action diffused my anger, but did not extinguish it.

"It was at Orlando Morrison Air Field that we were issued our brand new B-24 Liberator bomber, No. 40288S," said Dee. "It was built in San Diego, California by Consolidated Aircraft. While our pilot, Frank Fuson, was off somewhere, the crew decided to give the plane a name. The name we chose was the *Bad Girl*."

"When I returned to the plane," quipped Fuson, "the crew had given the plane the name *Bad Girl*. They had pooled their money together and hired a local artist to paint a naked lady, with a balloon covering her most sensuous attributes, on the nose of the plane. This, of course, showed how proud the crew was to have her and how unified they were as a combat unit. Needless to say, I was pleased, even though I was not part of the decision."

"The *Bad Girl* was one of ten specially equipped aircrafts to carry a secret weapon," said Colonel Fuson. "It was equipped to deliver the AZON bomb that the Air Force was developing in 1942 and 1943 with the Rand Corporation. This weapon was the forerunner of today's high tech smart bombs, used so successfully in the last few years against Iraq in *Desert Storm* and in *Kosovo*. Because we had done well in our training at Tonapoh, we were chosen for the AZON project, along with nine other crews," Fuson explained proudly.

"The AZON bomb was radio-controlled," said bombardier, Fielding

Washington. "The 1000-pound bomb had a radio receiver installed in its tail unit which was bolted to the payload end of the bomb. When the bombardier was over the target, he released the bomb and a flare ignited, spewing out a colored smoke trail from the rear of the bomb. Red, white, green and yellow flares were used for this purpose. Each bomb had a different color flare so that the bombardier could distinguish between individual bombs. The bombs could be guided in azimuth (left and right) as it approached the target. While watching the flare, the bombardier could keep the bomb in sight and remotely steer it toward the target. It was an exciting concept and its deployment was top secret."

"Last minute preparations were made to our plane at Morrison Field," said Dee, "and on April 1, 1944 we flew her to Pine Castle Field (now Orlando International Airport), just south of Orlando proper. When we arrived at Pine Castle we joined the nine other AZON-equipped B-24s, *Kiss Me Baby, Shack Time, A Dog's Life, Table Stuff, Miss Used, Lassie Come Home, Bachelor's Bedlam, Royal Flush* and the *Howling Banshee.*"

"Our training emphasis was on AZON bombing," said Colonel Fuson. "Our targets were floating platforms off the west Florida coast in the Gulf of Mexico. For a solid month we made practice runs from an altitude of fifteen thousand feet. The key man in this training operation was our bombardier, 2nd Lieutenant Fielding Washington, who successfully completed fifteen AZON training missions in the Gulf of Mexico. As each of the ten AZON-equipped B-24s completed their AZON training, they were given their combat assignment and took off for Karachi, India. We had finally received our shipping-out orders," said Fuson.

"During these training missions I was still fuming over the loss of my Sergeant stripes," said Dee. "I performed my job as radio operator, but with little enthusiasm, and apparently it showed. After a week or so had passed Lt. Fuson was fed up with my attitude. One day after we had landed he took me aside in private, apart from the rest of the crew, and gave me a low key, but firm lecture that went something like this."

"Look, DaBramo," he said firmly, "neither I nor anyone else in this crew was responsible for getting you busted. That was all your own doing. Your performance for the last week has not been what I would call exemplary. In fact, it was poor. Now, DaBramo, I want you to get over it now! Do you understand?"

"Yes sir," I replied, with somewhat of a lump in my throat. I got the feeling he meant business. It was this kind of leadership that endeared him to me and the rest of the crew. Like a good leader that he was, he disciplined you in private and commended you in public.

"On or about May 1, 1944, Lt. Fuson received orders for our overseas combat assignment," Dee recalled. "We were issued orders to fly to Karachi, India (now part of Pakistan) with our permanent crew. This meant that only six of the original ten-crew members would make the trip together--Fuson, Kotowitz, Washington, Jamerson, Simoneaux and me. The four gunners that made up the rest of the crew--Sgt. C. Bedard, Sgt. F. Underdahl, Sgt. F. Coppa and Pfc. W. Parr would fly to Karachi aboard an Air Corps Transport, and rendezvous with us in Karachi. The rationale for the decision to split up the crew was to allow for more fuel weight to be loaded aboard. Our orders were to start the long flight to Karachi on May 4, 1944.

"A few days before we were to leave we picked up a passenger, Sergeant Andrew E. Reeves. Sergeant Reeves was a technician assigned to the AZON bomb maintenance group. "Thanks to Lt. Fuson, my spirits were lifted by the restoration of my Sergeant stripes just before we left.

"In the early morning hours of the fourth of May, 1944, we took off for the British Caribbean Island possession of Trinidad, located a short distance from the northeastern coast of Venezuela," said Dee. "Our flight to Trinidad was about 1,800 miles and took about nine or ten hours. Since the airports we were flying into were new to us, we wanted to be sure to arrive during the daylight hours. Trinidad was the first Caribbean Island any of us had ever visited. I remember climbing out of the plane and stepping onto the tarmac and feeling the intense heat. It was like stepping into a blast furnace. The month of May is one of Trinidad's hottest months. We were surprised to find out that the main industry of Trinidad was producing and refining oil, which made it an important refueling station for ships and planes alike. As I can best remember, sleeping that night was not very comfortable. Air conditioning in those days was not the popular thing. We refueled that evening, and early in the morning of May 5, we took off from Trinidad on our second leg, a 1200-mile flight to the city of Belem located on the northeast coast of Brazil. We were glad to get up into the cooler flying altitude and get relief from the intense heat we had experienced on the ground. We knew, however, that the next two stops were going to be very close to the equator and the heat and humidity were going to be stifling.

"On the way to the city of Belem we crossed the equator and flew over the Amazon Delta, which, from our altitude vantage point, was quite a sight. Our first observation over Belem was that it appeared to be a busy shipping port. The city is located south of the equator in the Amazon River Delta area. As we had predicted, Belem was very hot and very sticky indeed. We refueled that evening and spent the night in a barracks at the U.S.-operated airstrip.

"Early on the morning of May 6, we flew southeast following the east coast of Brazil toward our next destination which was the U.S. airstrip at Natal, Brazil. From Belem to Natal was a distance of 900 miles. Natal is located on the most eastern tip of the South American Continent, about five degrees south of the equator. In 1942, the airport at Natal was built by the U.S., for the specific purpose of shortening military flights to Africa. Up to the time the base was built, Natal was almost non-existent.

"The routine at Natal was the same as it was at the other airports. We arrived on May 6, refueled that evening and took off in the early morning hours of May 7. Our destination this day was Ascension Island, a British possession in the middle of the South Atlantic Ocean off the coast of West Africa. This leg of the journey would be a 1500-mile jaunt directly east over the open ocean waters of the South Atlantic. Again, the early morning take-off-time was essential to insure that we arrived at Ascension Island during the daylight hours. Their time was especially important since the time zone they were in was about four or five hours later than that of Natal, Brazil. This leg of the trip would be a good test of the navigation skills of our Navigator, William Jamerson.

"To make the vast ocean crossing, Fuson, Kotowitz and our navigator Jamerson, used radio navigation beacons transmitted from Allied ships stationed at given intervals along our route across the South Atlantic. For the last leg to Ascension Island, they honed in on the radio beacon transmitted from the island's airport. After landing on the British possession, we were surprised to find that the airport was operated by Americans. We were welcomed by our fellow compatriots and were treated very well during our short two-day stay.

"On May 9, we bid farewell to our American hosts on Ascension Island and flew in a northeasterly direction toward the African coast to our next destination, Accra, Ghana, 1,200- miles distance. When we approached the African coast near Accra, we ran into a thunderstorm system and had to divert our route and fly around it. We didn't have radar in those days to guide us through, so we took no chances and gave the storm a wide berth.

After landing in Accra that afternoon, we learned that another U.S. plane enroute to Accra, was lost in the storm we had circumvented. We were saddened by the news and thankful that we had made it.

"Almost immediately after touching down at the airstrip, I delivered a radio message to Lt. Fuson that I had received from the control tower, telling him that an Air Operations Officer would be meeting our plane on the runway, and we were not to leave the plane until he arrived. The A.O. arrived and handed Fuson a secret message. The text of the message read as follows:

SECRET
HEADQUARTERS
STATION NO. 3
CENTRAL AFRICAN WING
AIR TRANSPORT COMMAND

Under the authority ATC Radiogram 0537 the following O (officers) and EM (Enlisted men) are routed to UK and upon arrival they will report to the Commanding General, Eighth Air Force, United Kingdom

B-24, 44-40288 FD-----AF2A
2nd Lt. Frank C. Fuson, 0693666 (P),
2nd Lt. William J. Kotowitz 0760636(CP)
2nd Lt. William Jamerson, 2nd Lt. Fielding L. Washington, 0701663 (B) S/Sgt. Ulgers
B. Simoneaux, 38267516 (AMG)
Sgt. Emilio Dabramo, 32741278 (ROMG)
Sgt. Andrew E. Reeves, 38397442 (ET). APO 16038-AF2)

"We now knew that we were going to be flying missions over Europe and would be in the thick of it all. As for our four gunners with whom we had trained for the last few months, they were on their way to Karachi and would not be joining us in England. The thought occurred to us that we may never see them again, and as it turned out, we never did. Other AZON bomber crews got as far as Egypt before they were diverted back to England.

"We learned that Accra had been the capital city of the British Colony of Ghana since 1901. Forty years of British rule certainly had an influence on its citizens. We were all taken aback a bit when we heard the Ghana citizens speaking English with a British accent. We were shocked to observe that most of the young kids had no clothes or shoes. One of the joys of Accra, however, was the abundance of fresh bananas sold to us by the local kids.

"On the morning of May 10, with our plane refueled and our passenger, Sgt. Reeves aboard, we took off on an 1,800-mile flight to Marrakech, in West Central French Morocco in North Africa. A few hours north of Accra we were flying over the Sahara Desert. In a sense it was like flying over the South Atlantic Ocean, but instead of seeing waves of water we were seeing waves of sand and barren mountains below us. Flight time to Marrakech was about ten hours. When we arrived in the late afternoon at the American-operated base, we were all a bit tired and weary."

The crew learned that Marrakech was a large city with a history dating back to the ninth century. It was the home of the famous Koutoubia mosque and its 220 foot high minaret. For the crew, it was the first time any of them had experienced an Islamic city. Their only previous experience with Morocco was with Humphrey Bogart and Ingrid Bergman in the famous 1942 film, *Casablanca*.

Morocco became a French protectorate in 1912. It remained loyal to the French Vichy Government after the fall of France to the Germans in 1940, but in November 1942 the Allied Forces landed on the Mediterranean beaches of French Morocco and all resistance collapsed.

"Early on the morning of May 11, we left Marrakech and began the longest leg of our trip, a 2100-mile flight to Ireland," said Dee. "Our flight plan to Ireland routed us across the Mediterranean to Gibraltar, then north along the coast of Portugal. From there we crossed the Bay of Biscay off the east coast of France on a direct course to Ireland."

"One of my fondest memories of this long and arduous trip," said Fuson, "was when Dee picked up some down-home American music on his long-distance receiver and piped it throughout the plane."

"Our visit to Ireland was very brief," said Dee. "We refueled that evening and early on the morning of May 12, we took off for Rackheath, England, the home of the 467th Bombardment Group. This was a one-day stay and on May 13, 1944, we flew on to Horsham St. Faith Airbase near Norwich, England, close to the southeast coast. Horsham was one of about fifteen bases located in that immediate area. We were to be part of Squadron 753 attached to the 458th Bombardment Group. It was at Horsham that we were assigned our four new gunners--Bauch, King, Harris and Large.

"Our stay at Horsham was equally as brief," said Dee. "We barely had time to unload our baggage from the plane and get to our barracks when we had to pack up again and head back to Ireland for Combat Orientation Training at a facility near the city of Dublin. This training was designed to indoctrinate the new crews in the combat routines, flight and emergency procedures that our pilots and navigator had to follow. Our instructors were experienced pilots and crewmembers that had completed their required missions. Needless to say, they were the best instructors we could have had under the circumstances. They pulled no punches and told it as it was. We listened with purpose and comprehension to every word spoken by them. The course was to have been two-weeks duration, but we were summoned back to Horsham on May 21, after only one week had passed. We knew now that our first mission was to come up in the not too distant future, and we could feel the tension building. Unbeknown to us at the time, D-Day, June 6, 1944 was only sixteen days away.

"Once we settled in at Horsham and got into the routine, we began to explore the City of Norwich, England," Dee reminisced. "The people of Norwich were very appreciative of us. They had already survived four years of war and had made many sacrifices of their own, including the ultimate sacrifice of losing their loved ones at home and in faraway lands. One of my favorite hangouts in Norwich was *The Cat and Fiddle Pub*. At the pub I befriended Mr. and Mrs. Clark, an elderly English couple, and we got together often. They were like parent figures to some of my friends and me. They often expressed their concern about our welfare. When it was obvious that we were flying the next day, they would say things like, 'We will be waiting and praying for your safe return.' Such lovely people those Clarks were. Many years after the war was over, I traveled to Norwich and had a wonderful reunion with them.

"Besides frequenting the pubs, the Norwich social clubs organized dances, and families invited us to their homes in an effort to provide us with a touch of home. In return, we reciprocated by bringing them gifts of cigarettes and foodstuffs that were nonexistent at the local market places."

"One of the things I liked to do for relaxation in Norwich," said Frank Fuson, "was to go to one of my favorite pubs and play cribbage with some of the older English gents. During those days I smoked a pipe and had unlimited access to good pipe tobacco. One of the old gentlemen with whom I played cribbage, smoked a pipe too. When I got to the table he would be sucking on a small clay pipe empty of tobacco. After I sat down and he got out the cribbage board, I would offer him some of my pipe tobacco. Immediately he would remove the small clay pipe from his mouth and stick it in his vest pocket. Then he would pull out a pipe with a much larger bowl, fill it with my tobacco, and light up. I would chuckle to myself, and I am sure a slight smile came to my face. He was a proud man and would never ask me for tobacco. Recognizing this fact, I made sure to offer him tobacco each time we met, and he would carry out the same ritual."

"Our first seven or eight days in Horsham were taken up with training flights," said Dee. "It was important for our pilots and navigators to know the flight procedures in and around Horsham. After all, there were thousands of planes stationed at fifteen combat airfields in the area. They had to learn how to marshal up on the runways before taking off for a mission. Then they had to practice how to rendezvous over England, first with their squadron, then with their group and, finally, with the other groups that were to participate in the same raid. Then there were landing procedures and emergency landing procedures. There was a lot to learn. In addition, on May 31, our Bombardier 2nd Lt. Washington got his chance to hone his skills in guiding AZON bombs at a target range in England, given the code name *Stack Yard Green*. Our plane made 10 practice runs that day."

From the Bombardier Mission Reports that Fielding Washington had managed to save for nearly sixty years, it is known that the first combat mission for the crew of the *Bad Girl* took place on June 14, 1944, eight days after D-day.

From George A. Reynolds book, entitled, <u>458th Bombardment Group IV</u>, 1996, ten AZON planes, each loaded with five 1000-pound bombs, were given six bridges as targets that day all of which were in France behind the German lines. The planes returned with all their bombs still in their bomb bays. Bad weather had obscured the target enough to make the weapon ineffective. Fielding Washington's records confirmed this.

"On June 15, the same planes were given the same targets," said Washington. "On that day our bomb bays had been loaded with three AZON bombs. I launched each of them against the targets and the results were negative. In addition, one bomb's flare did not ignite, so I could not guide it to the intended target."

The Crew of Bad Girl at the 8th Air Force Bomber base at Horsham, Norwich, England. Front row left to right: Bauch-gunner, U.B. Simoneaux-FlightEengineer and Crew Chief, King-Gunner, Harris-Gunner, Large-Asst. Flight Engineer, Emilio DaBramo-Radio Operator. Back row left to right: 1st Lt. F. Washington–Bombardier, 1st Lt. M.J. Kotowitz-Co-pilot, 1st Lt. F. Fuson-Pilot, 1st Lt. W. Jamerson-Navigator. Photo taken just before a mission. (Courtesy of Dee DaBramo)

During my interview with Dee, I asked him, how he felt before his first mission.

"I felt very patriotic," he replied. "We all did. After all, we were well-trained as a crew and we never gave a thought to the fact that we might get hurt, or killed for that matter."

Then I asked him how he felt after his first two missions.

"As I recall, the first two missions were not very far into enemy territory. We were on AZON missions in support of our troops that landed at Normandy a few days earlier. Our targets were bridges behind German lines that were being used to transport supplies to their troops. Since we performed well as a crew and returned safely, without injury, it gave us a feeling of invincibility and pride in being an American," Dee remarked. "As I reflect on those feelings today, I am convinced, as horrible as this may sound, that wars are best fought by young people because of their feelings of invincibility."

During my interviews with Dee, his recollections of his combat experiences, after more than fifty years had elapsed, were often sketchy. When I pressed him a little bit by asking him to describe some of his mission experiences, he became melancholy and reluctant to talk about them, so I dropped the subject for a while. When I returned later to the subject of his mission experiences, he just flat-out told me he didn't want to talk about it. Respecting his feelings, I never broached the subject again, and recorded only those stories he volunteered to describe. Since his combat experiences played a major part of his being in subsequent years of his life, I set out to find as many of his crewmates that I could to fill me in.

Most of the information that follows comes from interviews with Pilot, Retired Lt. Colonel Frank C. Fuson Jr., Bombardier, Retired Lt. Colonel Fielding Washington and Crew Chief, Staff Sergeant U.B. Simoneaux.

Like Dee, Co-pilot William Kotowitz did not want to talk about his combat experiences.

"That's a part of my life that I have put behind me and I don't want to bring it up again," he said emphatically during my attempt at a telephone interview with him.

He did, however, give me some background information regarding his life before WWII and after he was discharged. I respected and honored his wishes and never called him again.

Pilot - Retired Lt. Colonel Frank C. Fuson Jr.

"Dee was a very likable person. He got along with everyone in the crew and with everyone in general. In fact, he was the clown of the crew, or as the British would say, he was the *court jester*. We all loved him. It doesn't surprise me that Dee did not want to talk about his combat experience, since it was a very traumatic experience for him. Unlike the other members of the crew, Dee was least directly involved in a combat operation. As radio operator, his station was a cubbyhole just aft of and below the cockpit. Directly above him was the top turret and all he could see were the feet and legs of the top turret gunner. He had no window to look out of to observe what was going on. He was physically isolated from the action, and was helpless to respond to what was going on around him.

The pilots were flying the plane, the navigator was getting the plane over the target and back home again, and the bombardier was sighting in on the target and dropping the bombs. The four gunners were looking out for enemy fighters or shooting at them. At the height of air combat, he could only sit and hear the explosive chatter of the 50-caliber machine guns reverberating throughout the plane from stem to stern, as the gunners fired at German planes attacking the group formation. Over the target, it was the out-of- rhythm explosions of the German anti-aircraft fire bursting all around the plane, and feeling the plane being jolted out of position with every close burst of flak, and shrapnel penetrating the skin of the plane. It was not an enviable position to be in," Frank Fuson said with conviction.

"I think every member of the crew had a souvenir piece of flack that had penetrated the skin of the plane during one mission or another," Dee told me, as he displayed the piece he had saved since the war.

"Dee's main job was to man the array of radio equipment he had in front of him," said Fuson. "He was trained in radio procedures and took orders from the co-pilot and me when we needed him to contact our home base or other planes in the formation.

"He also had some other emergency activities to perform," said Fuson. "For example, Dee was our First Aid Specialist. He had the only portable oxygen equipment for use in getting around the aircraft to administer first aid to a wounded crewmember. As a qualified gunner, he was required to take the place of a gunner that had been wounded or killed. He was also responsible for dropping a wounded crewman out the bomb bay doors when it was deemed crucial to saving his life. For example: If a crewman was badly wounded, and it was quite certain that he would not make it to our home base alive, then the decision would be made to drop him into enemy territory where he might have a better chance of getting medical attention. This practice was later verified to be effective by several prisoners of war survivors. To get the job done, Dee's responsibility was to attach a thirty-foot tether to a D- ring on the individual's parachute, and gently drop him through the open bomb bay doors. The thirty-foot tether was to insure that the man cleared the plane before his parachute began to open. Fortunately for our crew, Dee never had to perform this task. He had one other emergency task to perform. When the bombardier could not open the bomb bay doors, from his remote station below the cockpit, Dee was in position to open and close them manually."

"The first time I had to open the bomb bays," recalled Dee, "I botched it. As I opened the doors I could see, hear and feel the flak bursting below us and in close proximity to the plane. In my rush to get them opened, I didn't quite finish the job. I reported the doors open, but they weren't open all the way. The result was that when the bombs were released, the doors went with them. This mishap was not an unusual occurrence in the Group. There were always two possible consequences that could result from this mishap. First, shrapnel from German flak had an open path into the fuselage of the plane. We were lucky on that day and we weren't hit. The other consequence was inevitable; the crew froze from the cold on the return trip home in spite of the fact that we all had electrically-heated flight gear. At 20,000 feet altitude and above, the air is very cold, perhaps 30 to 50 degrees Fahrenheit below zero. I took a ribbing from the crew for a few days after that incident."

Crew Chief - Staff/Sergeant U.B. Simoneaux.

"My combat station was in the upper turret that was positioned above Dee and his radio station. I was constantly on the alert once we got over hostile territory, which, for the most part, kept my mind off being frightened. When the shooting did start, I didn't have time to think about being afraid. I was not envious of Dee's position. I am sure he was scared most of the time we were in the air."

Bombardier - Retired Lt. Colonel Fielding Washington.

"The radio operator in a B-24 was totally closed from the world around him. He sat at his table working the radio equipment. He does not man a gun and he can't see what is happening outside the plane. He is in his own little world. He is blind and cannot see anything except the feet of the top turret gunner, and that's about it. I can understand how a radio operator could suffer more from nerves than the rest of the crew. But I don't know of anyone in the crew that didn't suffer from nerves. Before we took off on a mission we were all issued a box lunch. On several occasions I can recall Dee remarking, jokingly, 'I hope I get the opportunity to eat this lunch.' He always had a feeling of uncertainty, and this was his way of expressing it."

The Flak Farm

"To help the combat flight crews deal with battle fatigue after a number of missions, the Air Corps provided rest homes, or *flak farms*, as the combat crews called them, where they were given some time off, perhaps three to five days," Dee explained. "Exactly what the formula was for determining when you went and how long you stayed, I don't remember. A flak house," Dee described, "was usually a large manor house in the beautiful English countryside. The one we frequented was called the Coombe House. It was fully staffed with housekeepers, chefs, servers, drivers and even a butler. There was usually a staff member in charge of recreation who organized individual or group activities, such as horseback riding, tennis, golf and croquet and trips to the countryside. Some of us even partook in *the ride to hounds* in a country fox hunt. We dressed for dinner, and the food and service were excellent. It was a time to relax and enjoy some of the finer things of life. But, regardless of how wonderful it was, the inevitable thought of going back to Horsham and flying again was omni-present. Life was like being on an emotional roller coaster."

"One very funny thing I remember about the staff at the Coombe House," Frank Fuson said, with a broad smile on his face and a slight chuckle, "was the staff's pet weasel that they had trained to hunt rabbits. On occasion, some of us guys would take the weasel out onto the grounds and put it to work catching rabbits in their burrows. The weasel was quite good at hunting those rabbits."

The Coombe House Hotel was located about 100 miles southwest of London. The train ride from London to Semlely Station, which was about two miles from Shaftesbury, took about two and a half hours.

Excerpts from the historic report of Coombe House Hotel, Shaftesbury, Dorset, AAF Station 523, written by RC "Dick" Harris, Jr., former adjutant at Coombe House and C. O. Ebrington Manor.

"All guests were picked up at the Semlely Station. There was a grass airstrip nearby at Zeals, which could accommodate two-engine aircraft and was often used by guests, some just dropping in for lunch or tea.

"The main building is a large stone structure having enough rooms, baths and outside facilities for 40 guests. The original Coombe House structure was built in 1886, by a Vinegar millionaire, Mark Hanbury Beaufoy, and resembles a medieval manor. An addition to the Manor was built in 1911 and was known as the Library. The area surrounding it consisted of 50 acres. It is 700 feet above sea level and 2 ¼ miles from Shaftesbury. The name Coombe originated from the fact that the house was situated above three hollows or coombes. It had a magnificent ballroom with a huge fireplace and an indoor badminton court which was popular with the guests during cold rainy days. It had a large garage, stalls for horses, and a large lawn in front where many athletic games took place. A skeet-shooting range was located in the southeast corner and was a very popular activity.

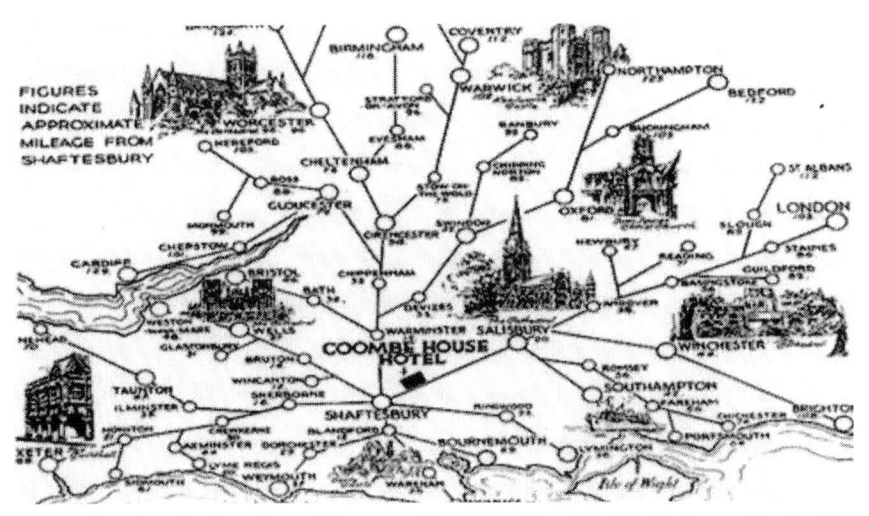

Map showing the location of the Coombe House Hotel in Shaftesbury, England. (Courtesy of 2nd Air Division Memorial Room, Norfolk, England)

"Numerous recreational, athletic, and outside activities were available, including golf, horseback riding and tennis. The tennis courts were located in Shaftesbury 2 ½ miles away to which many of the guests rode their bikes. Tours were made available to Stonehenge, 28 miles away via Wilton, and to Wardour Castle 7 ½ miles distance.

"The facility housed a "Little Giant PX" which was always well-stocked and open daily for all guests. Now, after 50 years, it can be told that ration cards were always observed or looked at, but rarely checked or stamped. A wet bar was provided when spirits were available.

"The food was extra good. All guests were served three meals a day, plus afternoon tea. Snacks were also served after the evening movie. It was the habit of the resident butler to awaken each resident guest with a glass of juice or tea in hand, and usually gave a hint about the breakfast menu and tell them that they should be on time if they wanted to eat. Food was allocated from authorized hospital funds and often supplemented with Red Cross funds. Life at the House was informal. There was no set schedule, and the guests could wear whatever clothes they chose. Civilian clothes, called 4-F clothes, were provided to the guests if they wanted them. Some guests even had their own civilian clothes.

COOMBE HOUSE WAS A FLAK FARM

FLAK HAPPY ISN'T THE WORD FOR IT
by Ann Newdeck, ARC
27 January 1944

It's January in England, so sun just rising is rare and welcome. Breakfast smells like bacon and eggs. Apparently the grapevine knew it too because half the house is up for breakfast, 20 or so combat flyers disguised in sweaters, slacks and sneakers. Plans are afoot for golf, tennis and shooting skeet in the back yard, but the loudest conversation and most uproarious kidding center around the 4 who are going to ride to hounds in a country fox hunt. On a rainy day there's almost as much activity at Coombe House—the badminton court in the ballroom is our chief pride. But nevertheless the Army calls it Rest Home. It looks as English as the setting of a Noel Coward play, but even as you approach the house you discover that actors and plot are American. You meet a girl in scuffed saddle shoes and baggy sweater kneeling

The U.S. 8th Air Force rest and recreation facility at the Coombe House Hotel in Shaftesbury, England. (Courtesy of 2nd Air Division Memorial Room, Norfolk, England)

"At first, the Air Force ran these rest homes alone. After two had been established, a large part of the responsibility was transferred to the American Red Cross to make them as un-military as possible," wrote Ann Newdeck, ARC in her article of 27 January 1944, which appeared in the 8th Air Force News of February 1978. The staff at Coombe House was made up of British officers who administered the facility with AAF military personnel under their supervision and American Red Cross personnel. The military personnel maintained the facility and provided the services to the guests. The Red Cross personnel saw to the recreational needs of the guests and the AAF to their medical and psychological needs. There were as many as thirty staff members in all."

Entrance to Coombe House Hotel. Horseback riding and bicycling were popular with the crews. (Courtesy of 2nd Air Division Memorial Room, Norfolk, England)

*Front view of the Coombe House Hotel.
(Courtesy of 2nd Air Division Memorial Room, Norfolk, England)*

Combat missions.

The following excerpts are recollections of combat missions described by Pilot, Retired Lt. Colonel Frank C. Fuson Jr., Bombardier, Retired Lt. Colonel Fielding Washington, Crew Chief, Staff Sergeant U.B. Simoneaux, and, to a lesser degree, Dee DaBramo. In addition, information was drawn from the book 458th Bombardment Group IV,

1996, written by George A. Reynolds. This book is a history of the 458th Bombardment Group that included Squadron 753, of which Dee and his crewmates were a part.

From the book, 458th Bombardment Group IV, by George A. Reynolds, 1996.

"The ten AZON planes were under the command of Colonel Robert W. Vincent. The group inherited the name of the Buck Rogers Boys because of the space-age nature of the AZON bomb itself. Thirteen AZON missions were flown from May 31, 1944 through September 9, 1944. The main mission of the group was to destroy bridges leading to the Normandy beachhead, to cut off the flow of German troops and supplies reinforcing the defenders opposing the Allied Forces at Normandy. The results were mixed. Three of the missions were aborted because of poor weather over the targets, and only seven of the thirteen missions were considered successful."

Pilot - Retired Lt. Colonel Frank C. Fuson, Jr.

"Two factors affected the success of our AZON missions," said Fuson. "One was the weather. If the bombardier did not have a clear view of the target, his chances for successfully guiding the bomb to the target were small. The second factor had to do with the density of the flak over the target. Not only did the flak obscure the target from the bombardier, it also was a distracting element. If the bombardier flinched, he could easily lose sight of the flight path of the bomb. When we were training in the Gulf of Mexico, the element of flak was not a factor and our success rate was very good."

From the book, 458th Bombardment Group IV, by George A. Reynolds, 1996.

"The project was discontinued after the raid on the Flensburg oil refinery near the city of Mulheim, Germany on the 13th of September 1944. The ten AZON planes were fully integrated into the regular strategic bombing plans of the 458th Bombardment Group."

Pilot - Retired Lt. Colonel Frank C. Fuson, Jr.

"Before the AZON missions were abandoned, we also flew regular bombing missions with Squadron 753 when our AZON capabilities were not required. We did not always fly the Bad Girl. Plane assignments were given the day before a mission, and we flew the plane that was assigned to us."

Bombardier - Retired Lt. Colonel Fielding Washington.

"From the Bombing Mission Reports that I managed to save from my flying career in Europe, our crew flew missions in at least fifteen different B-24s, but our hearts were always with the Bad Girl."

Pilot - Retired Lt. Colonel Frank C. Fuson, Jr.

"We flew some memorable and historic missions in the nine months we were at Horsham. The most historic ones took place on July 24 and 25, 1944. By this time we had five AZON missions and at least a half dozen strategic bombing missions under our belt. We had struck at the Baltic Sea Port of Keil in northern Germany, Saarbruken and Koblenz on the Mosel River and La Grande Vallee in northeastern France."

The Disastrous Raid on St. Lo, France.

"By the last week in July, 1944, the Allied Forces had driven from the beaches of Normandy to a line in France between St. Lo and Poeles," noted Colonel Fuson. "Our mission at St. Lo was to carpet-bomb the defending German Forces east of this line. This was where the American troops, under the command of General Leslie McNair, were to make the break-through from the Normandy Beachhead in an offensive called *Operation Cobra*. The objective of *Operation Cobra* was to open the way for Patton's Third Army tanks to drive into Brittany and onward to Brest. On July 24, the 8th Air Force was to put up every available aircraft into the raid. The sky was black with thousands of planes, B-24 and B-17 heavy bombers along with B-25 medium bombers and fighter escorts. On the way in our bomb run, we could see the massive number of allied vehicles, tanks, ambulances with their red crosses, and thousands of troops along the road leading to St. Lo. Our group had our bomb bays loaded with fifty-two 100-pound, anti-personnel bombs, which was the maximum that we could carry. We were to fly at 10,000 feet so that we could better see the target and avoid dropping our bombs on our own troops. Our usual bombing altitude was above 20,000 feet, which helped us avoid some of the German flak. Flying at 10,000 feet made us a bit nervous. As we approached the target zone, the visibility got worse and worse, and the groups lowered their altitude accordingly. Finally, the raid had to be aborted because of poor visibility, and we all returned to England. What was startling about this aborted raid was that we did not encounter any German anti-aircraft fire. Apparently we had caught them by surprise.

"That evening at Horsham, I sent Jamerson, our navigator, to snoop around the flight line to try and ascertain what our mission might be the next day. His objective was to find out what kind of bombs and how much fuel was being loaded aboard the planes. This was a common practice by all the pilots. It was our way of getting some idea of what type of bombing raid we were going on the next day. Jamerson reported that we were carrying the same anti-personnel bombs and the same amount of fuel as we had on the twenty-fourth. This meant that we were headed back to St. Lo the next morning.

"To no one's surprise, on July 25, 1944 the 8th Air Force again launched every available plane in their arsenal and we were headed back for St. Lo. The only problem for us was that the Germans more than likely knew it too. When we approached the target area, at an altitude of 10,000 feet, the anti-aircraft fire was intense. The Germans were waiting for us, all right. The sky all around us was black with exploding shrapnel. It just so happened on this day I had Dee up in the cockpit, using him as an extra pair of eyes to help us keep track of the thousands of planes in the skies around us. On that day we witnessed planes in the lead group exploding as they were hit by flak, and the bodies of their crewmen hurtled through the air like rag dolls. Some crewmen managed to get their chutes open, but they were on fire. We saw them frantically kicking their legs as they plummeted earthward. Even those whose parachutes didn't catch fire, were in grave danger as they descended into that dark cloud of flak and our anti-personnel bombs that were exploding a few feet above the ground. It was a horrible sight, and Dee witnessed most of it from his position between the pilot and co-pilot seats. Our group, the 458th, was very lucky that day as we didn't lose a single plane. But not all went right on this mission. We witnessed a terrible mishap. When the lead bomber in the lead group opened its bomb bay doors, the bomb release mechanism malfunctioned and their bombs were jettisoned prematurely. Since the lead bomber controls the drop for the rest of the group, they followed suit and dropped their bombs as well. That meant that fifty-two 100-pound anti-personnel bombs from each of about 30 planes, dropped on the American side of the front line. Our group, thank God, realized the mistake and held our bombs and dropped them into the German defenses. At that time we had no idea as to the damage inflicted on the German and American forces.

"When we returned to Horsham, I went to the customary after-mission intelligence briefing where I first heard the details of the tragic mishap. The briefing was conducted by a two-star general who told us that General Leslie McNair, Commanding General, Army Ground Forces, who had gone up to the front line to observe the raid, was killed immediately, along with hundreds of his troops, by the bombs from the lead group. We found out later that the U.S. 47th Infantry's Third Battalion had 111 killed and 490 wounded in the raid, and had to be replaced in the front line with a reserve battalion. The U.S. 30th Infantry Division lost 25 soldiers killed and 131 wounded. On the positive side, he told us that most of our bombs landed on the Germans. This had a significant impact on the ability of the American troops to break through the German lines in *Operation Cobra*. The break-through the German lines at St. Lo assured the Allied victory in Europe, because the Germans had no chance now of turning back the assault at Normandy. A few days later Patton's tanks rolled through the German lines, routing them. In August of 1944 we flew eight missions in Germany and occupied France. One of our targets was the Clastres Aerodrome in French-occupied territory. In September, the 458th flew only six combat missions, and we flew one of those on the thirteenth of September in what we considered to be our own plane, the *Bad Girl*," said Colonel Fuson. "It would be our last bombing mission flying the *Bad Girl*."

Air- mailing fuel to General Patton's 3rd Army tanks.

Pilot – retired Lt. Colonel Frank C. Fuson tells of the mission. "After September 13, 1944 all bombing missions were cancelled in order to modify each B-24 bomber for a special mission. That mission was to ferry fuel to Patton's Third Armored Division that was spearheading the attack against the German Army in France after the break-through at St. Lo in *Operation Cobra*. At the time, the missions were not widely publicized, nor do I believe that the U.S. public knows of it today.

"All aircraft were stripped of all non-essential equipment and personnel to make weight available for gasoline. Fuel tanks of varying shapes and sizes were fitted into the bomb bays of each plane and loaded with as much fuel as they could carry. Our flight crew was reduced from six to five members, the Pilot, Co-pilot, Navigator, Crew Chief and Radio Operator. Since we weren't carrying bombs, there was no need for a Bombardier or the four gunners. Our Bombardier, Fielding Washington, did fly with us once or twice as an observer.

"Three recently captured airfields in France were selected as our drop points. They were Lille (the hometown of General Charles DeGaulle), Clastres, and St.Dizier. All were located close to the border between France and Belgium. How ironic it was for us to be landing at the Clastres airfield unloading fuel, when on the ninth of August, we had bombed the hell out of the place when the Germans were still occupying it. I remember staying at the Grand Hotel in Clastres, while the plane was being unloaded, and the French people telling me that several French civilian workers had been killed during that raid. I felt very sorrowful and avoided telling them that we took part in the raid. They spoke of the incident, but did not display any animosity toward the Americans because they knew it had to be done to rid their country of the German occupiers. This attitude helped to put my mind at ease."

British and Canadian troops unloading gasoline from B-24 bombers in France for General Patton's 3rd Army tanks. (Rare Photograph, courtesy of S/Sgt. U.B. Simoneaux.).

Crew Chief - Staff Sergeant, U.B. Simoneaux.

"We flew about a half dozen of these missions in September 1944. The three French airfields used for these missions to deliver fuel to Patton's forces, were fairly close to the front lines. At night we could hear the artillery firing and could see the gun flashes just over the horizon. There were also other Allied aircraft in the air, supporting the ground troops and covering our operation.

"The scene at the airfields was a mixture of order and chaos. Our planes would land and queue up to wait to be unloaded. The British and Canadian troops, occupying the area at the time, unloaded each plane. The unloading operation was makeshift and primitive. They would drain the gasoline from the bomb bay tanks into five-gallon Jerry cans, using rubber hoses. The Jerry cans were then loaded onto trucks and driven off to catch up to Patton's tanks.

Dee, with Crew Chief S/Sgt. U.B. Simoneaux, waiting for British and Canadian troop to unload the fuel from their B-24 Bomber. (Rare Photograph, Courtesy S/Sgt. U.B. Simoneaux).

"There were no mess facilities at the airfields, so you had to bring your own food. Before leaving Horsham we were issued "C" rations, but we didn't like them very much. So, Dee and I located a storeroom at Horsham that had some "K" rations of beef stew and other tasty items, so we managed to acquire them from *midnight stores* (we stole them).

Dee and I figured out a clever way to cook the "K" rations with as little fuss as possible. We would empty the contents of the "K" ration cans into our mess kit. Then we would fill the empty "K" ration cans with sand and soak the sand with gasoline. The cans were buried level with the ground and lit with a match. We placed our mess kits over the flaming cans and cooked us a hot meal.

"If our plane was to be unloaded soon after we arrived, then we would stay with it and take off for Horsham as soon as possible for another load. If we were going to be required to stay over night, sometimes we would sleep on the ground near the aircraft. On some occasions, when we were unloading at Clastres, we would all stay overnight in town at the Grand Hotel. The French people treated us very well, especially since I'm a Cajun and speak French quite well.

"On one run from Horsham we had a very close call. We were carrying the maximum load of cargo fuel and a minimum load of mission fuel. The fact of the matter was we were overloaded on all of these missions. In extraordinary circumstances, like war, you perform extraordinary feats. This meant that we flew at a very low altitude of a few hundred feet. One foggy morning, after taking off from Horsham, we emerged from the fog to see some high-tension wires strung between two pylons directly in our path. Because of our heavy load we could not gain altitude fast enough to climb over them, so Lt. Fuson flew under them. One could only speculate as to what the outcome would have been if we had struck those wires with a full load of fuel. Some crews would rather have flown bombing missions than fuel missions because of the imposing danger of the operation.

"On a return trip from a fuel run to France, we were approaching Horsham and could see a huge column of smoke off the far end of the runway on which we were to land. After landing we found out that one of the B-24 bombers loaded with fuel lost an engine on takeoff and crashed. The entire crew was killed. None of the so-called *Trucken Missions* were counted toward our original thirty-mission quota," said U.B.

From the book, <u>458<u>th</u> Bombardment Group IV</u>, by George A. Reynolds, 1996.

A total of 494 aircraft were dispatched in this operation, and six were lost. One crashed on takeoff, killing all aboard. One left for St. Dizier, and wasn't heard from again. Four were damaged and placed in salvage.

A total of 727,160 gallons of fuel were airlifted to Patton's Third Army in September 1944.

October of 1944 was a very interesting month for Dee and his flight crew. After completing their *Trucken Missions,* carrying fuel to Patton's Third Army in France, the 458th group planes were converted back to carrying bombs.

"On October 2, 1944 the crew experienced one of the saddest moments of our combat career at Horsham," said Dee. "On this day we were on stand-down, and a new crew had just arrived from the States, and they were assigned to the *Bad Girl* for a training flight. Upon take-off, No.1 engine failed and the pilot had to make an emergency landing and crashed the *Bad Girl.* The damage was so heavy that we would never fly her again. Losing her was like losing a member of your family. It wasn't until that day that we realized how strongly we identified with that plane, and what an important role she played in our lives. The loss weighed heavy on our hearts," Dee remarked in hushed tones and a saddened face. "Of course, we could just as easily have been the crew that day, taking off on a mission with a full load of bombs. God only knows what might have happened to us," he said sorrowfully.

"I have never forgiven them for crashing our plane, even to this day," (56 years later) mourned former bombardier, Retired Lt. Colonel Fielding Washington.

As I listened to the heart-breaking comments from Dee and the other crewmembers about the fate of the *Bad Girl*, I wondered how the incident happened and who were involved. I wondered who the pilot was and what story he reported of the incident. I began my investigation with a call to Air Force Historical Research Agency at Maxwell Air Force Base, Alabama. It was from this source that I received my answers from Archivist Dixie Dysart.

The following is the report filed by the Flying Control Officer at Horsham. It tells of the incident in a most concise manner, which is appropriate for its purpose, but tells little of what actually happened in the cockpit of the plane while the event was occurring.

> AT APPROXIMATELY 0945 HOURS 8-24J-288 "S" PILOTED BY LT. AKINS CRASHED ON THE AIRFIELD. #1 ENGINE WAS ON FIRE AND HE WAS GIVEN PERMISSION TO LAND ON R/W 05. UPON LANDING THE AIRCRAFT SKIDDED OFF THE R/W

TO THE LEFT AND CRASHED. NONE OF THE CREW WERE
INJURED. SEVERE DAMAGE WAS DONE TO THE AIRCRAFT.
WEATHER NE AT 15 M.P.H. – 8 MILES VIZ.

>Jesse Halpern
>1st Lt., Air Corps,
>Flying Control Officer

For information of what actually happened in the cockpit, I had to find the Pilot's Report. I received the actual report written by the pilot, 1st Lt. Arthur C. Akin Jr., from the Archivist. Fortunately, most of the print from the microfilm of the report was legible, but some of it was not and I have indicated this.

Subject: Crash Landing of Ship 288   October 6, 1944
The takeoff runway was 23, with a formation taking off on a training mission. I pulled off to the right side of the runway to avoid filling the runway with prop wash from my engines. On the green light I advanced the throttles and began rolling down the runway. Number one engine suddenly revved up and pulled one ---*not intelligible* ---off the runway but was straightened out without difficulty. I was ---*not intelligible* ---off the ground and making my turn to Sal –*not intelligible*-- 5 when I noticed a great pressure on the right rudder. At about the same time my engineer tells me that number 1 engine is on fire. The co-pilot and I –*not intelligible* for number I being – *not intelligible*--prepared to cut the engine and try to feather it but the oil tank exploded blowing a hole in the top of the engine and there was no oil pressure. We made a turn back to the field and called the tower for landing instructions and were told to use runway 05. Our altitude was too low to allow the crew to bail out safely and I didn't believe there was any danger of the empty auxiliary tank exploding and advised the crew to jump if they liked, but I thought their chances were better if they stuck with the ship. I dropped ten degrees of flaps to gain altitude and was pulling ____ inches of manifold pressure, 2450 RPMs. When I turned on the approach I had reached

800 feet. I let down on the field, making a high approach. I cut off all power by this time and *–not intelligible--* the rudder trim. The landing was with a slight wind from the left, so when I landed I thought the wind was pulling us to the left and I applied full right rudder but it continued its merry way to the edge of the runway, hit a pile of sand and tore off the nose wheel and the left main landing gear immediately afterward. The plane then slid along on its belly and left wing tip and the propeller and nose section of No.1 engine were torn off. On landing at the time, I found a hole burned through the rudder, and it blew out when it hit the runway. -----*the rest of the report was not intelligible.*

Lt. Arthur C. Akin Jr.

October 6, 1944. The wreckage of the Bad Girl at the 8th Air Force Base, Horsham, England. (Courtesy of Dee DaBramo)

What Lt. Akin did not mention in his report, but was mentioned in the Engineering Report of the accident was, "The fire was immediately extinguished by ground personnel." This, of course, meant that the plane was on fire when it landed and the crew's lives were in peril, but all survived unhurt.

My curiosity concerning Lt. Arthur C. Akins did not end with the finding of these reports. I searched George A. Reynolds Book, <u>458th Bombardment Group IV</u> for other evidence of his service with the 458th.

I was deeply saddened with what I found. On November 24, 1944, less than two months after the crash of the *Bad Girl*, Lt. Akin and his crew were killed when they crashed into downtown Norwich. The crash site has been preserved as a memorial to the crew and the civilians killed in the crash. This fact was unknown by Dee and his crewmates when I interviewed them.

From Fielding Washington's Bombardier records, we know that on the October 3, 1944, the crew flew their twenty-third mission to Gagganau, France. The twenty-fourth mission was flown to Hengelo, Netherlands on October 7. Mission number twenty-five was to Osnabruck, Germany on October 12, and the twenty-sixth mission was to Cologne, Germany on October 14, 1944.

Dee and his crew members were rapidly closing in on the magic number 30 and, to date, not one had been wounded or hurt, thanks to the skillful piloting of Frank Fuson and William Kotowicz, and a favorable nod from *Lady Luck*.

On October 17, 1944, the crew flew back to Cologne for their twenty-seventh mission. It was on this day that *Lady Luck* abandoned them, but the skills of Pilot Fuson and Co-pilot Kotowitz did not.

Bombardier - Retired Lt. Colonel Fielding Washington.

"I do not have record of this mission to Cologne in my collection of reports. Under the circumstances, I did not file a report on that raid. What was the point?" he told me with a sense of amusement in his voice."

None of the crew could remember the number of the plane or if it had a name, but the events of the day were recorded in their collective memories.

Pilot - Retired Lt. Colonel Frank C. Fuson, Jr.

"As I recall the events, we dropped our bombs from an altitude of about 27,000 feet. We knew from the raid on October 14, that the flak over the city was going to be intense, so the higher we could fly, the safer we would be. Within minutes after the drop, we were hit with flak and lost two engines. One of the consequence of losing those engines was that we lost electric power to our gyroscopes. Now we had no compass to guide us home. I immediately called the group leader and informed him that we were losing altitude and would proceed back across the French border and look for a field to land on. Then we called up the fighter escort squadron flying cover for us. Within a few minutes two P-51 fighters had positioned themselves at our wing tips. We made radio contact and they proceeded to lead us across the French border into Allied occupied territory. I ordered the crew to dump everything from the plane that wasn't permanently attached to the bulkheads, including the guns and ammunition. I told them to use the fire axes to break them loose, but be sure not to cut any cables or hydraulic lines.' The objective of this action was to lighten the plane as much as possible. B-24s didn't fly very well at high altitude on two engines. However, I did tell DaBramo to keep his radios because we were going to need them before the day was over. During all this time we were losing altitude and the weather was closing in on us. As soon as the fighters assured me that we had crossed the border into Allied occupied France, we began to look for a field to land on. I didn't care if it was an airfield or a pasture, just as long as it was level enough and long enough to allow us a decent chance to make a safe landing. The weather was not good and only on occasion could we see the ground through breaks in the cloud cover. We sighted an open pasture through a hole in the clouds that looked fairly decent for making a landing. I contacted the pilots of the P-51 escort planes and asked them to go down and take a look for us. They peeled off and made a very low altitude run over the site and returned within minutes. One of the pilots called us on the radio and told us that it looked pretty good and was worth a try. This is when I contacted the crew on the intercom and told them what the fighter pilot had said.

"Now, we have just a few minutes before I make my approach. If any of you want to jump, now's the time. They all made the decision to stick with the plane. I don't know if it was because they had confidence in me and Kotowicz or they were afraid to jump. We were all in this together now. Perhaps that is the way it was meant to be. The conventional wisdom in this situation was to make a belly landing, but I made the decision to make a wheels-down landing to soften the impact. As I was making my final approach toward the field, and into the wind, I told Kotowitz to be sure to pull the crash bar once we were settled on the ground. This action would shut off all electrical power to all engines and minimize the chance of a fire. Everything was looking good until a few hundred feet from the edge of the field. At that moment we were hit by a blinding rain squall and we couldn't see the field in front of us. I knew instantly that I was going to overshoot the field. Again, I recalled my B-24 flight training, which told me that a B-24 did not have enough power to climb out of an aborted landing with two engines. I immediately raised the landing gear to reduce the drag and give us more air speed, and at the same time I reached over to the turbo charger switches, and as quickly as I could I turned them into the *red zone*, beyond maximum power. The engines surged and the plane was able to climb to about 1000 feet. I did not think we could make a 360 degree turn and approach the field into the wind. So, to be sure we had a second chance at the field, I made a 180 degree turn and lined the plane up with the landing site and started a down-wind approach. The problem with a down-wind approach is that the landing speed would be greater than normal. Normal landing speed for a B-24 was about 90 mph. We dropped the landing gear, which lowered our landing speed somewhat. I could tell we were really sailing when we flew by the pasture fence. Our speed had to be 120 to 130 mph. As I neared the ground I cut the power to the two engines and we touched down. Kotowitz, apparently sighted a ditch or crater on the field ahead of us and slammed on the brakes. The result was that the nose wheel sheared off and we slid a good ways on our belly. Dirt and mud were jettisoned into the plane through the open nose gear well, and at the same time the joystick went limp and struck me in the chest and knocked the wind out of me. Kotowitz pulled the crash bar to cut electric power to the engines, as I had ordered him to do, and for the moment at least we avoided a fire. When I recovered from the blow to the chest, in perhaps a very few seconds or so, I looked out the left side of the plane and there was the crew frantically running in all directions away from the plane. In a few seconds I was out of the plane and fleeing like the rest. We were all afraid that the plane would blow up like those we had seen at Horsham. We all got out alive, thanks to those P-51 pilots. In the melee of the day I never did get their squadron designation or the names of the pilots, but still remember them fondly as our saviors on that day in October, 1944.

"As soon as we were certain that the plane was not going to catch fire and blow up, I sent Dee back in to send a message to Horsham telling them that we were all okay and the ship was not salvageable, and that we would be returning as soon as we could arrange transportation. I also had Dee tell Horsham that no one was to divide up our belongings as if we were missing in action. It was the custom that when a plane went down and the crew was missing in action, killed or taken prisoner, the other crews in the squadron would take possession of their uniforms. Personal items were sent home to their families. By some miracle, the radio worked fine and the message got through.

"Our crash landing did not go unnoticed. It was observed by a contingency of British and Canadian Forces and, of course, the local French people. Ironically, we had come down in a pasture near Lille, France where a month or so earlier we had ferried fuel for Patton's tanks. First to arrive at the scene was a British Army halftrack with a machine gun mounted on it and several troops. They greeted us and inquired if we needed medical assistance. A minute or two later a Major from the Canadian Forces arrived in a jeep with a few of his men. Some of these guys most probably had participated in the unloading of gasoline at the Lille airfield a few miles away. The Major shook our hands and asked about our well-being, and he invited us to their quarters at a French Chateau that they had commandeered. The Canadians were great. They treated us royally with plenty of food, beer and, of course, French wine. I and the crew had a chance to unwind from a very traumatic experience, to say the least. Our hiatus at the chateau lasted three or four days."

Crew Chief - Staff Sergeant U.B. Simoneaux.

"Within a few minutes after the British and Canadian soldiers arrived, dozens of Frenchmen from a nearby village came running toward the plane with buckets and other types of containers swinging from their arms. The troops surrounded the plane, making sure they did not get into it. Since I spoke French I could communicate with them. They told me that they wanted the gasoline from our fuel tanks for use in their vehicles. Gasoline was very scarce, if not impossible for them to obtain at this time in the war. I told Lt. Fuson what they wanted and he spoke with the Canadian Major. Apparently they felt it could do no harm, and he gave me the order to help them out. Being the flight engineer I knew how to get access to the gasoline. I explained to the Frenchmen what it would take to safely extract the fuel, and I opened the petcock to the wing tanks and they drained every ounce of fuel from the tank."

Radio Operator -Technical Sergeant Emilio DaBramo.

"The Canadian Major had asked Lt. Fuson if our radios were still operating. Fuson told him they were and offered them to the Major, which was what he was after. He also told the Major that his men could have whatever else they could find of interest to them. Lt. Fuson sent me into the plane to remove the radios and turn them over to the Major's men. Some of the Canadians took parachutes for souvenirs. Everyone went to the Chateau where the Canadians were housed, except U.B. and me. Because he could speak French he was a hit with the town's people. They invited us to go into town with them. The two of us ended up at a Café in town where we were wined and dined until the wee hours in the morning. We spent that night and the next couple of days with a French family in the village. The morning of the third or fourth day we ran into a Canadian MP in a jeep and he drove us to the Chateau where the rest of the crew had been housed by the Canadian Forces."

Pilot - Retired Lt. Colonel Frank C. Fuson, Jr.

"I will admit that we were not in too big a hurry to get back to Horsham, but I knew I had to at least make an obvious effort to return. Our first offer for a return trip back to Horsham was from an American aircraft salvage officer. He had come to France to salvage a B-17 that had made an emergency landing at the Lille airport. Somehow he had heard that we were in the area and he looked me up. He wanted us to fly the B-17 back to England with our crew. I refused the offer because we had no experience flying a B-17.

"The Canadian Forces finally were able to arrange for our transportation back to Horsham. On or about the 25th of October we were given a lift to an operating B-26 medium bomber base in France. From here we were flown to a base in England, about forty miles from Horsham. From there we were transported to Horsham by bus."

Bombardier - Retired Lt. Colonel Fielding Washington.

"When we returned to Horsham, the first thing I had to do was collect my belongings. Apparently the word did not get out to everyone that we had landed safely in France and I was not missing in action. I retrieved them all."

For me, as author, the missing link to the story of the crash-landing in France was identifying the P-51 fighter pilots that saved Dee and his crew members on that fateful mission over Cologne. Without this, the story lacked closure. During the writing of this chapter I made numerous attempts, via the internet to locate the P-51 fighter squadron that was responsible for this heroic event. I even had hopes of identifying the pilots by name. After two years of trying, with no results, I finally gave up hope. Then, one day in June of 2005, in my resident town of Nashville, Indiana, one of the most astonishing events of this whole writing experience occurred most unexpectedly. I was on my way to lunch at one of my favorite eateries, the Artist Colony Inn. As I approached the hotel check-in-desk, on my way to the dining room, I was confronted by a small sign announcing the Reunion of P-51 Fighter Squadron 357 from WWII. It grabbed my attention immediately, and my dimmed hope of ever locating that fighter squadron that saved Dee and his fellow crew members was suddenly renewed. My first thought was this couldn't be it, or could it? If it is them, this would be the miracle of all miracles. But what did I have to lose? With great anticipation I approached the clerk at the desk and asked her where the group was meeting. She directed me downstairs to the conference room. As I started down the stairs, I consciously attempted to dismiss the thought of this being the members of the squadron I had been seeking for years that might provide closure to the story of the mission over Cologne.

I entered the room where several members of the group were sitting around a table reminiscing. As I approached the table they looked up at me and acknowledged my presence. I introduced myself and told them the story of my search for the squadron, and perhaps the pilots, that helped to rescue Dee's plane and crew members on that fateful day of October 17, 1944. None of them could recall the incident or whether their group had been involved. One gentleman, Rich L. Spicer, did promise to search the group's mission records when he returned home and send me whatever information he could find. My hopes were dimmed, but I had a wonderful experience reminiscing with them about their flying days in WWII. From the literature they gave me, I chronicled the following historical information about their fighter group.

The 357th Fighter Group was activated on December 1, 1942, at Hamilton Field in California and began a year-long training regimen. Hamilton Field was the same location where the original crew of the *Bad Girl* had been assembled.

The 357th arrived in the British Isles on November 30, 1943, and were the first P-51 Fighter Group assigned to the Eighth Air Force at Lewiston, England. Their first mission was flown on February 11, 1944. During fourteen months of combat, their primary mission was bomber escort (313 missions in all). During this time, 596 enemy aircraft were destroyed in the air and 107 on the ground. Forty-six pilots of the 357th became Aces with five or more air victories.

The squadron's most prominent Aces were C.B. Bob Anderson with sixteen kills, the famous Test Pilot Chuck Yeager with thirteen and Bill Overstreet with ten kills. These three ace pilots had trained together since the beginning of 1939. Bob Anderson and Chuck Yeager were not in attendance that day at the Artist Colony Inn but the eighty-three year young Bill Overstreet was.

The 357th Fighter Group received the Distinguished Unit Citation twice and the French Croix De Guerre. Individuals from the group won multiple Distinguished Flying Crosses and Air Medals. Their group's greatest victory came on January 14, 1945 when they shot down fifty-six enemy planes on a mission over Berlin. Eighty-two pilots of the 357th lost their lives in the air war over Europe.

Of the many combat stories I heard that day, the most extraordinary one was told to me by Ace Bill Overstreet.

"While flying high over enemy territory an enemy anti-aircraft shell pierced my cockpit and, unbeknown to me at the time, cut the hose to my oxygen mask. Soon I could not breathe at the altitude that I was flying and I passed out. The plane was flying by itself. Finally, after about an hour and a half of flying on its own, the fuel tank I was flying on ran out of fuel. Once the fuel ran out, the plane began to spin out of control toward the earth. Miraculously, when the plane reached an altitude where oxygen was available to me again, I regained consciousness, only to find that I had run out of fuel and was in a tail spin heading earthward at a rapid rate of descent. I had enough consciousness that my rote memory from my long hours of training kicked in, and I quickly recovered from the downward spiral, switched to the full fuel tank and restarted the engine. By then the plane was skimming the tree tops and I picked up a few leaves by the time I pulled out. Then I was worried, as I had no idea where I'd been heading during my one and a half hours of unconsciousness. I figured I had to head northwest to get back to England, so I did and found the English Channel. I got to the Fourth Fighter Group Base, and I landed rather rapidly since I wasn't as steady at that point in time. After I landed, the medics slapped me in the hospital for a few days."

Bill later downed his own plane when a train he was strafing blew up in his face and he had to bail out over enemy territory. He was captured by the Germans, but later escaped.

Pilot - Retired Lt. Colonel Frank C. Fuson, Jr. tells of the resulting psychological wounds of combat.

"When we arrived back to Horsham from our ordeal in France, we had three missions to complete our required number of thirty. Several of the crew's nerves were wearing a bit thin. Dee was one of them that showed signs of mental fatigue. Nevertheless, we still had three missions to go and the prevailing attitude was that we would all make it together. We couldn't have been back at Horsham more than a couple of days when the word came down from Eighth Air Force Headquarters that all crews would fly thirty-one missions. Now we had four missions to go before the nightmare was over.

"One of the leading contributors to crewmen being declared ineligible for combat, due to extreme stress, was the policy decisions made by the commanding general of the Eighth Air Force, related to the number of missions we were required to fly. When the first B-17s arrived in England in 1942, the crews were told that they would be required to fly twenty-five missions before they were permanently taken off the line. The number twenty-five was, at best, an educated guess since no one had any idea of the circumstances the crews would be faced with when in combat over Europe, and what the stress limits would be. In the early part of the air campaign, few B-17 crews made it through to their twenty-fifth mission. They were either shot down over Europe, killed or taken prisoner or crash-landed at the first base they came to in England. Some who were shot down in Europe managed, somehow, to get back to England, with the aid of the underground forces.

"We all remember the story of the *Memphis Belle* that was a celebration of its crew's completion of their twenty-five missions. Now the setting of the number twenty-five was okay in the sense that the combat crewmen had a mindset and they knew that when they completed twenty-five missions, they were through. The fact of the matter was that in 1942 and early 1943, the average number of missions completed was fifteen.

"As the war progressed, the German Air Force became less of a threat and fewer of our bombers were being lost. The introduction of the P-51 and P-47 long-range fighter escort planes had a lot to do with this fact. The fighter escorts, however, did nothing to reduce the enemy flak over the targets. We still had to fly into the flak on a steady course to drop our bombs with any degree of accuracy. Taking flak over the target was the most stressful of all our operations. The end of war statistics showed that more bombers were lost due to enemy flak than to enemy fighter action. The net result of the decrease in bomber losses was that the number of missions was steadily increased over time.

"As I mentioned earlier, when we arrived in May 1944, the number of missions we had to fly was up to thirty. Well, that was an accepted fact, and everyone set his mind on the number thirty. Each crewman was in the countdown mode right after the first mission. To quicken the countdown, some individuals even volunteered to fly with other crews when their regular crew wasn't flying. Our bombardier, Fielding Washington, missed two missions with us when he was ordered to attend navigator school. To make up the two missions lost, he volunteered to fly as a waist gunner on two missions with another crew. What upset the apple cart was when the commanding general added one more mission to the count and then another and another. Before we had reached thirty-one, we were required to fly thirty-five missions. The sum total of those decisions was a serious breakdown in flight crew morale, and the onset of debilitating stress that led to many being disqualified for combat duty and sent to rehabilitation centers for treatment. Our crew was no exception. I lost three members of my crew to debilitating stress, and Dee was one of them.

"Dealing with stress was also an individual thing. Dee dealt with his personal stress with his wonderful sense of humor, which in a way, helped us all. As I mentioned earlier, he was the *court jester* of the crew. Almost everyone drank too much and smoked too much. These were, of course, only a temporary diversion from reality, and we had an almost unlimited supply of both.

"In retrospect, I can also sympathize with the Eighth Air Force Command. They were under tremendous pressure to get the war over with, and often had to make unpopular decisions, and, after all, they did get the job done."

I asked Colonel Fusion why was it that with all the responsibility he had as CO that he did not succumb to the pressures. He thought for a moment before responding.

"First of all, I was so busy doing my job that I didn't have time to think about it and, secondly, up to that point in my life, I had not yet learned to cry.

The last four missions, according to Fielding Washington's bombardier reports were:

(1) on October 30, 1944, to an oil refinery at Harburg, Germany, (2) on November 4, 1944, to an oil refinery at Misburg, Germany, (3) on November 5, 1944, to a canal at Minden, Germany and (4) on November 10, 1944, to an Air Base at Hanau, Germany.

Pilot - Retired Lt. Colonel Frank C. Fuson, Jr.

"During one of these four missions, and I don't remember exactly which of the remaining four it was, we came the closest to being killed than any of us had experienced during all the time we had been flying together, including our crash landing in France. Strangely as it may sound, enemy flak over the target or German fighters played no part in the incident. In fact, the incident occurred on our return flight to Horsham. The weather during the month of November 1944 in England and Europe was not good for bombing or flying. The sky over the targets and that of our home field at Horsham were under a constant overcast, making flight operations very dangerous. Thirteen days in November were stand-down days due to bad weather. On the particular day in question, we were on our way across the English Channel heading home from our mission. The weather was very bad, and we had quite a few planes in the air flying in formation to our right, left and above us. As I often did during bad weather, I had Dee position himself between the pilot and co-pilot seats as an extra pair of eyes. He was an extra lookout, so to speak. The weather was so bad that the group had to continuously lower its altitude to stay below the cloud cover to see where we were heading. As we approached the English coastline we couldn't have been more than a few hundred feet above the water of the English Channel, flying in broken clouds and fog. As we passed over the English coastline and broke out of a fog bank, suddenly Dee shouted out, 'TOWERS AT 12 O'CLOCK,' pointing directly ahead of us with his arm fully extended. There they were as big as life itself," said Fuson. "I had only one choice of direction to choose from, and that was to pull up and try to fly over them. As I nosed the plane upward and increased power we immediately ran into a cloud, and I lost sight of the towers. To make things worse, I lost some of my instruments when the Picot tube froze up. This meant I had no altimeter or speed indicator. I quickly reached up above my head on the instrument panel and turned on the Picot tube heater to defrost it. My instruments were restored within a few seconds, although it seemed like an eternity, but I still had no idea where I was in relationship to the other planes in the formation or to the towers. I just kept climbing, hoping I would not hit the towers or one of the other planes in the formation. Thankfully, by sheer luck, we avoided both. After leveling off, I spotted a nearby airfield. I had Dee radio Horsham to tell them that we were landing the plane at another airfield and I would see them tomorrow. We landed safely, and I got a room at the BOQ and went to sleep. That's how I handled the stress of that incident.

"After thirty-one missions, Dee and two others of my crew were removed from the active combat flying schedule with extreme stress symptoms and sent home for rehabilitation. Some of us went on to fly thirty-five missions before leaving the European Theater of Operations in January of 1945.

"During the nearly nine months of combat, the original crew of the Bad Girl had flown fifteen different B-24 bombers. Of the fifteen planes flown, six survived the war, one was lost over Germany, one was lost over France and seven were lost in crashes in England. We were involved in only one of those incidents –that, of course, was when we crash-landed in France. Not one of our crew was killed, wounded or hurt. Indeed, we had a lot to be thankful for when it was all over," Fuson said thankfully.

As I read the letters that Dee had written home to his family and friends, I could detect the progressive changes in Dee's state of mind as he was engaged in the thirty-one missions from June 14, 1944 through November of 1944. Excerpts from these letters, courtesy of Julia Czerenda, Dee's niece and daughter of Dee's sister Aida, follow:

Letter written to family on June 14, 1944, the day of his first mission. (8 Days after D-Day)

Dearest Mom, Dad, Aida and Sadie,

I am now sitting at my dayroom where we write letters and so forth. I have now been over enemy territory and it's sure thrilling. The first time I was over enemy territory I was scared to death but a guy gets used to it I guess. If you ever see the movie <u>Memphis Belle</u>, you can see what I go through but I can not tell you. I sure hope that this war is over soon so we can all come home again. Occupied Europe seems to be very peaceful to me but it really isn't when you get near places where you should not be as far as they (Germans) are concerned.

I went to a show a couple of nights ago and it was the USO from the U.S.A. building up our morale. They are sure doing a good job, so always donate to the Red Cross and USO. I want you all to for my sake.

Letter written to family on July 1, 1944 after completing several missions.

Dearest Mom and Dad,

Just a few lines to let you know that everything is going okay. I just got paid and I am going to send you $75.00 this month as I do not need it at all. Please use this money on buying new dining room furniture or a new car or something but don't go put it right in the bank as I want you to use it for several things. Honest Dad, I want to come home with nice new furniture and things like that so we can all enjoy them together. Money doesn't mean anything to me, but seeing that you are all happy means more to me.

Letter written to family on July 9, 1944.

Dearest Mom and Dad,

………..Mom, if it is possible send me a nice St. Mary's medal with a chain to wear around my neck. I lost my other one so I carry my Rosary Beads on every mission which is just as good.

According to Catholic legend, Mary appeared to St. Catherine Laboure in Paris and asked to have a medal made in honor of her Immaculate Conception. Mary promised that all who wear it will receive great graces.

Letter written to family on July 21, 1944.

Dearest Mom and Dad,

Mom and Dad when I come home I have an experience that will make you really listen. I have never been through anything like that before but it is a good thing to go through I guess.

Letter written to family on July 28, 1944.

Dearest Mom and Dad,

Just a few lines to let you know I am now on a two day pass and will not have a chance to write you for a few days or so. It really is wonderful to get a pass so you can rest in peace without having someone waking us up at all times and say, You are now wanted at – for a certain reason.

Mom, I have finally found a nice family in town here and every time I go to town they always invite me to their house and I have loads of fun. They have a daughter 20 years old and she is very nice. She is married to a British soldier and I just kid the heck out of her. I promised to get her some good American lipstick. So send me in your next package a couple of tubes of lipstick and she said to make it an orange shade. The girls over here can't get anything so I will do them that favor in return for showing me and my buddy a good time at their home.

Letter written to family on July 30, 1944.

Dearest Mom and Dad,

Today is Sunday and I am going to go to confession so I can receive Communion today. We all think a great deal of our new Priest as he is forever cheering us up and he insists that we go to church.

I haven't heard from anyone for a few days and it is very hard to think of stuff to write. I thought when I came back from my two day pass I would have loads of mail but no such luck.

Letter written to family on August 6, 1944.

………I have been receiving mail from you regularly and I cannot say how happy I am to receive mail. I received a Pawling newspaper today for the first time and it really was good to see the old home town paper. It really had a lot about Dewey in it but he came from the home town so I will excuse it this time.

Things are really going good over here now as you know. The Yanks are really on the move and hope the hell we have Paris real soon. When I come home I will tell you some real good stories about the war.

Daddy, I really have a lot to tell you after I see you again and you will really be surprised to hear some of these things.

Letter written to family on August 24, 1944

Dearest Mom and Dad,

I now have 19 missions to my credit and keep praying that I finish all of my missions without any trouble to anyone of our crew.

Letter written to family on September 1, 1944.

Dearest Mom and Dad,

Mom, I still have 21 missions to my credit but hope to put in a few more soon. I hope you are all going to church lately as it makes me feel much safer.

Letter written to family on October 4, 1944.

Dear Mom & Pop,

Thanks a million for praying that me and crew finish our missions without any trouble at all. I only have 8 more missions to go and I will be finished.

Tell Aida or Sadie to light a candle in the church every Sunday for me as it makes me feel much better. This war really makes a guy religious if he wasn't before he got overseas.

Letter written to family on October 10, 1944.

Dearest Family,

............I now have 24 missions to my credit and have 7 more to go. Don't forget to keep praying and lighting candles that we finish soon and in the best of health. I now have another Oak Leaf Cluster to my credit so that makes three Oak Leaf Clusters to my Air Medal so I feel prouder each day. I guess I don't deserve any of it, but who cares so long as I get home some day.

Letter written to family on Oct. 13, 1944.

Dearest Mom and Dad,

............I now have twenty-five missions to my credit as I put one in yesterday. Just keep praying that the Dearest Lord continues to guide our lives as he has and we will come home in the next 6 to 8 months. It is almost sure we won't be home before next February so don't be disappointed if you don't see me sooner. I am sending you a Sacred Heart medal I bought in church last Sunday so have it blessed and have someone in the family wear it around.

Letter written to family on Oct. 17, 1944.
Dearest Mom and Dad,

............I don't know whether or not I told you that I now have 26 missions to my credit. I put my last one in over Cologne but I guess you read all about it in the daily news. I have six (6) more missions to go and I will be finished with my tour but I guess it will be ages before I get to come home. I hope you are doing me the big favor and inviting a couple of soldiers to dinner each Sunday as they would appreciate it.

Letter written to family on October 27, 1944. (Letter after crash landing in France)
Dearest Mom and Dad,

I still have five (5) missions to go so it will be ages before I finish. Don't forget to keep praying that our whole crew finishes all of our missions soon and in the best of health. We all keep our fingers crossed as we are very close to finishing. The Lord had really guided us so far and hope he continues. Mom and Dad, after I come home you will never have to worry about your son going to church. I will never miss Mass under any condition. I am not kidding one bit either.

Letter written to friends at home in Pawling, on October 27, 1944. (Letter after crash Landing in France)
Dear Friends,

I now have 27 missions to my credit and have only four (4) to go and I will be finished. Don't forget to pray that I finish all of my missions in the best of health. I just can't wait to see that good old U.S.A. On my last mission we crashed landed in France so I visited some more of

France. Brussels is also a very nice place. If I only knew Mr. Fynant's address I could have visited his family there as we were in no hurry to getting back to England.

We are all wishing the war is over soon so we can come home for Xmas and New Years. No one can realize how lonesome a fellow gets after being away from home so long.

Letter written to family on Nov. 5, 1944. (Letter after crash landing in France)

Dearest Mom and Dad,

Well Mom and Dad, I now have twenty-eight (28) missions to my credit and only three (3) more to go. The Lord is still guarding my crew's life. I hope it continues as we haven't got much further to go and we will be finished. Don't forget to keep lighting a candle for me in church each Sunday and I will be home next May, I hope.

Letter written Nov. 18, 1944. (Letter after crash landing in France)

Dearest Mom, Pop, and Sisters,

I have been so happy lately that I wasn't able to write you a letter and let you in on some very good news. I have completed my tour of missions and was awarded the Distinguished Flying Cross. Honest, no one knows how it feels to be relieved from combat. It is no joke to get up nearly every morning at three o'clock and prepare for a mission. One of my raids it was 46 below zero, so it is good to get away from that. I will not be coming home for at least six months or more so don't get crazy. There is no use in getting home to soon or I would be in the South Pacific before you could say, Boo. As long as Jerry never gets another shot at me, I don't care.

Don't forget to say a nice prayer of thanks to God in church this Sunday but continue to light candles for me. If it wasn't for the Lord, I would never have been so lucky.

Your loving Son, Emilio

For their combat achievements, the original members of the crew of the Bad Girl were awarded the Air Medal with three Oak Leaf Clusters, the Distinguished Flying Cross and the European, African, and Middle Eastern Service medals.

A sketch of the lives of the crew of the *Bad Girl* after WWII had ended and their return to the United States.

Pilot – 1st Lt. Frank C. Fuson Jr.

After completing thirty-five missions in January 1945, Pilot, 1st Lt. Frank C. Fuson Jr., returned to the U.S. and made a career in the USAF. He served in the USAF for twenty-two years, many of which were as a pilot in the Strategic Air Command, flying mid-air refueling tankers for B-52s. He attained the rank of Lt. Colonel prior to retirement in 1964.

In 1954 he met Naoma Coleman while stationed at Lubbock, Texas. They married on January 9, 1955. Over the ensuing years they raised two sons.

In 1965 he entered the University of Oklahoma in Norman, Oklahoma and graduated with a B.S. Degree in Education and a M.S. degree in the Natural Sciences. He served as a High School Science Teacher until his retirement in 1985. In addition, for many years he and his brother operated a peanut farm near their hometown of Wellington, Texas. He passed away on July 22, 2007, at his home in Norman, Oklahoma.

Co-Pilot - 1st Lieutenant William J. Kotowitz.

After completing thirty-five missions in January 1945, Co-pilot, 1st Lt. William J. Kotowitz, returned to the U.S. and was discharged. He became a successful businessman with a major steel company, married and raised a family.

Bombardier – 1st Lt. Fielding Washington.

After completing thirty-five missions in January 1945, Bombardier 1st Lt. Fielding Washington, returned to the U.S. After being discharged he married Jacqueline Young on May 23, 1945.

He attended George Washington University School of Law and received his Law Degree in 1949. He practiced law in Washington D.C. for one year, and then in 1950 he rejoined the Air Force as a Military Lawyer with the branch of the Judge Advocate General. He retired from the USAF in 1971 with the rank of Lt. Colonel. Upon retirement he founded his own law firm in Sequin, Texas and practiced law until 1991. He and Jacqueline had one child, their daughter Jacqueline.

Crew Chief - Staff Sergeant Ulgers B. Simoneaux.

Crew Chief, Staff Sergeant U.B. Simoneaux completed thirty-five missions in January of 1945 and returned to the U.S. and was discharged. U.B. picked up where he left off before the war. He started and operated a very successful sugar cane plantation in Louisiana. On May 4, 1947, he married Opal Kern and together they raised a daughter and four sons.

Navigator, 1st Lt. William S. Jamerson.

1st Lt. William S. Jamerson returned to the U.S. after completing thirty-five missions and was discharged. He immediately enrolled in law school at the University of Texas and graduated in 1948 with his law degree. During this same period of time he served as a member of the Texas House of Representatives from one of the El Paso legislative districts. He joined the USAF Reserve and served with the Troop Carrier Squadron from 1945-1966 and retired as a Major.

Technical Sergeant Emilio "Dee" DaBramo and his life-long friend 1st Lt. William Jamerson. (Courtesy of Dee DaBramo)

He was in private law practice in San Saba, Texas from 1949 to 1956 and was elected Mayor of San Saba. In 1956 he was employed by the Southern Union Gas Company and served as staff attorney until 1971.

In 1961, he married his wife Maurice, and they were married for 37 years. In 1972 he was employed by Supron Energy Corporation and served as Vice President and General Counsel until he retired in 1982. He died on March 29, 1998 in Dallas, Texas.

"Before Bill died," said Dee, "I visited him at his home in Dallas. He had had a major stroke and was incapacitated in a wheelchair. We spent our time talking and talking. Most of what we talked about was our time together in the Army Air Corps and all the hell we went through and survived it all. 'Look at me now,' he would say, 'after all we went through and I should end up like this. I can't even walk.' His spirits were quite low at that time and I was deeply saddened with his condition. That was the last time I spoke to him. God bless his soul. When Bill passed away, I attended his funeral in Dallas, Texas."

An Army Air Force, Lt. Colonel, presenting Technical Sergeant Emilio DaBramo with Distinguished Flying Cross on November 11, 1944. (Courtesy of Dee DaBramo)

As author, Tom Brokaw wrote in his book, <u>The Greatest Generation,</u>

1998, "They came of age during the Great Depression and the Second World War and went on to build modern America--men and women whose everyday lives of duty, honor, achievement, and courage gave us the world we have today."

The men of the Bad Girl can aptly be identified with the Greatest Generation that author Tom Brokaw has described so well.

CHAPTER 5

Homecoming

CHAPTER 5
Homecoming

Back in Stone House and Pawling in 1944, an aura of uncertainty prevailed over the community as the war dragged on. The local newspaper published the events of the war daily, along with comings and goings of the community members of the Armed Forces and, of course, the casualties. But life in the main went on as usual, untouched by the ravages of war.

"On a day-to-day basis my crewmates and I were unsure of what was in store for us as we continued flying our combat missions not knowing if we would survive the next mission or not," said Dee. "Several of my friends had already paid the ultimate price of war. Three were high school teammates. Private First Class Benjamin D. Utter was killed in action in the Italy campaign in August of 1944, and is remembered with his name on the bronze plaque in the Pawling town square, as is the name of my other teammate Jack Holiday who was killed in the sinking of the U.S. Navy Destroyer, the *USS Jacob Jones, DD 393*, by a German submarine off the coast of New Jersey on February 28, 1942. My friend Francis Sprague joined the Merchant Marines after graduation in June of 1943 and was reported killed in action in April of 1944. Since he was a merchant seaman, his name does not appear on the bronze plaque in the Pawling town square honoring the dead of WWII. It was as if merchant seamen hadn't put their lives on the line like the rest of the men who died serving their country in the Armed Forces. It was a very saddening thought, knowing that when I returned home I would never again be able to enjoy their company and play the game of baseball with them. Two other friends who served in the air war over Europe did survive with me.

Eugene Frink and Louis Francis Taney were shot down over Germany and spent several years in a German Stalag."

Dee's boyhood friend Louis Francis Taney, U.S. Army Air Corps was shot down over Europe and became a prisoner of war in Germany. (Courtesy of Dee DaBramo)

The people of Stone House and Pawling were probably more aware of the cost of the war, in human terms, than most communities. It was kept fresh in their minds by the omni-presence of hundreds of living casualties of the Army Air Corps personnel that were housed and cared for at the Army Air Corps Convalescent and Rehabilitation Center in Pawling. The main physical facilities of the Center were located at the private boys prep school, known before the war as the Pawling Boys School and today as the Trinity-Pawling School. At the beginning of the war the school was commandeered by the Army Air Corps and was used as a Technical Training Center. Later in the war it was converted to a Convalescent and Rehabilitation Center. In addition, the nearby Green Mountain Lake Farms, then a holiday camp for Consolidated Edison employees, became part of the Center and were used to house single officer patients. Today it is a YMCA Conference and Vacation Center, owned and operated by the YMCA of Greater New York.

Pawling Boys School before WWII. It was commandeered by the U.S. Government and converted, first, to a technical training center and later to a Convalescent and Rehabilitation Center for returning wounded Airmen from WWII. The School is known today as the Trinity-Pawling School. (Courtesy of Trinity-Pawling School).

The July 17, 1944 issue of Life Magazine explains the function of the Center.

AIRMEN CONVALESCE

To speed the recovery of its casualties, the U.S. Army Air Force has enlisted the therapeutic power of life in the open country. At Pawling (Thomas Dewey's hometown), the AAF has taken over 700 acres of rolling Dutchess County land, including the grounds and buildings of a private prep school. Here it has set up a Center for convalescent airmen who no longer require formal hospital treatment. Coming from the indoor doldrums of hospitals, the patients get a tremendous boost toward recovery simply by being given the run of a place equipped with tennis courts, bridle paths, trout streams and a full bucolic roster of cows, chickens, pigs, barns, farmland and gardens. More than 90% of Pawling's patients return to active duty, physically and psychologically restored. Set up as an experiment, the Center has made such a good record that it may become the model for a whole group of similar institutions across the U.S.

"Our thirty-first mission over Hanau Air Base in Germany on November 10, 1944 was my last," said Dee. "The crash landing in France during our twenty-seventh mission flown on October 17, 1944 and the succeeding four missions had taken their toll on me. I had the constant image in my mind that I was falling out of the sky, like the crewmen I saw dropping like rag dolls from their downed planes during the disastrous raid over St. Lo, France. I had no control over it. My medical report read as follows:

> *Anxiety state chronic. Mild transient IMS manifested by tremors, insomnia, restlessness, tenseness and emotional instability. Extended precipitaltery stress, moderate. 31 missions as radio operator on bomber including one crash. Predisposition, no disability. Prognosis good.*

"I was temporarily removed from flight status and was never authorized to return. I spent the remainder of November and December 1944 at Horsham. One of my last memories of Horsham was Thanksgiving Day 1944, and the thousands of my fellow airmen waiting in line for a traditional American turkey dinner.

The chow line for Thanksgiving dinner November, 1944 at the Eighth Air Force base at Horsham, England. (Courtesy of Dee DaBramo)

"On January 8, 1945, I boarded an Army transport ship for home, the name of which I don't remember," Dee told me. "But I do remember it was loaded with hundreds, if not thousands, of walking wounded. It was during this trip that I realized how lucky I was to return home in one piece. The sixteen-day voyage home with a thousand or more wounded men did not do much for my emotional state of affairs. Our ship docked at Pier 51 in New York City Harbor on January 25, 1945. I did not inform my family that I was coming home. This act of lack of concern for them, I am sure, was the result of my emotional state of mind."

From the Sandy Hook Pilot's Day Logs I discovered that the ship that Dee arrived home on was the *USS Mount Vernon AP-22*. The day and time of the ship's arrival matched perfectly with Dee's account. The log read as follows:

> *On January 25, 1945 at 2300 hours pilot A.G. Peterson boarded AP-22, the Mount Vernon, at Sandy Hook and piloted it into New York Harbor where it was received at Pier 51, North River.*

According to the January 25, 1945 issue of the <u>New York Times</u>, the day of Dee's arrival in New York City, the city had just endured a heavy snowfall a few days prior to his arrival and was in the throes of removing the snow with 8,000 employees and 700 pieces of equipment out on the streets. The forecast for the day was: Partly cloudy today, highest temperature near 36 degrees, fresh to strong winds.

On Broadway *Carmen Jones* was playing at the Broadway Theater, and at the Metropolitan Opera House, Mozart's *The Magic Flute* was being performed. At the Roxy Movie Theater *Sunday Dinner for a Soldier*, starring Ann Baxter and John Hodiak, was showing. On stage at the Café Zanzibar Revue were Bill Robinson, Maurice Rocco, The Delta Rhythm Boys and Louis Armstrong and his Orchestra. *Billy Rose Presents 7 Lively Arts* was playing at the Ziegfeld Theater, starring Bert Lahr, Beatrice Lillie, Benny Goodman and Anton Dolan. New York City was in full swing in spite of the war.

None of these New York City bright light amenities attracted Dee's attention. He was dead set on getting home to Stone House to see his Mom, Dad and sisters Aida and Sadie. Dee slept aboard ship that night since it was early in the morning when the ship finally docked.

"As I can best recall," said Dee, "my orders allowed me a twenty-five day furlough and then I was to report to the Army Air Corps hospital at Atlantic City, New Jersey on or about February 20, 1945.

"My main objective was to get home to Stone House to see my family and my girl friend," said Dee. "I did, however, make a short visit to Dr. Haberman and his wife Bess at their Manhattan apartment. Dr. Haberman and his wife were good friends of our family. For many years my father was their groundskeeper at their summer home at Whaley Lake. When I was old enough I would work there with my father. Dr. Haberman took it upon himself to provide the DaBramo family with free dental care during those many years, and we became close friends. They were surprised, if not shocked to see me, since I had not called them in advance. They opened their hearts to me and made me feel at home. After an hour or two, I said my goodbyes and left their apartment for Grand Central Terminal in downtown Manhattan to catch a train home to Pawling."

"It was Bess Haberman who later described Dee's state of anxiety and stress during his short visit to their Manhattan apartment," said Sadie.

"Dee had great difficulty concentrating and jumped from one subject to another," said Bess. "While sitting on the sofa he was constantly fidgeting with the lace doily on the arm of the chair with his fingers. All signs pointed to him being in a state of great anxiety and stress."

"When I arrived at the N.Y. Central Railroad Terminal I bumped into a high school friend of mine from Pawling," Dee said. "She was as surprised to see me as much as I was to see her."

"I didn't know you were coming home," she told me.

"I just arrived by ship to New York City from overseas," I told her. "I wanted to keep it a secret so I could surprise everyone," I confessed.

"Then I asked her how my girlfriend was. Unbeknownst to her, she dropped a bomb on me. She told me that the girl whom I had been dating before I left for the Army, had become engaged to be married about a month before my return. I was devastated at the news, and I could feel tears welling up in my eyes, which I struggled to fight back. I didn't know what to say, so I broke off the conversation by telling her that I had to catch a train. In retrospect, I know now that my heartbreak emotions were a product of the anxiety and stress conditions that I was experiencing at the time. When my girlfriend and I parted after my Christmas furlough in December of 1943, we had not committed ourselves to each other. Certainly I had been dating other women during my sixteen months of training and nine months in Norwich, England. I was also a poor letter writer, which didn't encourage a binding relationship either. She had been dating other men as well. She had been working as a nurse at the Air Corps Convalescent Center in Pawling and met a patient with whom she fell in love. Nevertheless, for whatever reason, I was devastated and feeling pretty sorry for myself which brought me to tears."

The following excerpt of a letter, dated Novermber 1, 1944 from Dee's former girlfriend confirms their breakup, which Dee, in his state of anxiety, seemed to have forgotten or refused to acknowledge. (Letter courtesy of Julia Czerenda)

> *Dear Emilio,*
> *..........As I said in my last letter, I was getting smarter. Well Dee, I'm through, (and have been for some time), trying to make myself believe you ever really loved me. I realize now that you are still, and always have loved XXXXXXX. Well, I think it's wonderful. I expect to see you two together a lot when you return. She is a lovely girl. I know by now you must have heard that I am or have been going with XXXXXXX.*

I met him last May at the USO but we have been going together since the June prom.

"I have no recollection of the time I spent on the train ride to Pawling," said Dee. "The train arrived at the Pawling station early in the afternoon. I do remember that the weather was cold and blustery as I stood on the corner, where, when I was a kid, I stood hundreds of times to hitch a ride home from Pawling High School after practice. There I was in full uniform with tears in my eyes, my B-4 bag at my feet and my thumb out looking for a ride over the mountain to Stone House and home. The first car that came along stopped and offered me a lift.

"Where ya headed, soldier?"

"To Stone House," I replied.

"Throw your bag in the back seat and hop in," he offered with a broad smile that reflected his pleasure to be of service.

"The depth of my despair manifested itself in uncontrollable tears that flowed from my eyes. Crying in those days was not a manly thing and crying in front of another man was even less manly."

"What's wrong, my friend?" he asked with a saddened look on his face and a tone of voice that expressed sincere sympathy.

"I opened up immediately and told him I just returned from overseas and was on my way home to see my family who had no inkling of my coming, and that I had learned that my girlfriend had become engaged to be married just a month or so ago. I don't remember his reply to my tearful confession, but I suspect it was sympathetic.

"The ride from Pawling to Stone House was only five miles, and before I knew it I was home."

"You're home, son," was the next thing I remember the kind gentleman saying, as he slowed his car to a stop in front of my parent's house.

"I got out of the car, retrieved my B-4 bag from the back seat and shook his hand through the opened window and thanked him. He drove off and I stood there at the side of the road for a moment with bag-in-hand, made sure my tears were wiped from my face, composed myself, conjured up a smile and bounced up the porch stairs, two steps at a time, to the front door. I knocked briefly to alert those inside that someone was about to enter, pushed open the door and stepped inside. My mother Josephine was the first to see me. She was so overwhelmed with joy that she fainted to the floor before anyone else could break her fall. They revived my mother and the whole family welcomed me with open arms and with tears of love and joy in their eyes. Mom recovered from her shock and wasted little time in preparing one of her well-known Italian feasts, and we all sat around the table and ate, drank my father's home-made red Italian wine and talked for hours. I did learn that my mother had been quite ill a few months prior to my arrival and was in a weakened condition. This, of course, concerned me and the suggestion was made that perhaps I could convalesce at the Pawling Center instead of elsewhere to be near her.

"Later that evening I retrieved my 1931 DeSoto Coupe that my father had been caring for during my absence, and drove into Pawling to round up some of my friends. It didn't take long to find them and we partied most of the night."

"The bond between my brother Dee and my mother was very strong," said Dee's sister Sadie. "I'm sure that if Dee had been killed in the war she would have died of a heart attack. She had suffered the tragic loss of her brother, whom she loved dearly, when she was a kid. One summer he and two of his friends drowned in a river near her family home in Italy while taking a swim break from tending their sheep. The memory of her agony and that of her mother still burned deeply in her mind's eye.

"When Dee came home in January of 1945, my sister Aida was a month from turning eighteen and I was sixteen years old," remarked Sadie. At our ages we were quite aware of what was going on around us and I remember how my brother dealt with his anxiety and stress. Our home was small and Dee's room was next to Aida's and mine. At night we could hear him stirring restlessly in bed and sometimes crying out in a state of terror. This occurred frequently during the days he was home on furlough. At first, he also had difficulty remembering some of his friends that he had known all his life."

"While on furlough, I spent a lot of my time partying with my friends, most of whom were veterans home on leave," Dee confessed. "We were all using booze as a cover-up for our state of anxiety and stress. In fact, this behavior was a continuation of my well-learned behavior practiced in Norwich, England, to cope with combat stress.

"I also managed to inquire into the facilities at the Pawling Convalescent Center that was operated by the Army Air Corps, in hopes that I might one day be transferred there for rehab.

"Two notable events occurred during my furlough. The first was the family's celebration of Aida's eighteenth birthday on February 7, and the second was my twenty-second birthday on February 17. On many occasions, during my time in England, I had doubts that I would ever survive to celebrate my twenty-second birthday.

"On the twentieth of February, I arrived at the Atlantic City, New Jersey hospital and was given a thorough physical and psychiatric exam. With the exception of my poor state of anxiety and stress, I was found to be in good physical health. Citing the poor health of my dear mother, I took the opportunity to request a transfer to the Pawling Convalescent Center. My request was granted on February 27 and I was admitted at the Pawling Center on March 2, 1945. I was home to stay.

"The routine at the Pawling Center was simple enough. I was required to be on the site most of the day, but was free to leave in the afternoon. I attended various therapy sessions on a regular basis and was encouraged to participate in all of the planned social and sporting events. One of the things I enjoyed most was playing baseball, since it was one of my favorite sports at which I excelled. As usual I played hard, and according to my medical record, on June 13, 1945, I fractured my left ankle while running the bases. This put me out of action for a short while."

"Although it was nice having Dee at home again," Sadie recalled, "it was not the best thing for him. The problem with the situation," she went on to say, "was that Dee was home with his cronies, the guys he grew up with, some of whom were returning veterans like him, and the new friends he made at the Center with whom he spent a lot of time in the local bars. Not only did they drink a lot, they were drunk a good part of the time. This situation did not escape the notice of my parents and especially our mother."

"I was interned at the Pawling Center for about six months," said Dee. "During these six months three extraordinary historical events occurred. The first event occurred on April 12, 1945. On that day, President Franklin Delano Roosevelt died of a cerebral hemorrhage while visiting Warm Springs, Georgia. My family and I and most of my friends were stunned and shocked by his death. He was our Commander and Chief, and we felt the loss deeply.

"The second event of great historical significance occurred on May 8, 1945. On that day we celebrated VE Day, (Victory in Europe) signifying the unconditional surrender of the Axis powers in Europe. I felt a deep sense of pride when I heard the news."

The records from the USAF Museum summed up the cost of the European air campaign.

The air offensive conducted by the AAF in conjunction with the RAF against Germany and Italy was of tremendous value in bringing about victory in Europe with the final defeat of these two nations. It was costly, however, for the AAF losses from all causes totaled 27,694 aircraft, including 8,314 heavy bombers, 1,623 medium bombers and light bombers, and 8,481 fighters destroyed in combat. Total AAF battle casualties were 91,105 personnel –34,362 killed, 13,798 wounded, and 43,035 missing, captured or interned.

"The third event of great historical significance that occurred," Dee remembered, "happened on August 14, 1945. This was the day that the Japanese signed the unconditional surrender document on the deck of the Battleship *Missouri BB-63*. WWII was officially over.

"On September 2, 1945, I was ordered to report to the separation center at Fort Dix, New Jersey and on September 4, 1945, I was honorably discharged from the Army Air Corps. I was once again a civilian and my military life was officially over, but its impact on my life would be everlasting, good and bad. I had served with the best guys I had ever met. We had a camaraderie that has never been duplicated in my civilian life. It is an experience that only the stress and anxiety of combat can produce. In many cases this feeling of camaraderie is the reason why many men make the military a career. In my way of thinking, these experiences can only help make one a better person for having had them.

"In addition to receiving the cherished Honorable Discharge Certificate, I was also made the recipient of $406.85 in mustering-out pay. Little did I realize at the time that this money would help me launch a whole new life. My level of anxiety and stress at the time I was discharged was, in my estimation, moderately reduced. The nightmares continued, however, and on occasion, even today, sixty or more years later, they occasionally occur.

"During the six months at the Pawling Center, I had not given much thought to my future. I was just having fun with lots of time on my hands and money in my pocket. It was at this time that my poor mother had had enough of my drinking antics. One morning she found me asleep on the front porch, fully clothed, where in the early morning hours I had passed out drunk in my own vomit. She was bound and determined to do something about my behavior. The next day she ran into the one person outside our family that she knew might still have some influence on me. That someone was my former high school principal, Mr. Earle Norton. In her Italian accent she spoke to him with a sense of desperation in her voice, 'My- a- son Emilio has become a bum. He drinks too much and is always drunk. Before he went into the Army he was-a- nice-a- boy, now he's a bum. Can you talk some sense into him?' she pleaded.

"Now, Mr. Norton, as Principal, was no one to fool with," said Dee. "He had conditioned me to respond to him in a positive way when, as a student at Pawling High School, he more than once took me on trips to the boiler room for some behavior modification with the rubber hose. So, when he called me and asked me to meet with him at his office at the school, I responded without hesitation. Can you imagine me, a grown man and a WWII veteran, responding in this way? I did exactly that. I had a great deal of respect for him and liked him very much. I knew that if he wanted to talk to me, it was going to be in my best interest. Now, mind you, I had no idea my mother had talked to him. I found that out after-the-fact many years later.

"The meeting with Mr. Norton was a cordial one. He greeted me with a hardy handshake and praised me for my military accomplishments and courage. He was genuinely proud of one of his ex-students, and it showed sincerely on his face. We sat down together, and he began to question me."

"Dee, what plans do you have for your life now that you have been discharged?"

"I hemmed and hawed around for a few seconds, trying to think of an appropriate answer, but in the final analysis I had to admit that I had no idea what I wanted to do for the rest of my life. Mr. Morton listened intently to my spiel, but of course, from his experience in dealing with thousands of young adults during his career, he most likely deduced what my final answer would be before the truth spewed from my mouth."

"I really don't know," I told him.

"Well," he uttered, "have you ever thought about becoming a gym teacher? With all your success as an athlete in soccer, baseball and basketball during your years at Pawling High, I think it would be a natural profession for you," he said with sincerity.

"He must be kidding," I thought to myself. "My high school average of just above 65 % was not going to get me into College--no way."

"What do you think?" he pressed on looking me straight in the eye.

"I knew he was looking for a decision, and right now. I was taken aback a bit at his suggestion, but pleased in a way that he had confidence in me to suggest it."

"Well," he repeated patiently, "what do you think?"

"I have never given it a thought before, but I like the idea," I told him.

"Good," he responded positively.

"But my grades were barely passing," I blurted out, "and besides, where would I go to college?"

"Dee, that part I think I can handle," he said convincingly. "What you have to do now is make the decision, yes or no," he said as he sat back in his chair with his arms folded, waiting for me to make a decision.

"Yes," I said hopefully.

"Okay then, I'm going to call the president of Cortland State Teachers College to find out if the college will accept you," was his quick response.

"Without hesitation," said Dee, "he picked up the phone and dialed the president of Cortland State Teachers College, Dr. Donnal V. Smith. He introduced himself to the president as the Principal of Pawling High School."

"Dr. Smith, I have here in my office the first boy from our high school that has been discharged from the Army Air Corps."

"I'll never forget the phrase he used to describe me, as the first boy from our high school," Dee said with a chuckle.

"Mr. Norton explained to the president that I was a decorated veteran who was just discharged from the Army Air Corps and wanted to attend his college in the physical education program. He listed my athlete accomplishments at Pawling High School and told him that I would make a great gym teacher and coach some day."

"I want to recommend him to you," Mr. Norton went on to say. "Can you tell me what he has to do to enroll at Cortland for the fall semester?"

"As I remember," said Dee, "the two men spoke for several more minutes before Mr. Norton hung up the phone.

"Dee, as of this moment you are a college freshman," he said with an enthusiastic smile. "The president said you should report to Cortland in four days and you will be the thirty-fifth G.I. to register for the fall semester."

"Mr. Norton then went on to explain to me all about the financial benefits of the G.I. Bill, recently passed by Congress, to insure that veterans were given an opportunity to better themselves with a college education. He also told me that Cortland College provided free tuition to all their students. The projected post war need for new teachers in the state of New York was enormous. To meet this need the New York State Legislature responded to the crisis with legislation that provided free tuition for qualified students attending the eleven state teachers colleges.

"Everything happened so fast that I felt I was caught up in a whirlwind. It took awhile for the events of that meeting to sink in, but as soon as it did, I felt relieved that a major decision had been made, not necessarily by me, but for me. Mr. Norton was a clever man. He was also a strong authority figure in my life, and I feared I dared not cross him. Later in life I often wondered if the whole deal wasn't a setup. Had he indeed called Dr. Smith for the first time on that day, in my presence, or were all the arrangements for admitting me to the college made beforehand and the only deciding factor was my decision to say yes or no? Whatever the truth was, it really didn't matter. The fact of it all was it changed my life forever.

"I naturally had some apprehension about attending college, but was ready for the challenge. The challenge, I thought, couldn't be any greater than what I had already endured. Self-confidence was one of the great benefits I obtained from my military service. I no longer exhibited the characteristic of the petulant kid. I'm sure Mr. Norton and the college officials realized that I was now a mature and responsible individual.

When Dee got home that afternoon he told his mother, father and sisters about the meeting with Mr. Norton.

"He literally picked up the phone and called the president of the college right there while I was sitting in his office," he said, "and I don't have to take an entrance exam or anything. My family was delighted, especially my mother, who had tears in her eyes after I made the announcement. I am sure she was pleased with herself as well, having been the one that initiated the whole affair when she spoke to Mr. Norton days earlier. She used her inherent instinct of a birth mother to do something to protect the future of one of her children. Michael, my father, was equally as proud, for he had accomplished one of his long-time goals regarding the education of his children. In June, my sister Aida had graduated from Pawling High School with honors, and had been accepted at Albany State

Teachers College to study to be a Latin and mathematics teacher. Now my father had two of his three children in college. Sadie, the youngest of his daughters, would be entering her senior year at Pawling High School.

"I didn't have much time to get ready to leave for Cortland. It was the fifth of September 1945, and I had to be there on the ninth of September. I remember my sister Sadie taking money from her savings and buying me two suits to take to college. She had a heart of gold. Everyone in the family was scurrying around, in an atmosphere of hope and great joy, getting me ready to leave for college. I was finally ready to go with $406.85 in mustering-out-pay in my pocket, the security of knowing I had the G.I. Bill to live on and free tuition, books and fees at Cortland State Teachers College. Everything was tilted in my favor. Now, the rest was up to me. My task was to study hard and pass my courses and get my degree."

CHAPTER 6

A New Beginning

CHAPTER 6
A New Beginning

By mid-August 1945, World War II was over and the U.S. Armed Forces were beginning the process of downsizing. The first wave of WWII veterans entering university would begin in the fall of 1945. For the new Cortland College President, Dr. Donnal V. Smith, the timing couldn't have been more perfect. President Smith came to the college in 1943. He was a young man of 42 with ambitious ideas for the growth of the College and the raising of its academic stature. Leonard F. Ralston, author of the book, <u>Cortland College, An Illustrated History</u>, Cortland College Alumni Association, 1991, best explains President Smith's ambitions for the College at that time.

"President Smith faced a pressing need for more students in 1943. Only with a larger student body could he recruit a stronger faculty and expand campus facilities. Obviously the war was partly responsible for the low enrollment, since so many young men had been called into military service. Also responsible for the low enrollment was a 1930s Regents' mandate limiting the number of graduates each year --to only those who could be placed.

"The end of the war in 1945, and the flood of returning servicemen with veteran's benefits, provided Smith with new opportunities to increase enrollment. Smith was happy to welcome the homecoming soldiers to Cortland. The Board of Regents approved a temporary revision of enrollment quotas for the teachers' colleges, and some veterans enrolled as early as the fall semester of 1945."

The ambition of President Smith to expand the college in enrollment and facilities, and the patriotic spirit of the time helps to explain, to a great degree, why Dee and the other thirty-six veterans were readily accepted at Cortland College without having to participate in the usual entrance exam process. But regardless of the reasons for being accepted to the college, these veterans were given an opportunity for a college education, which many, Dee included, may never have had otherwise. Dee has never forgotten how this opportunity came about and how it changed his life forever. Many years later he would introduce a proposal to Cortland College Admissions Department that would provide the opportunity for the admission of marginal students from impoverished neighborhoods and dysfunctional families.

When Dee left home on September 9, 1945 for Cortland to begin his college career, he had no idea of the type of environment he would be entering. His lifestyle during the last six months in the Air Corps, rehabilitating in Pawling, was nothing short of foot-loose and fancy-free. This was about to change.

Cortland College was in a transition period too, with the new president bent on change. Yet some of the old social rules still existed on campus. To illustrate this point, I once again refer to Leonard F. Ralston book, <u>Cortland College, An Illustrated History</u>, Cortland Alumni Association, 1991.

"All women had hours or curfews, regardless of where they lived. Freshmen women were required to be in by 10 p.m. on weekdays. Upper-class women could remain out an hour later on weekdays, but all were required to be in by midnight on Fridays and Sundays, and 1 a.m. on Saturdays. All women had to sign out when going out of the residence after 8 o'clock on any evening. An elaborate set of graduated penalties for repeated violation of curfew hours led to "campusing," or confinement to the residence during evening hours for some period of time. Women wishing to leave the city had to have travel permit forms signed by parents on file and carry cards showing the level of freedom to travel. There were also detailed regulations governing women's dress. Men were almost completely free of the type of restrictions placed on the women. Men were expected to keep "reasonable hours," reasonable being understood as one hour after closing hours for women, but there were no penalties for violations."

In the fall of 1945, the total enrollment at the college, according to Leonard F. Ralston, was 577, with a freshman class of 256. This was the highest enrollment since 1940 when there were 596 students enrolled. Of the 577 enrolled, 514 were women and 63 were men. Of the 63 men, 37 were veterans, while the others were high school graduates or transfers.

Even with a cursory look at the numbers, one can easily see the potential for social conflict. The administration and faculty weren't sure what to expect when the first veterans began to arrive. After all, they were used to dealing with high school graduates, and for the past few years the college was mainly a women's school. Suddenly they were faced with a whole new breed of cat when the veterans arrived on campus. In addition, many young married couples also appeared for the first time. It would be a new challenge for the administration and the faculty to deal with a whole new set of conditions and problems. Never before in the history of Cortland College would the challenges be as demanding and socially fragile as it would be with the influx of a totally new type of student – the WWII veteran.

Trouble at the train station.

"My sister Aida and I would start our college careers at the same time, but at different universities and under radically different circumstances. She was off to Albany State to study to be a mathematics and Latin teacher, and I was off to Cortland to study to be a gym teacher. Of the two of us, you can be sure that she knew more about what college life would be like than I. Her high school academic record was superb, whereas mine was marginal at best. For four years she had been anticipating and planning for the occasion. My planning time was four days.

"On Sunday morning, September 9, 1945, with my mind still spinning in a four-day whirlwind, I bid my family goodbye as I boarded the bus in Pawling for Poughkeepsie, N.Y. and leaving my mother behind in tears of joy. I am sure that in her mind she was saying to herself, 'my son- a is a good- a boy.'

"The twenty-five mile bus ride to Poughkeepsie was uneventful. The scenery along Route 55 held no special interest to me since I had traveled it scores of times before. Thoughts of my impending arrival in Cortland, and what lay ahead for me in the coming weeks, made the trip evaporate in time."

"Poughkeepsie Train Terminal," shouted the bus driver as he approached the terminal.

"This announcement woke me from my thoughtful state, and I grabbed my Army B-4 bag from the overhead rack and exited the bus. The Poughkeepsie to Syracuse leg of my train trip would begin in about 20 minutes. This trip would be my first as a civilian. Without my uniform, with its array of combat ribbons, silver wings and sergeant strips that adorned it, I would be just another nondescript person traveling in civilian clothes. I stepped off the bus and entered the Poughkeepsie train station with some of the other bus passengers and walked straight to the ticket booth to purchase my ticket to Syracuse. While I was engaged in purchasing my ticket, a commotion broke out in the waiting room of the station. At first I didn't pay much attention to it. When I turned from the ticket booth to look for a seat to cool my heels while waiting for the train to depart, I saw the source of the commotion. It was a middle-aged man and a woman shouting at each other. The people in the station took cursory notice of what was going on, but turned away in an obvious attempt to extract themselves from the situation as best they could. They just didn't want to get involved. Well, I didn't either. This was no time for me to involve myself in a situation that might jeopardize my college career, especially since I hadn't gotten there yet. So, I sat down in a seat as far from the fray as I could find. Within seconds after I sat down, the confrontation began to escalate. The man slapped the woman in the face and knocked her down. She got up screaming and crying. As she tried to fight back he hit her again, only this time with his fist. She fell to the floor once again and no one nearby stepped in to help her. Not only did they not get involved, they turned away as if the tragedy wasn't happening. I could feel myself quickly becoming incensed with rage, not only with the guy beating up the woman, but also with the insensitivity and uncaring of the people witnessing the event. My sense of indignation overcame me, and I walked over to the guy and punched him in the jaw and knocked him out, sending him tumbling backwards to the floor. Now, the crowd gathered around me looking down at the guy lying motionless on the floor with blood all over his face.

"Good for you, the SOB deserved it," one guy told me.

"Others were patting me on the back and congratulating me for the action I had taken to help the woman being abused. Several people kept telling me that I had better get out of here before the police arrived to arrest me. That suggestion set off the survival bell in my brain in much the same way as I had experienced during the scores of missions I had flown over Europe. I kept hearing my subconscious self repeating in my head, 'how the hell did I get into this mess.' Now, I am sure that if I had been in uniform the police would not have arrested me under the circumstances, out of deference to my service to my country. But, that was not the way it was. I was just another civilian just like the rest of the uncaring people in the station, and I would most likely be arrested for assault and battery or worse. It was time to extricate myself from the situation. Somehow I managed to get on a train going south in the opposite direction from what I had intended to travel. I didn't buy a ticket at the station ticket booth in fear that the ticket agent would tell the police where I was heading. I purchased a ticket to Harmon, N.Y. directly from the conductor on the train. Harmon was about 49 miles south of Poughkeepsie. When I arrived there I got off the train and boarded the first train back to Poughkeepsie. Again, I purchased my ticket from the conductor on the train and not the ticket agent at the station. As the train approached the Poughkeepsie station, I was really sweating it out. 'Gosh,' I said to myself, 'I hope there are no police waiting there to arrest me.' The train stopped at the station and disembarked some passengers and embarked others. All seemed quiet, and best of all, there were no police to be seen. The whole affair was like I was playing out a role in the present day TV program The Fugitive. It wasn't until the stationmaster hollered, 'All aboard,' and the doors closed and the train started moving that I could relax for the first time that day. The conductor came by and checked my ticket to Syracuse, and I was on my way at last. The experience was emotionally draining, but I felt vindicated by the fact that I had at least made an attempt to right a wrong. After all, hadn't I just participated in punching Adolf Hitler in the nose to right a wrong?

"By the time I had traveled from Poughkeepsie to Harmon and back to Poughkeepsie again, about three hours had passed. My original plan was to arrive in Syracuse early in the afternoon and catch a bus to Cortland. With that plan having gone awry, I would have to play the rest of the day by ear. The hours of riding were taken up with periods of catnaps and observing the beautiful passing scenery of up-state New York. I did manage to get a bite to eat in the dining car, which was the first food I had had since eating breakfast with my family. The train pulled into the Syracuse station late in the afternoon, and I immediately walked to the ticket booth and purchased a bus fare to Cortland. Since Cortland was only 30 miles south of Syracuse, the ride would take an hour or less. The bus to Cortland followed a route through wide glacial valleys and rolling hills, typical of the beautiful Finger Lake Region of central New York State. It made stops at the city of La Fayette, the quaint little towns of Tully and Preble, then passed Little York Lake, to Homer and then on to

Cortland. I remember that the trees were just beginning to change the countryside into a kaleidoscope of color, made vivid by the red rays of the setting sun low in the Western sky. It was much like trees back home in the mountains surrounding my family's home in Stone House. I felt a sense of serenity by it all.

"The bus pulled into the Cortland station on the east side of town. The station building was an ordinary looking structure, typical of bus stations in most rural up-state towns. In passing, I was not impressed, although I didn't really expect anything better or had given it much previous thought. In any case, I had arrived, and after the way the day began I was thankful to have made it to Cortland a free man. I left the station and walked to the YMCA where I had a reservation for the night. It was here that I met several other veterans who would be my classmates for the next several years."

Freshmen orientation.

"On Monday, September 10, 1945, the other veterans and I were to meet with Dr. Ben A. Sueltz, Coordinator for Veterans Affairs for the College. Dr. Sueltz was short in stature, but not short in intelligence. He projected an air of great authority like some of the colonels I had met, except he wasn't wearing a uniform. His responsibility that morning was to inform the assembled veterans of our G.I. Bill benefits, which he did with the meticulous care of a true mathematician, which he was. Dr. Sueltz was a brilliant man, there is no question about that and he must have had some inkling of what was in store for the college before the veterans enrolled, which probably accounted for how he approached us in our first meeting. He instructed us in the filling out of the forms for our G.I. Bill benefits which provided us with everything free of cost, except of course, beer and cigarettes. Since I was a physical education major, my benefits included all sports equipment that was required for my sports activity courses. They included tennis rackets, skis and golf clubs. I could not believe my good fortune. It was great. I pocketed more money and benefits from the G.I. Bill than I did my first year as a teacher.

"We veterans, however, all left the meeting with the feeling that this little man was the law unto himself, and I am sure this was the image he intended to project. He wasn't dictatorial in the true sense of the word, but he did project the image that he was a no-nonsense person and definitely in charge. He laid down the law, so to speak, and you had better follow it and you had better remember what he told you the first time because he wasn't going to repeat it. Of course, we all had been conditioned to authority figures during our military service, so it wasn't like this was our first encounter with one. Some of us also had the feeling that he resented the fact that we were receiving all the G.I. benefits. Our attitude toward him at that time was, 'Look Dr. Sueltz, or whatever your title is, we veterans have been there and done it all, and you aren't going to dictate to us or push us around.' Later, with time and a more mature understanding of the man, this feeling eroded and we had enormous respect for him.

"On the same day, the freshman class, of which we were included, met in the auditorium for the beginning of orientation. The first thing that impressed us vets when we arrived at the auditorium was the number of women in the freshmen class. The ratio of women to men was about four women to one man. The ratio of women to men in the whole college was about nine to one. To some of my veteran friends, who had never had a steady girlfriend before, this was like dying and going to heaven.

"At the top of the orientation agenda was a welcoming address by President Smith. He made a special effort to welcome the veterans to the campus and wished us the best of luck in our endeavors at Cortland State. He then turned the program over to other administrators and professors. We were lectured on the rules and regulations of the college and what was and wasn't acceptable behavior in the world of academia. For the veterans, as one might imagine, some of the rules, like curfew hours for the women, were viewed as puritanical.

"We were pleased to find out, however, that the men had no such restrictions, and I am sure if we did we would have figured out some clever way to circumvent them. Then they passed out the freshman green beanies that were designed to distinguish the freshmen from the upper classmen. Needless to say, the veterans were not going to have any part of that childish nonsense. The upper classmen, the overwhelming majority who were women, never attempted to enforce the rule on us, and the green beanies never became an issue or showed up on our heads.

"Next on the agenda was housing. Campus housing was almost non-existent. With the exception of two fraternity houses and five sorority houses that were already filled with members, non-members had to go out into the Cortland community to find lodging. The College provided us with a list of approved housing and weekly rental costs, which ranged from four to five dollars a week per student. When I was registering for my classes, I met a seventeen-year-old non-veteran student, Eugene "Nick" Nicolato. We decided to hunt for an apartment together and become roommates.

Nick Nicolato describes the meeting with Dee and their subsequent life together, dating from September 1945 to January 1946.

"When Dee told me his name, I remembered who he was," Nick recalled. "I had grown up in Dover Plains, a small town about 15 miles north of Pawling where Dee went to high school. Dover Plains and Pawling were in the same athletic league and, although I was four years behind Dee in school, I remembered him as an outstanding basketball player of our day. During our conversation we realized that neither one of us had found a place to live and decided to hunt for one together and be roommates. The apartment we chose was on the third floor of a building on Central Avenue across the street from the high school. Down the road a bit was a Brockway Truck assembly plant, which, at times, was very noisy when they would test truck engines all night long. The first floor housed a beauty shop, operated by a woman named Mary. She also managed the building, and was the person who showed us the apartment. The apartment was essentially two large rooms, a kitchen, a bedroom and a bath. As I remember, she was a sweet and caring person.

"During our stay together, I found Dee to be a very eager guy, hardworking and bright. He had a bubbling personality, smiled easily and always enjoyed people. As I recall, during the time we were roommates, he was very serious about his schoolwork. Like me, he was trying to get his bearings in the college academic environment.

"As a seventeen-year-old, and being away from home for the first time, I found the veterans very paternalistic towards us non-veteran high schoolers. Dee and I became good friends and we double-dated on occasion.

"After a short time on campus, Dee hitch-hiked home and picked up his 1931 DeSoto and drove it to Cortland. During holiday breaks, Dee would transport three or four students, me included, to the Hudson Valley, and we would share in the expense for gas. The rides home were always memorable, since we all joked, laughed and just had a good time traveling Route 17 southeast. It was on this first trip home that I met Dee's parents and sisters Aida and Sadie. They were delightful and humble people.

"There was a downside to living with Dee as well, which was not of his making, but as a result of his wartime experiences. He often had nightmares in which he relived his experiences when flying bombing missions over Europe. I would have to wake him up and settle him down before he and I could get back to sleep. Dee would never speak openly of these experiences."

"Nick and I found a small apartment with one bedroom, a kitchen and a bath," said Dee. "For furniture," he recalled, "we had two single beds, two small desks, a table and some chairs and various lamps. It had no fire escape from the third floor. I don't remember the exact cost, but it was somewhere in the neighborhood of eight to ten dollars a week for the two of us.

"My advisor was Dr. George Anderson, professor of Anatomy and Physiology. He assisted me in making out my first semester course assignments prior to registration. I was given twelve core-course credit hours that included English, Education, Chemistry 1 and Biology 1. I had twelve physical education sports activity courses that accounted for six credits. It was a full load, like every other freshman in the physical education program. As I recall, the veterans got credit for such courses as Personal Health and Safety. For those who were officers and had matriculated at a University ROTC or a Navy V-12 officer program, they received credits for some of the science courses they had completed in those programs. Our advisors were given total discretion in making decisions on previously earned credits.

"Another professor that took an interest in me was Professor Anthony P. Tesori, better known as "Tony" Tesori. Tony was one of us. He had been an officer in the Navy during the war and understood the veterans quite well. He could speak to us at our level of understanding, unlike Dr. Ben Sueltz, and because of this we all respected him. I am not sure how this incident came about, but Tony, who was part of the faculty of the Physical Education Department, had reviewed my high school transcript, and, needless to say, he was not impressed. Tony was a tall handsome guy, better than six-feet tall and very athletic-looking. His physical stature alone commanded our respect. He had a plan for me that he felt would bring me success. As part of my orientation, Tony interviewed me. The interview went something like this."

"Dee," he said, "I have in my hand your high school transcript and, from the looks of it, if you are left on your own, you're not going to make it through this college."

"With those words I could feel my face flush red, partly from embarrassment and partly from anger."

"Unless you are given some strict guidance and support," he quickly interjected.

"My anger subsided with those words, and I anxiously waited for the next shoe to drop."

"Now, the plan is this. You are going to have to study a minimum of two hours a night at the Cortland City Public Library, downtown. This is the only way you will have a chance to make it academically."

"Again, I could feel the hair on the back of my neck stand up at attention from a feeling of indignation. I didn't like the idea of someone telling me, a seasoned veteran, that I had to do something that seemed childish.

"Well sir," I responded respectfully, "as you know, each physical education major has to play a varsity sport as part of the requirement for graduation and I have soccer practice every afternoon."

"Let's see now," he paused thoughtfully with his eyes turned upward and his brow furrowed in seemingly deep thought before continuing his sentence. "Soccer practice goes from four o'clock to six o'clock. That should give you time to take a shower, have dinner, and still get to the library by eight o'clock. Since the library stays open until 10 o'clock, you will have a good two hours to study."

"I had no counter argument to his logic, and his suggestion stood. What I didn't know at the time was that Tony was a native son of Cortland. He had graduated from Cortland High School, and then from Cortland College in 1939. He knew everyone in town, including the folks that ran the library. He had chosen the town library instead of the college library as the place for me to study for two good reasons. First, there would be fewer distractions from the 514 coeds and the other veterans. Secondly, he could better monitor my study program. I was required to sign in at the librarian's desk when I arrived and sign out when I left. And besides that, the night librarian could keep tabs on me. As it turned out, the public library was only a block or two from my Central Avenue apartment. Tony had me wired in for success."

The silence of the library.

"I will never forget the first evening I arrived at the library. This was truly a momentous occasion for me since it was the first time I had ever entered a library with any serious thought of using it to educate myself. My days in the Pawling High School Library were few and far between and without purpose, except perhaps to get out of a class.

"I signed in as instructed, and sat at a big round table near the librarian's desk. At first, I just sat there and observed my surroundings. It was a strange experience. People practically walked on their tiptoes so they would not make noise and disturb others. They spoke in whispers when requesting help from the librarian, or when they spoke to each other at the tables. There was no slamming of books or eating or drinking on the premises. It was about as sterile and sanctimonious a place I had ever been in, except of course, for the Catholic Church. For the first day or two, I more or less put in my time for record purposes. Finally, I decided that as long as I had to be there, I might as well study. One evening I brought my biology book with me and began to study. Lo and behold, after a few weeks or so I began getting "Bs" and "Cs" on my quizzes. It was the first time I realized I had a brain that could master the academics. Once I learned that success at the college level meant that you had to be self- motivated, my daily trips to the library became more meaningful to me. This experience was unlike the training philosophy of the military in which you were regimented, spoon-fed the subject matter in small doses, given practice time to reinforce your learning, and constantly motivated by the fact that your life and those of your crewmembers depended on you for survival. Tony Tesori knew what he was doing. There is nothing like success to encourage success.

"All of our professors, and many of our fellow students, were mindful of the problems that some of the veterans were experiencing with the academic side of life, me being one of them. They literally bent over backwards to help us."

Antoinette Sposito, a sophomore coed at the time, remembers how it was when the veterans enrolled on campus.

"Being a super athlete that he was, Dee excelled in every phase of the physical education training program. However, the academic aspect of the program, for a time, was more of a problem for him and other veterans. Being Dee, he was able to develop fabulous relationships with his teachers and other students, who were extremely understanding and willing to encourage him and the other veterans. Most students and teachers were aware of where they could assist, and did so. The faculty was exceptional in this regard. At times, Dee and I would be assigned an academic project requiring library research. He would do the socializing in the library, and I would do the research. He would receive a grade of "A" and I would garner a "B" on the very same project.

"The veterans were very welcome, to say the least, and were treated by the faculty with understanding and patience. Most instructors and coaches enjoyed having them on campus and in their classes. The veterans, in turn, treated the faculty with respect and with a high level of appreciation for their concern and patience. Certainly the student body was appreciative as well, for college life became more interesting, more vital and more meaningful.

"As for the male general education students, it was difficult indeed. Due to the concentration of physical activity and all the out-door action on the campus grounds, with the individual and team sports constantly in the limelight, it was natural that some could have felt that they were treated as second class citizens."

The wonderful coach, Fred T. Holloway.

"My soccer career began within two or three days after registration," said Dee. "Fred T. Halloway was the coach. He was a Scottish-born, naturalized U.S. citizen who was hired by the college in 1937. He had played soccer at Springfield University in Massachusetts. He knew the game of soccer quite well. This would be the first men's varsity sport since 1940.

"Coach Holloway was a tall slender fellow. His coaching style was unlike most coaches. He was soft-spoken and did not go into wild tantrums when his players made mistakes. He was a thinking coach, and, best of all, he was a teacher. He liked to demonstrate how to play rather than tell you how to play, and often took to the field to do just that. He was also inventive. In the fall season at Cortland, it got dark early in the evening, and toward the end of practice time, it became difficult to see the brown leather ball. That was not a problem for him. He would take the brown leather balls and paint them with whitewash so we could see them better when it got dark, thus we could practice longer. I remember several times when his wife would come to the field after dark to fetch him for dinner. She would holler out to him, 'Fred, are you aware that it's dark outside?' His whitewashed soccer balls were the forerunner to white leather soccer balls used today around the world. His demeanor was professorial, from which came the derivation of his nickname, "Prof Holloway." Because of his professorial demeanor, at first meeting him, one would think he could be easily bamboozled, and, as veterans, sooner or later we would test that theory.

"The team he put together was made up of mostly wise and older, all-knowing and macho veterans, most of whom liked to drink and carouse a bit, me included. The remainder of the team was made up of recent high school graduates. One of these high school graduates was Charles "Chuck" Miesenzahl. Chuck was a farm boy, raised on a dairy farm near Honoye Falls, New York, in the Finger Lake Region along Route 20A."

Chuck describes his first meeting with Dee.

"I met Dee at the first soccer practice in the fall of 1945. The practice field was a makeshift arrangement in an open lot across the street from Old Main. It measured about 200 feet by 200 feet, far short of a regulation field. Crisscrossing the field of trampled grass were two well-worn foot paths that led in two directions from the road out front. The designated goal at one end of the field was between a telephone pole and a guide wire. The goal on the opposite end of the field was staked out with whatever was handy to use as indicators. It was not an ideal practice field, to say the least. It was more like a playing field that you would find in an empty lot in any U.S.A. town or urban city in those days. Luckily for us, it was not the field we played our games on. That game day playing field was behind and to the left of Old Main. The football club was given priority of that field for their practice. It was anticipated that the next year the college would have a varsity football team. As for me, I was not a soccer player. My game was football. The only thing I knew about soccer was that the only guy that could use his hands on the ball was the goalie. I had planned to go out for football, but my roommate, John Clark from Franklin, New York, was a soccer player and he argued his point convincingly.

"Why do you want to go out for football?" John asked. "They don't have a team. What they have is a football club and no playing schedule. The soccer team has a fixed schedule with other colleges in the state, and we will be doing some traveling."

"But, John," I pleaded, "I have never played soccer in my life and don't know the first thing about the game."

"Now, Chuck, you don't have to know anything about the game. You can run, can't you?"

"So, there I stood in an empty lot across the street from Old Main with a bunch of soccer players, most of whom were veterans. Coach Holloway ran us through all the drills he had planned for us that day, and then decided to have a short scrimmage to see what we were capable of doing. He got us all together and began calling out playing positions.

"I need some wings," he called out.

"Wings, I repeated to myself. The only wings I knew about were on birds and airplanes. I didn't know one position from the other, except goalie. Some of the guys raised their hands and stepped aside in a small group of wings."

"I need some forwards," he called out again.

"Again, some of the guys raised their hands and stepped aside in a small group of forwards. I just stood there with my mouth shut because I didn't know what he was talking about. Finally, there were only two of us left when he called for goalies. I ended up as the goalie, defending the goal at one end of the field. After the scrimmage was over, Coach Holloway came over to talk to me."

"Son, you're not a goalie, are you?"

"No sir, I'm not," I admitted rather sheepishly. "Sir, I have never played soccer in my life. Actually, I'm a football player."

"Well," he said thoughtfully, "why don't you work with the forwards, and let's see how things turn out."

"I was assigned to Dee for instruction. Dee taught me the fundamentals of trapping, dribbling, passing and, most importantly, positioning on the field on offense and defense. It was a great learning experience for me. He did such a hell of a good job with me that I was one of the starters in our first game against R.P.I. My roommate, John Clark, was right. Being a farm boy, I could run.

"One of the wonderful things about my experience with the veterans was that we had a mutual respect for each other," Charles Miesenzahl continued. "They did not look down on us as kids. Much to the contrary, they were role models for us, and were more like big brothers away from home. They were always there to help us when we needed help. Since they were older, they hung around with each other more, and we, as younger students, right out of high school, tended to hang out together. But, when we were altogether as a team, there were no discernible divisions between us.

"Being with the veterans at that time had its sad side as well. During my first semester, I roomed with three other students, one of whom was a veteran. Each night he would frequent a local bar and drink a few beers to dull his mind so he could sleep. I found out later that he had been a bombardier during the war, flying bombing missions out of England, as Dee did as a radio operator. As a result of this experience, he had difficulty getting to sleep at night, because, in his mind, he was never sure if the bombs he had dropped had killed enemy troops or women and children. Sadly, he ended up dropping out of school."

"Coach Holloway was faced with potential problems not characteristic of high school athletes attending college for the first time, and I am sure he must have been aware of this," said Dee. "It didn't take long for the veterans to put him to the test. The occasion arose in late September during a trip to Troy, New York, where the team was to play its first game of the season against Rensselaer Polytechnic Institute (R.P.I.). The bus ride, via Route 11 and old Routes 5 and 20, was about 160 miles. At about the halfway point in the journey, we made a rest stop. The stop was a roadside restaurant that had a bar. With exception of Coach Holloway and the bus driver we all piled out of the bus and into the establishment. Well, we had struck gold, a bar. It didn't take long before we were all bending our elbows at the bar with a mug of beer. Needless to say, the bar owner was elated to have the business. Coach Holloway and the driver waited and waited for us to return to the bus. I don't remember how long it was before Prof decided to investigate our tardy return, but he finally did. He stepped through the door, and there we all were drinking our beer. The fact that he caught us in the act didn't faze us a bit. For that matter, the prevailing attitude among the vets was we really didn't care. Coach Holloway appeared unfazed with what he had discovered or with our apparent arrogant attitude. Then he did the unexpected. He called the bartender over to him, laid several bucks on the bar, and in an uncharacteristically loud voice shouted, 'Bartender, another round for everyone.'

"Wow! What a guy, was our immediate reaction," said Dee. "In one simple act he won our respect and admiration. But he wasn't finished with us yet.

"We continued on our journey to Troy, and arrived at the R.P.I. campus in mid-afternoon. The game was the next day. After we settled into our accommodations, we went to dinner. After dinner Coach Holloway got us all together for our pre-game strategy meeting. He explained the game plan and emphasized the fact that the team we would be facing the next day was an experienced team, and we were going to have to play our best game in order to win. Just when we thought the meeting was over is when he dropped the other shoe. The ensuing conversation went something like this."

"Oh!" he said, "incidentally, I want to make one thing perfectly clear. I want you guys to know why I bought you all a beer at the bar. All of us on the staff at the college are very proud of you veterans and your accomplishments during the war. While you were sacrificing your lives for us, we, here at home, were safe and out of harm's way."

"I don't remember all of his speech," said Dee, "but it impressed and humbled us all. Then, he uttered the punch line."

"I bought you that beer today out of respect for what you guys accomplished during the war, but I am sure you all are bright enough and smart enough to know that if you didn't drink beer you would be better off," he began. "But, effective, as of this moment, gentlemen, the war is over. Don't you ever again repeat what you did today while you are playing for me. We are a team, and we have team rules, and you will all honor those rules. This doesn't mean, however, that I am going to send people out to spy on you to see if you're drinking beer or not."

"We sat there speechless as he quietly turned and walked from the room," Dee remembered vividly. "We all got the measure of the man, and we respected him immensely. We went out the next day and played hard with a determined and positive attitude. We really wanted to win for Prof Holloway. We lost the game 6-2, but we were now a team. The team had a mediocre season in 1945, but we had the makings of a very good team in the years to come. We ended the season with 2 wins, 1 tie and 3 losses. The bar scene was never repeated again."

Dating the Cortland College girls.

"For most of the men at Cortland, getting dates was not a problem," said Dee. Being out-numbered nine to one by the women in the first semester was like living in paradise. The older veteran students tended to date the older girls in the junior and senior classes. The non-veteran students, who were seventeen to nineteen years old, tended to date the younger freshmen and sophomore girls. Consequently, there was never a conflict of interest between our two groups when it came to dating."

Antoinette Sposito, a sophomore coed at the time of the arrival of the veterans to the campus, describes the impact of their arrival.

"To say life and times had changed dramatically when the service men arrived after WWII would be the understatement of the century. The appearance of thirty-seven sophisticated men, who viewed the world in a different light, into the predominately male-free world of Cortland College, was, to say the least, exciting and earth-shaking.

"Everything changed at the college, the classes, the sports, the teams, the town, the sororities, and even the bars. All these, and much more, came alive with a new energy and the maturing of many new friendships among the men themselves and among the women of the college. Many fell in love, married and, to this very day, share time and memories together at reunions on an annual basis. Friendship and activities were food for the soul for the veterans. Dee, being one of the more outgoing, friendly, and extremely handsome young men, it quickly became evident that he was to be a hit on the campus. Dee brightened up the lives of many young women. For him, life was beautiful, interesting and motivating. He was a fun-loving person and more than a bit prone to being a jokester at times, which eventually got him into some difficult situations. It was the veterans that stole the limelight, and the thought of dating them was exciting. Most general education male students were much younger than the veterans, and I don't recall any animosity toward them."

Carole Welsly Philips, a sophomore coed at the time, describes the impact that the arrival of the veterans had on the lives of the women on campus.

"When I arrived on campus as a freshman in the fall of 1944, the Allied invasion of Europe was in its fourth month of operation, and there were very few men on campus, perhaps twenty or so, and almost three hundred and fifty women. That was a ratio of about 18 to 1. That ratio was not too exciting for the women, but certainly great for the men.

"Most of the women who didn't have a steady boyfriend dated local fellows from Cortland and surrounding areas. And, of course, most of these men were not of draft age, which meant that they were younger than us. But we were used to dating younger guys, because that's all that were available when we were at home.

"In addition to dating local men from the Cortland area, we also dated guys from Cornell and Colgate Universities. These were usually ROTC midshipmen. Many of us girls were invited to the midshipmen balls at Cornell that were quite nice. One of the highlights of the balls was the presence of a big name band like Jimmy Dorsey and others at Barton Hall on the Cornell campus.

"I can remember several occasions going to Colgate with some of my sorority sisters to a weekend dance on the Colgate campus. Unlike today, the fraternity houses in those days had housemothers, and we felt quite safe staying on campus. Usually two fraternity houses would host the dance. In this way, the rooms of one frat house were reserved for the girls, and the guys would make arrangements to sleep in the other house.

"In the fall of 1945, when the veterans arrived on campus, Dee being one of them, we girls were delighted. To us, they seemed very mature and sophisticated. The university administration and faculty accepted the veterans with open arms. They bent over backwards to accommodate them in every way possible, and the veterans responded in kind.

"As students, we knew that they had been through hell, and we did all we could to assist them academically. English seemed to be the one subject that they needed help in the most. We girls would hold study groups with the veterans we knew, Dee included. We would review all the material that had been covered during the period, prior to the test, and they would absorb as much as they could by listening and asking questions. They were always very gracious and grateful for our help.

"Dee, however, was a special person. It just so happened that I was his first date after he arrived on campus. We first met one evening at the Tavern, a local hangout. The Tavern was popular because they had a jukebox and a wooden dance floor that was typical of taverns in those days. Women were forbidden, by state law, from sitting at the bar, so the proprietor had small tables positioned around the dance floor and several booths at which we could congregate. They served beer and Coke for ten cents a glass. The waiters and waitresses were usually fellow students working their way through school. Dee was good-looking, a good dancer and had a very sweet way about him. Perhaps the better words are, smooth way about him. Because of his outgoing personality, he was easy to get to know. We dated and double-dated on many occasions, but never started a serious relationship and have maintained our friendship to this day.

"Dee was very popular with the girls and had dates with many of them. I remember one time when a sorority sister of mine jumped from the roof of the sorority house to meet Dee after hours."

"The only conflict that I can remember, that was apparent on the campus, was with the men from nearby Cornell and Colgate Universities," said Dee. They were much more affluent than the Cortland men. Many of them had nice cars and would pull up to the sorority houses dressed in their fraternity jackets, white shirts and ties. They would stroll into the sorority house with an air of superiority, without acknowledging the presence of the Cortland men who were waiting for their dates. For some strange jealous reason, the Cortland men considered the Cortland girls to be their exclusive property, and resented the outsiders. God only knows, there were more women to go around than the Cortland men could ever handle. Nevertheless, the resentment prevailed. We didn't hesitate, however, to take our dates to dances at Cornell's Barton Hall when the Big Bands would come to play. All animosities were conveniently set aside for these occasions. A bit of hypocrisy, I would say.

"I can remember having more than one date in an evening," said Dee. "If I happened to date an underclass woman with a 10 p.m. curfew, I would escort her to her residence, and then leave and pick up an upper-class woman with an 11 o'clock curfew, or pick up a date with a girl from town."

Home for the holidays.

"Our first break in the semester came at Thanksgiving," remembered Dee. "Classes ended on Wednesday, November 21, 1945, and there was a mass exodus from the campus. In those days the chief mode of transportation for most of the male students was to hitch-hike home. If you were lucky and had a friend or a parent with a car heading home in your direction, you would share the expenses. The objective, of course, was to save money. The women took a bus or train home, or their parents came to pick them up. Since I had my 1931 DeSoto coupe, I offered three or four students, who lived in the Hudson Valley, a lift home. Those were memorable trips, especially that first Thanksgiving Holiday. We couldn't wait to get home and share our college experiences with our family and friends.

"My first Thanksgiving at home was something special. Aida, my oldest sister, was home from Albany State College, and we spent much of our time together talking about college life. Sadie, my youngest sister, was a senior in high school and attentively listened to our conversations. My mother, Josephine, prepared a Thanksgiving feast fit for a king and queen, and the five of us spent the afternoon stuffing ourselves with her gastronomic delights and my father's home-made Italian red wine. My parents were overwhelmed with pride and joy with our accomplishments. Later that evening, I drove over the mountain to Pawling to visit with some of my friends. In a way it was like returning from the service in January 1945, only under much happier circumstances.

"I did manage to visit my former principal, Earle Norton, to bring him up-to-date on my progress and activities at Cortland. It was my way of thanking him for what he had done for me. He was all smiles, and I am sure, gratified with the fact that he had influenced my life in a very positive way. Christmas 1945 was much the same. Regardless of how much I enjoyed coming home and visiting with my family and friends during the holidays, I was always anxious to return to my new life at Cortland, which was symbolic of my life's new beginning.

"When the first semester ended, I had managed to pass all my courses, although English was still my nemesis. The mandated two hours of study each night at the Cortland City Public Library had paid dividends. The second semester would be easier for me, because the soccer season was over, and I could concentrate more of my energy on my studies.

Second semester, 1946.

"At the beginning of the second semester, I heard about the accelerated academic program. This program allowed a student to complete the four-year curriculum in three years by attending three summer secessions. Some of the veterans saw this as an opportunity to start their careers one year earlier. I signed up for the program almost immediately. For me, it meant that I would graduate in August 1948 instead of May 1949. The benefits of the G.I. Bill of course, made this possible. We didn't have to work over the summer to save money for the next school year, as many of the non-veteran students, by necessity, had to do.

"The second semester saw a greater influx of veterans than the first semester. About a hundred or more veterans were enrolled, and a number of them were married. This group of veterans was welcomed and whole-heartedly accepted by the student body. Again, for the administration, the social dynamics of the situation changed with the introduction of married students.

"Sadly, my roommate, Nick Nicaloto, left school at the end of the first semester and joined the Navy. Nick turned eighteen years old on February 25, 1946 and was going to be drafted, so he decided to enlist."

Dee's former roommate, Nick Nicolato, described the situation he found himself in near the end of the first semester.

"In 1946 the draft was still in effect, and all eighteen-year-olds were subject to call up. Before I received my draft notice, I decided to join the Navy. In a way, I was both happy and sad. I was, admittedly, somewhat envious of the benefits that the vets were getting, and decided that I could serve my time and return to school with the G.I. Bill. Like many of the students at Cortland, we had to work to make it through school, since most of us were from blue-collar families. I was sad because I had made so many wonderful friends, Dee being one of them.

"When I came home on leave from the Navy, I would travel to Cortland to visit Dee and other friends I had left behind. As always, they were pleased to see me and would throw a party for my homecoming."

"There were other veterans and non-veteran students that dropped out of school at the end of the first semester for various reasons," Dee recalled. "With Nick gone, I needed to find a new roommate, and besides, I did not relish living alone. Like most events in my young life, they just sort of happened and finding a new roommate was no exception."

Dee's former roommate and long-time friend, Ralph Whitney, tells of their meeting.

"I arrived at the Cortland campus in January 1946 with the second wave of veterans. On the first day on campus, I was walking toward the steps of Old Main. Bouncing down the steps in front of me came a guy that looked familiar. He raised his head, and, as was the tradition in those days on campus, we said "hello" to each other. Before we took another step, we both realized that we had met before. Lo and behold, we recognized each other from our high school days. I had attended Amenia High School and he had matriculated at Pawling High School. Our two high schools were in the same sports league. Everybody knew "PI" as he was called in high school. (PI is short for the Italian word Paesano, meaning brother or pal). He was not only the star of Pawling High School he was also the star of the whole league. We chatted for a few minutes reminiscing about our high school days, and then he told me that he was looking for a roommate and asked if I had chosen one yet or had a place to live. Of course, I hadn't had time to find a roommate or a place to live. So, for me, it eliminated a lot of anxiety and the time and trouble looking for a roommate and a place to live. I stopped what I had intended to do at Old Main and we walked downtown to his apartment. You should have seen the place! It was on the third floor of this old house across the street from Cortland High School. It was small and compact, consisting of a bedroom, a kitchenette and a bathroom. There were no dorms on campus, so his place looked good to me. When my father came by to visit me at our apartment a few weeks later, his reaction to the place was rather funny. Being a very practical thinking man, my Dad realized that there was no fire escape from the third floor. So he went out and purchased a thirty-foot rope and tied it to the iron radiator for us to use as a fire escape in case we needed it. I am sure my father never described the apartment to my mother, knowing full well that it was not what she would have chosen for her only son. Dee has never stopped kidding me about that. My father and Dee would meet again a few years later under entirely different circumstances.

"To say the least, living with Dee was an adventure. Like during our high school days, he was friendly and full of fun. Little did I know what the next eight months would be like. Let's face it, I was living with a "heller," but he was so much fun to be with.

"Dee loved a party, and often we would end up at one of Cortland's local beer joints with a group of friends playing drinking games. The allowable drinking age at that time was eighteen, so this meant that all or nearly all the students were legal drinkers. One of his favorite games was the *Horse Race Game*, especially when a new coed was present in the party. The game went something like this. With a half dozen or more of us students drinking beer at a table, Dee would suggest that we play the horse race game. Of course, more than likely the new coed had never played the game. Dee would assign names of horses to each of the contestants, like War Admiral, Sea Biscuit, and other famous Kentucky Derby winners. The new coed was given the horse name of *Hoof Harted*. Each participant had to call out the name of their horse, as fast as they could, in sequence around the table, with the new coed at the end of the line. If someone missed their turn or mispronounced the name of their horse, they had to drink up. By the third round of this antic, the new coed would realize that she was pronouncing her horse's name Hoof-Harted as *who farted,* and, of course, would have to drink up. Fun was had by all. He had four or five drinking games in his repertoire.

"A one-time prank he pulled off also comes to mind. As spring rolled around in 1946 and the weather warmed up, the girls at the Alpha Delta sorority house had their room windows open to take in the warm spring air. Dee, with my help, decided to give the girls a wetting down. We found a ladder in the sorority house garage and quietly leaned it against the house below one of the open windows. He grabbed a garden hose and climbed the ladder as I turned the water on. He sprayed the occupants in the room for a few seconds, soaking them down. Other than a lot of screaming and fussing, no harm was done and we made a quick get-a-way, leaving the ladder leaning against the building. Dee thought that the prank was such a success that he would repeat the act."

"Who would expect me to strike twice," he said, chuckling at the thought.

"I didn't accompany him this time," said Ralph. "As he was about to climb the ladder, with the hose in his hand and the water running, the girls were ready for him. They ran from the house after him. They were smarter than he gave them credit for. They chased him for a block or so, and he ducked behind a house (which is now the present president's home) and threw himself into a small rubber raft floating in the swimming pool. Although he escaped the frenzy of the Alpha Delta sorority girls, he got drenched in the pool as the rubber raft sank to the bottom under his weight.

"Being Dee's roommate had some sad moments as well. On several occasions I would be awakened in the middle of the night with Dee screaming and convulsing in his bed as he was reliving his experiences flying in combat during the war. I would have to wake him up and calm him down. Dee never spoke of his experiences, and it wasn't until many years later at a Cortland WWII Veterans Reunion that I discovered that he had won several medals and battle ribbons during his combat service."

"In the second semester," said Dee, "I was scheduled to take anatomy and physiology. This was considered to be one of the toughest courses for the physical education major. Our textbook was Gray's Anatomy. To start with, it was the largest book I had ever owned, let alone read. It was enough to frighten anyone. To obtain a good grade, it took a lot of memorization of each of the body systems and its functions -- such as the bones, muscles, vascular system, digestive system, and on and on. This is where my study time in the Cortland City Library really paid off. I did well in this course where others struggled. I can attribute my success in this course to two things. First, my mind was conditioned to memorizing and using Morse code as a radio operator in the Army Air Corps, and secondly, my mandatory requirement to spend at least two hours each night at the library.

"Strangely enough, one of the courses feared the most by the veterans was speech, with Professor Mary Noble Smith. It wasn't that we feared Mary Noble, but that we feared the thought of speaking in front of a group alone on stage. I, and most of my classmates, had had little or no experience standing before a group and delivering a speech. Ironically, we were all scared to death just thinking about it. Surely we had all faced more trying circumstances in our combat careers, and just couldn't figure out why we were so up-tight.

"Our first assignment was to prepare and deliver a three-minute speech before the class. When the time came to present our speeches, you could hear a pin drop in the classroom. No one would dare create a disturbance in the room in deference to our collective fear. Mary Noble Smith would stand in the back of the classroom to observe us, and take notes on what she observed for her critique later. One of her observations was that we were nervous as hell. After the first day's round of speeches, she addressed the class."

"Gentlemen, why are you so nervous?" she asked. "After all you have experienced in the war, certainly presenting a speech before a group should be very easy. Come on now, relax."

"Her observations helped us see our fear for what it was, the fear of the unknown and the fear of failure. Thanks to her, at the end of the second semester, I had achieved my first "B" grade in an English course. But, more significantly than that was it gave me great confidence in public speaking, which later played a significant role in the success of my career in informing and persuading people to my way of thinking.

"Early in the second semester, I pledged the Phi Beta Epsilon fraternity. This was a fraternity made up of only physical education majors. It was established on campus in 1924, and had a house at 15 James Street, a block or two from Old Main. My motivation for joining the fraternity was two-fold. First, like most students, I wanted to be part of a group with whom most of my friends were associated, and secondly, it would later provide me with the opportunity to live on campus. Since the Beta

House was located about a block or so from Old Main, I would no longer have to walk a half-mile or more from my apartment on Central Avenue to the campus in the freezing cold and blustery snowy days that Cortland County is famous for.

"As part of the ritual of joining the fraternity, each pledge had to go through several weeks of hazing and then "hell night." Chuck Misenzahl and I pledged at the same time."

Chuck Misenzahl recalls hell night at the Beta House.

"They naturally had hazing in those days, and we endured many stupid things. To begin with, we were stripped down to our under shorts and tee-shirts and crammed into a tiny room on the third floor. Actually it must have been a closet. Here we were made to smoke cigarettes and cigars. The objective was to get you to puke. If the cigars and cigarette smoke didn't make you puke, then the smell of the vomit would finally do the job. Then they blindfolded us and escorted us down to the second floor bathroom. Here we were obliged to crawl on our hands and knees with a blindfolds on and reach our hand into the toilet bowl, and grab what we thought was a turd. What it really was was a peeled banana. In the meantime, the pledge master was constantly paddling us on our rear-end as we moved from station to station. We endured several other minor tortures until the episode was over. At the end of it all, each pledge went through the formal induction ceremony, and was officially made a member of the fraternity. The next year Dee and I and some of the other members were instrumental in toning down hell night a bit."

A den of thieves.

"Time during the second semester seemed to fly by as I was consumed with classes and my daily trips to the Cortland City Public Library. Before we all knew it, we were faced with mid-term exams again. A day or two before mid-terms, the veterans would perform a feat that would seriously confront the college administration and faculty with a most unusual challenge. But, before I get into the details of the situation, let me set the scene for you.

"In 1945, the classroom facilities on campus consisted of one building, known affectionately today as *Old Main*. The only other building on campus was the wooden gymnasium. With just under six hundred students, it was easy for the students and the faculty to know each other on a personal basis. All of the professors had an open-door policy, and would bend over backwards to accommodate the needs of each and every student, especially the veterans. You rarely needed an appointment to have a conference with one of your instructors. In fact, I never heard the word conference used. When you met, it was a meeting, not a conference. In fact, few if any instructors had an office. What they had was a desk in the classroom where they taught their classes. It was from this fact that the birth of the incident evolved. As veterans, we were well aware of the fact that we stuck out like sore thumbs among the other students. We were sure that our social behavior and our academic achievements were being closely observed and monitored by the faculty and administration. I don't mean to imply by this statement that they were looking for negative things. Actually the contrary was true. They were looking for signs of our needs, so that they could step in early to assist us when we needed help or advice that would assure our success at Cortland. There, too, must have been a strong feeling of uncertainty among them, although they never let on. No one knew exactly what to expect from us, especially in the first year. We didn't know what to expect from them either, and the only way we knew how to find out was to test the system. In reality, as veterans, we were better equipped to handle uncertainty than they were, although we never overtly acknowledged this fact. Thus, we, as individuals, felt that we, in some respects, held the upper hand. It was this feeling that led us to conjure up a plan to rid ourselves of the uncertainty regarding the outcome of our mid-term exams. The answer to the problem was simple for us. We would steal the exams.

"When my bomber crew was ferrying fuel to France to supply Patton's tanks, we were issued "C" rations for our daily meals," Dee recalled. "We hated "C" rations, so we found a source of "K" rations on the base, and we stole them from the warehouse. Problem solved, yes! We were switching to our survival mode of operation that served us well so many times during our military careers. In one sense we had developed a mercenary mentality, a behavior that was not easily extinguished in a short period of time after being discharged.

"Six of us prepared a plan to get into the building late at night, after the custodians had cleaned up the classrooms and secured the building. We let all the vets in on the plan, and no one else. The plan went something like this. One of us would find out where the custodians kept the keys to each classroom. Another would unlock a window to one of the classrooms in Old Main. Each participant was given a specific room assignment. We already knew that the exams were stored on or in the instructors' desks. On the night of the caper, six of us drove two vehicles up to the hill and parked on a side street near Old Main. We carefully made our way in the dark, avoiding detection, to a spot just below the unlocked window. We boosted one of the guys up the wall to a position where he could open the window. He climbed into the building, shut the window behind him, and opened the front door to let the rest of the crew into the building. With our flashlights in hand we went to the custodian's room and picked up the keys to the classroom that was assigned to us. Our objective was to steal one copy of each test. Most of the professors had the tests stacked on their desktops or in an unlocked drawer. Some were less trusting and had them locked in their desks. The locked drawers did not pose a serious problem for us, only in the fact that it took more time to dismantle the desk, remove a copy of the test, and put the desk back together again. One or two professors had a more unique security system. They had their test sheets numbered. In this case, we would remove the staple and distribute a page to each guy and he would write the questions on a sheet of paper. We would then staple the test back together as if nothing had happened. The whole operation took about an hour or so. We left the building and met at Phi Beta Epsilon Fraternity house. Here we began looking up the answers from our notes and textbooks. Once we had the answers to each test, we distributed them to the other veterans. No one outside the veteran community was privy to this event. As I look back at this incident, I am reminded of the fiasco of the Watergate break-in during the Nixon era.

"The mid-term test period lasted three or four days. We were all relaxed with smiles on our faces, knowing full well we were going to do just fine. Like most thieves we could not restrain ourselves from bragging about what we had done. One afternoon a group of us was sitting on the steps of Old Main bragging about our success. What we failed to realize was a female student overheard our scheme. The girl was incensed with what she heard, and rightfully so, and quietly walked over to President Smith's office and told him what she had uncovered. The worst scenario that could have been imagined by the administration had come to fruition. President Smith was faced with the possibility of the worst scandal imaginable. If this story ever got out, the local newspaper may have read, *Scores of WWII Veterans Dismissed for Cheating at State College*. The situation called for very careful and thoughtful diplomacy.

"Within a few hours after the incident was uncovered, President Smith called for all veteran students to meet in the auditorium. We had no idea that our caper had been uncovered and we were about to get blindsided. He had us huddle around in a tight group in the first few rows of the auditorium. The conversation went something like this:"

"Gentlemen," he began with nervous hesitancy. "It has been brought to my attention that you, as a group, stole all the mid-term exams."

"With that announcement, we were all aghast," said Dee. "I'm sure, like me, most of the other vets felt a warm flushing of their faces, followed by a sense of great anxiety and humiliation. At that moment I thought we had had it."

"Don't try to deny it," he went on, "because I have proof. I will be handling this situation myself. I am not going to involve my instructors. I, as you can well imagine, have a tough decision to make. The easiest decision would be to dismiss you all from this college," he said, as he paused for a few seconds to let that statement sink in. "I hate to do that because I know what you guys have been through," he continued slowly.

"Then he began singling some of us out and telling the group of our combat experiences of getting wounded, experiencing the death of our fellow soldiers, etc. And then he pointed to me."

"DaBramo, you flew thirty-one missions over Europe, was shot down once and the recipient of the Distinguished Flying Cross."

"What he had done was review some of our military records and committed them to memory. Then he used this information to personally confront several of us to make his point," Dee clearly recalled. "Is this the kind of behavior your fellow Americans can expect from our war veterans that we so reverently look up to and admire?" he asked.

"The purpose of his rhetoric, of course, was to shame us for being petty thieves and cheats," said Dee. "And he succeeded. There was dead silence. He paused for a few moments to give his statements time to sink in, while at the same time he was shifting his eyes back and forth across the group to sample our reaction. Then he went eye ball to eye ball with each of us, called out our name, and asked each of us this simple question, 'Do you promise never to steal or cheat on an exam again?'

"We all answered this poignant question with a humble and sincere, 'Yes Sir.' Then, he paused for a few seconds to allow us to think about what his final decision might be before announcing it."

"Gentlemen," Dr. Smith began with a slow quiet whisper to his voice, "I'm a trusting person. You all, individually, promised me that you would never steal or cheat on an exam again. Is that right?"

"Yes sir, we repeated in unison, and nodded in the affirmative," Dee recalled.

"So, now," he went on, "I know that my instructors do not have to worry about locking up their exams. Is that right?" he asked.

"Yes sir, we repeated once again," said Dee.

"With that being the case," he paused for moment, "I'm not going to do anything about this, but now, gentlemen, you are going to have to study. And, remember this! When you become teachers, you will be required to teach your students values, values that you guys fought and sacrificed to preserve."

"With that final statement, Dr. Smith turned and walked out of the auditorium, leaving us there to stew in our collective embarrassment."

"Wow! That guy has class," someone blurted out.

"As a group, we pledged never to steal or cheat on an examination again," said Dee. "In Cricket terms, the final test match had been won by the administration. From here on out, the administration and we veterans had a mutual understanding. The thrusting and parrying between us was essentially over. The administration now held the trump cards. President Smith did a marvelous job of keeping the incident under wraps."

Charles Miesenzahl, who was not a veteran and not involved in the stealing of the tests, relates what the rest of the student body heard of the incident.

"We, non-veteran students, heard rumors that exams had been stolen. We did not know who stole them, and we didn't know what the outcome was. The vets knew and were aware of the situation, but there was no reason for them to tell anyone. The interesting thing about the attitude of the students at Cortland in those days was that we were not categorized as veteran students or non-veteran students. We were just freshmen, sophomores, juniors, seniors and men and women students. We were not identified as any special group. We all perceived ourselves as one student body. The bulk of the credit for this prevailing attitude fell mainly on the college faculty and administration. Their professionalism and dedication to the students was, in my way of thinking, one of the biggest neutralizers we had at Cortland. President Smith handled the test-stealing incident in much the same way that Coach Holloway handled the beer-drinking incident with the soccer team," said Chuck Miesenzahl.

"For me," Dee said, "the second semester ended well, grade-wise. Besides achieving my first "B" in an English course, thanks to Mary Noble Smith, I garnered two other "Bs" and a "C" in my core courses. Dr. Tesori took me off probation, and the nightly two-hour mandatory trip to the Cortland City Public Library was lifted. Needless to say, I was pleased with myself."

The first summer school session.

"Summer School was a whole new kettle of fish. Most of us had no idea of what it would be like to cram a whole semester course into six to eight week segments. We soon learned that we had to concentrate in class like never before and keep up with the daily assignments, or we would soon find ourselves sinking into a quagmire of despair from which there was no escape. Again, I called upon my military experience at radio school in Sioux Falls, South Dakota, in 1943. The course was very concentrated and intense, and, like summer school, you could not afford to fall behind and expect to survive.

"To say the least, the summer of 1946 was academically challenging, but it also provided us with some fun as well. Since most of the male students lived in town, we became part of the Cortland community. As veterans, we were well accepted by the residents and, as a result, we made many friends. We frequented many of the same churches, the same restaurants and many of the same drinking establishments. It wasn't long before we were asked to participate in the recreational activities sponsored by the town businesses. They had a well-organized summer basketball league, a baseball league and an industry fast-pitch softball league. Some of the veterans formed a softball team under the sponsorship of the Chocolate Shop and competed in the fast-pitch league. The Chocolate Shop was a popular ice cream parlor that most of the college students and town's people frequented. It was often a popular place to take a date after a movie, rather than a tavern.

"One of the fun highlights of the summer of 1946 was the VJ Day Parade, celebrating the first anniversary of the surrender of the Japanese on August 14, 1945. The word was out that it was going to be quite a bash, with several bands, a float competition and a large turn-out by the people of the city and surrounding Cortland County."

"Dee" fourth from the left in the first row, as a member of the fast-pitch softball team sponsored by the Chocolate Shop of Cortland. (Courtesy of Dee DaBramo)

Ralph Whitney tells the humorous story of how he, Dee and four other veterans got involved in the VJ Day parade.

"It was the custom for our softball team to stop into the Hollywood Grill after a game to get a bite to eat and down a few beers. On the evening of August 13, 1946, we were at the Hollywood after a game, and someone brought up the topic of the VJ Day Parade that was to take place the next evening. After a short discussion, some of us, Dee included, decided that the Cortland State veterans should participate in the parade, with a float representing them. Ordinarily it would take weeks or months to construct a decent float, let alone a winning float. We had less than twenty-four hours to accomplish the task. It had to be ready and in the parade line by 6 p.m. the following night. Six of us decided that if we could find a farmer's hay wagon, we could come up with some kind of float and tow it behind my 1929 Studebaker. At noon the next day, to the best of my memory, Dee, Clint Inglee, Bob Hudson, Jack Tuttle, George Keenan and myself met at the Hollywood Restaurant, and took off in my car and headed south in our quest to find a farm wagon. We took Route 11 south that follows the meandering Tioughnioga River toward Marathon. It didn't take long to get in the heart of the dairy country that surrounds the city of Cortland from every point of the compass. About three or four miles down the road we spotted a wagon in a hayfield in front of a farmhouse. I turned the car into the long driveway, that bisected a green field of hay on one side and a cornfield on the other, leading up to a typical-looking farmhouse sheltered under a canopy of sugar maples. I stopped the car about fifty feet from the walkway to the house. Dee, of course, was chosen to approach the occupants. He knocked on the door, and was greeted by the farmer. Dee turned on his charm and introduced himself and explained why he was there. We couldn't hear what was said, but we did see a smile break out on the farmer's face, which we interpreted as a good sign. After a few minutes Dee returned to the car and explained to us that the farmer liked the idea that the vets were going to participate in the VJ Day celebration, and graciously agreed to loan us his wagon for the parade. He did, however, have some stipulations attached to the agreement. We had to return the wagon by 9 a.m. the following day, clean and in good shape. The farmer helped us attach the wagon to the back of my car to tow it to the campus. On the way back, we spotted an old abandoned outhouse, a good two-holer. We decided that it would make a great centerpiece for our float. Since it appeared abandoned and remotely situated, we decided to load it on to the wagon and take it with us. There was no time to find the rightful owner and get permission to use it, as we did with the wagon. Exactly what we were going to do with it, we weren't quite sure. We were sure though, that by the time we got back to town one of us would come up with an idea. This was strictly an impromptu operation. It was now early afternoon, and we had to be in line by 6 p.m. We finally came up with a float theme, *Fun With Service Days*. To cover the wagon, I went to a funeral parlor and borrowed some artificial funeral grass mats. Someone else found a kid's pedal driven toy plane with wings and cockpit to represent the Air Corps. Another vet found a large wash tub and a canoe paddle to represent a ship of the Navy. A lawn chair was placed in front of the outhouse to represent how hard the Army worked. The outhouse was labeled the Officer's Club, and on the back of it we hung a pair of long johns labeled *MacArthur Wore These*. The float was ready, and we took our place in the parade line minutes before the six o'clock deadline. But, before we got started, we placed a case of beer inside the outhouse to provide nourishment along the parade route. To represent the Army Air Corps, Dee took his position in the pedal-driven toy plane, complete in a make shift uniform, that included a leather flying helmet with goggles. Clint Inglee with his sailor's hat and canoe paddle sat in the washtub to represent the Navy. Bob Hudson was perfect for the Army guy in the lawn chair, loafing on the job. Jack Tuttle and George Keenan sat in the outhouse with the door open.

"One of the highlights of the parade was when a World War I veteran named Earl, dressed in his WWI uniform of his day, his battle helmet and his combat ribbons, proudly marched along with us, to the delight of the onlookers lining Main Street. Earl was soon hauled aboard our float, and rode the rest of the way with us, to the cheers and applause of the crowd. What had been only an idea twenty-four hours earlier had become a rousing success with the crowd, to say nothing of the enjoyment we got out of it. The next morning we returned the outhouse to its original resting place and returned the hay wagon to the gracious farmer, sparkling clean and in "A-1" shape. Ironically the next day we read in the local newspaper, The Cortland Standard, that the Cortland State veterans' float was the winner of the "Humorous Division" trophy. Dee was selected by the group to collect the trophy and present it to President Smith as a token of our respect for him and all he had done for the veterans during our first year at the college.

The WWII Veterans manning their award-winning parade float celebrating the first anniversary of VJ Day in the summer of 1946 in downtown Cortland, N.Y. (Courtesy of Ralph Whitney)

"Truthfully, those eight months of rooming together with Dee, were not only the most fun-filled days of my life, but days that could never be duplicated," said Ralph. "I had never met anyone like him until I arrived at Cortland. He could be funny, he could be serious, he was smart, and if you were his friend, he would do anything for you. As I and many of his other friends learned later in life, he had many other fine qualities as well."

"Summer School flew by in a hurry and I did well academically," said Dee. "I garnered B's and C's, except in the written English course which I passed with a D. One of the great benefits of attending summer school was that it really honed your study skills. After summer school was out, I went home for a week or two to visit my parents and sisters and my friends.

Earl, a World War I veteran dressed in his original WWI uniform and helmet, rides with the WWII veterans on their award-winning parade float celebrating the first anniversary of VJ Day on August 14, 1946, in downtown Cortland, N.Y. (Courtesy of Ralph Whitney)

One of the interesting observations that I made when I returned home on that occasion, was that my old friends had less appeal to me than they did before I started my college career. It wasn't that I liked them any less, but it seemed that we had less in common, or perhaps it was the memories of my homecoming from the war in January 1945. I always felt anxious to get back to Cortland where I felt a sense of healing taking place."

My sophomore year (Fall of 1946).

"In the fall of 1946, I decided to take a room at the Beta fraternity house. It provided several advantages for me. First of all, it was practically on the campus, and I no longer would have to walk a good half-mile or so from my downtown apartment to Old Main in the dead of winter. Secondly, I would be with my fraternity brother friends with whom I studied, played soccer with and hung out with. Sports on campus flourished. Football became a varsity sport with head coach Carl "Chugger" Davis at the helm, assisted by Tony Tesori. The team had a seven game schedule. They won four games and lost three games. We even had a JV football team that played two scheduled games that fall, compiling a one and one record.

Old Main as seen in the winter of 1946. (Courtesy of Dee DaBramo)

"One of the great things about the members of the varsity sports teams in those days was they all supported each other. When there was a football game or a basketball game, the soccer players sat together as a group to support the team, and the football players and basketball players reciprocated when there was a soccer game. We were a very close-knit group of student athletes.

"All of our starters from last year's varsity soccer team were back in the fall of 1946. We had an eight game schedule. As a team, we improved a great deal and were able to win five of our eight games with no ties. Coach Holloway and my teammates were very pleased with our accomplishments that year. Two of my teammates, Suess and May, were elected to play in the North-South All-Star game at Sterling Oval in the Bronx, N.Y."

Charles Miesenzahl, Dee's teammate described the type of player Dee was.

"As Dee's teammate for three years, I can truthfully say that Dee put his heart and soul into every game. He was always very unselfish. He had the ability to go one-on-one with the other team's defenders, and he did many times. But, if he had a teammate open, he always passed him the ball. He was so unselfish that Coach Holloway would sometimes criticize him, asking, 'Dee, why didn't you take that shot?' But, that was Dee. That was not only the way he played soccer, it was also the way he conducted his life. Dee was also a leader on the team, both on the field and off the field.

"I remember once when we played Colgate University, a game we lost, and we were on the bus heading back to Cortland from the Colgate campus. Our bus was just a few miles from Colgate when a car sped up alongside our bus, and signaled us to pull over. The driver was the Colgate coach. He had come to talk to Coach Holloway. He told Prof that when our team left the visitors' dressing room, they were three towels short. Coach Holloway boarded the bus and explained the situation to the team. He asked us to examine our bags and see if we had any of the missing towels, and then stepped off the bus. Dee took the leadership role and the three towels were found. He collected them together and took them out to Coach Holloway. As a result of that action, we continued to play Colgate University the next year at Cortland and many years thereafter."

Antoinette Sposito, Dee's classmate, remembers Dee's athleticism.

"He was a fabulous athlete, amongst a field of many, involved in a demanding physical education program. Dee's athletic ability was combined with much style and grace on the one hand, and a no-rules barred attitude on the other hand."

"The spring and summer of 1947 passed in much the same way as that of 1946," Dee recalled, "and my academic success was assured."

Top row: Holloway, coach; Pryzybylo, Cocccri, Hall, Boland, DiBenedetto, Brown, Kleinspehn, Fletcher, Dick, Wright, Hubbard, Landon, Coombs, Underwood, Gietz, W. Williams, Mgr.
Second row: Mahon, Vertetis, Weit, McKinnon, Fletcher, Corlett, Croxs, Sennett, Meisenzahl, Troisi, Milliron
First row: Clark, DaBramo, R. Williams, May, Farrell

The 1947-48 Cortland State Teachers College Soccer Team
(Courtesy of the SUNY Cortland Alumni Association)

Emilio "Dee" DaBramo, the first All-American Soccer Player at Cortland State Teachers College. (Courtesy of SUNY Cortland Alumni Association)

My junior/senior year 1947-1948.

"In the fall of 1947, I entered my third and last year at Cortland State. This would be my last year on the soccer team and I was determined to make it our team's best year.

"We opened our season against the West Point Military Academy, overlooking the Hudson River. To play there was a thrill for all of us, especially the veterans of the team. We won by a score of three to one. Our only loss that fall was to the number one ranked team in the nation, Springfield College. We out-played them for three quarters, and victory seemed in our grasp, but in the fourth quarter they scored the only goal of the contest and won 1-0. We went on to win six games and had one tie and that was with Cornell University. With a great team-winning effort, and having my best year, I was selected as a member of the second team All-American Soccer Team.

"Our team success in the fall of 1947 was not the only highlight of my junior/senior year. The real highlight of the year was meeting a beautiful, young nineteen-year-old sophomore coed by the name of Celeste Cannizzo. Normally, upper classmen and especially veterans, dated junior and senior women who were closer to their age, but Celeste was the exception. One morning in late October or early November, I was entering the student lounge in Old Main, and there she was, sitting at a table with another coed that I knew. When I first set eyes on her, I remember saying to myself, 'Wow! she's a knockout.' She stood about five feet five inches tall, with fine facial features, high cheekbones and a sharp chin. Her eyes were a beautiful deep blue, which were accented by her dark eyebrows and brown hair. I sat down next to my friend, and she introduced me to Celeste. It was a brief encounter, but long enough to get her name and house of residence. In a few days we ran into each other once again, and I asked her for a date. She consented and our relationship got its start.

"Once we got talking to each other, we soon discovered that we had similar ethnic backgrounds. Her parents were immigrants from the town of Scoglitti, on the south coast of Sicily, who settled in Auburn, New York in 1928. Like my father, her father Ralph Cannizzo arrived alone in America in 1916 at age thirteen. He was processed at Ellis Island in New York City and transported to Auburn where he was provided employment as a laborer. When he was eighteen-years-old, he served three years with the U.S. Marine Corps, and was granted U.S. citizenship for his service.

"He returned to Auburn and was employed in the Anagenics Shoe

Factory. At age thirty he decided to return to his hometown of Scoglitti, Sicily and find a bride. Scoglitti, in those days, was a commercial fishing village and most of his family members were fishermen.

The Sicilian town of Scoglitti found a niche in the history of WWII. The Allied Forces Command selected the town as the landing site for the U.S. 45th Infantry Division's amphibious assult on southern Sicily.

"In July 1927, he met and married Celeste's mother Angelina, who, at the time, was seventeen years old. In December of 1927, Angelina, who was three months pregnant with Celeste, sailed from Sicily to New York City where she was met by Ralph, and they proceeded to their home in Auburn. Celeste was born on May 22, 1928. She and her two younger brothers, Sam and Ralph, were born and raised in the city of Auburn. In the 1940s, Auburn was a thriving manufacturing city with over 35,000 inhabitants who had prospered from the war. So, here we were -- a country boy and a city girl meeting and falling in love."

Antoinette Sposito, a classmate of Dee's, aptly describes Celeste.

"Celeste was a beauty, a homecoming queen, a delightful, sweet young lady with fabulously beautiful blue eyes and a charm that was very captivating. She and Dee were a stunningly handsome couple, and Dee was madly in love with her."

"My fall semester classwork went well," Dee remembered proudly, "and I was ready to participate in the student-teaching phase of my teacher training in the spring semester of 1948.

"My supervising professor for this phase of my training was my freshman mentor, Tony Tesori. I was delighted to be associated with him once again. My first practice-teaching assignment was in Bronxville, New York. Bronxville is a small and very affluent suburban town located just outside the eastern border of Yonkers, within commuting distance to New York City, and about sixty miles south of my hometown of Pawling. Normally I would have been very pleased to have had the assignment at Bronxville because of its proximity to Pawling and my family, except for the fact that Celeste was now the most important person in my life, and I shuddered at the fact that I would be 200 miles and six hours driving time from Cortland. There wasn't much I could do about the situation, so I set out to learn and gain as much experience as I could in the ten weeks I would be there.

Celeste Cannizzo (back row, third from left) with her Sorority Sisters at Sigma Sigma Sigma Sorority at Cortland State Teachers College in 1948. (Courtesy of Dee DaBramo)

"I, and another senior student, Antoinette "Toni" Sposito, were assigned to the Bronxville School System. The Bronxville School was comprised of grades K through 12. My master teachers at the Junior/Senior high school were Dan Mattiel, Art Lynch and Virginia Niles, and at the Elementary School, Dr. Janet Sorborn. Art Lynch and I hit it off right away because we had a common link. Art was a graduate from Cortland as a physical education major in 1926. Dan was the senior man of the group, and within a year or two of retirement. The school was well-equipped for conducting physical education, and physical fitness was held in high regard in the community. The program that these individuals had put together was outstanding. Besides the traditional varsity sports, they had gymnastics, folk and square dancing, and lifetime sports like tennis, golf and volleyball. Physical fitness was as important as many of the academic courses they offered. They set up my training program so that I would work with Dr. Janet Sorbon in the morning at the Elementary School and with Dan and Art at the Junior/Senior High School in the afternoon. Tony Tesori made visits on a regular basis to monitor my progress and provide mentoring when needed."

Antoinette "Toni" Sposito relates the practice-teaching experience with Dee at the Bronxville School assignment.

"Dee and I were assigned to the Bronxville School System for our first ten-week student teaching assignment, and what an experience it was!!! This "plum" assignment was located in the southern area of the county of Westchester. Bronxville was and is today a very high socio-economic area. It is a one-square-mile affluent village with storied wealth, excellent acclaimed schools with experienced professional faculty, and a very alert, interested, involved, and well-educated community.

"Residents were fiercely proud of their village and worked diligently to preserve its character. At this time Bronxville had only single-family homes, owned by an affluent community of high-powered professionals who commuted to New York City, ones who can readily afford to live in an area where the average cost of a home is more than a million dollars.

"Bronxville's village and school district boundaries are conterminous. Anyone living outside the village limits was in another school district. This is significant – Bronxville Schools are acclaimed, and are one of the village's greatest assets. The schools formed the social glue of the community.

"Dee and I could not have been more fortunate in being assigned to the Bronxville School System, for we were exposed to a physical education staff above and beyond our expectations. I recall Dr. Sorborn, Dan Mattiel, Art Lynch and Virgina Niles and others who were more than qualified for their positions. All were more than willing to support us as student teachers. They were outstanding in every way, extremely capable, caring professionals with a bent for teasing. Needless to say, they had a great time attempting to play cupid by teasing each of us. Dee had, by that time, fallen madly in love with Celeste, a relationship that I was aware of before being assigned to student teaching at Bronxville.

"Dr. Janet Sorborn, Director of Physical Education for the elementary school, was dedicated to her work and to the training of students for the future. She influenced us above and beyond imaginable. Her use of limited space for the elementary school children was truly inspiring. No group or class went without physical education because of lack of space. She used every corridor, every spare room to develop a program that was unmatched, and she encouraged me, in turn, to do the same, which I did. Dr. Sorborn taught us so much about using creativity and being the best qualified professionals possible. We still remember her today and always will. She was very special and truly a master teacher.

"The men's physical education program was highly respected, and the men seemed to take Dee under their wings, and taught him not only the organizational skills, but far more. Their program was a super one dealing with carry-over sports, attitudes and long-life involvement of life-time sports. Dee admired the men in the department. I'm certain that the philosophy of those men was often reflected in Dee's philosophy throughout the years. What better proof of their respect for Dee's attitude and working skills than for Dan Mattiel to have recommended Dee for a much prized position in Westchester County at Rye Country Day, in Dee's professional career.

"Another aspect that made life interesting at Bronxville was that I had the opportunity to live at home in Yonkers, while student teaching. Dee lived in Bronxville. Dee came to my family's home on occasion for dinner and to enjoy my family. He was always fun-loving and was a treat for my entire family. One evening when Dee came to the house wearing a coat, he asked, 'What do I do with my coat?' My sister told him to throw it in the hallway. We were all shocked when he literally threw it the length of the room onto the carpet in the hallway. To this day, 50-odd years later, we still recall and grin at some of those incidents."

"I enjoyed all the experiences I shared with Dee in Bronxville and from that a genuine friendship developed, though not active, throughout the years. It was quite evident that the physical education staff at Bronxville enjoyed us, and we enjoyed and appreciated them as well.

"Dr. Sorborn, always doing more than expected, prepared a lovely farewell dinner for Dee and me at her home in Bronxville, which was delightful in every way. This faculty was extremely generous, and we learned a great deal."

"By the time our ten-week assignment at Bronxville was over," said Dee, "Toni and I had experienced a wide variety of physical education programs that we had never dreamed were possible. I especially focused in on the lifetime sports programs, which I implemented and expanded on later in my career. I received good performance reports from my master teachers, and Tony Tesori was pleased with my development.

"During this ten-week period, I spoke often to Celeste on the telephone and visited Cortland as often as I could. However, as often as I could, was not often enough. I really missed her a great deal, and for the first time the thought of marriage crept into my mind. In those days a young lady did not spend weekends alone with their boyfriends, especially young ladies of first generation Italian-American Catholic families. Having her visit Bronxville, as a single girl, would not have been socially acceptable either. There were constraints from both ends of the social spectrum.

"My second ten-week assignment was at the Campus Elementary School at the College. The Campus School was all elementary education. The facility was housed in the north end of Old Main. I was very happy to return to the campus to be back with my friends, and most importantly, with the love of my life, Celeste. Neither of us was very happy with our ten-week separation, and we broached the subject of marriage often. I knew that next fall I would be taking a job, and we couldn't imagine being separated for any length of time.

"Tony Tesori was my supervising professor once again. My ten-week student teaching experience at the Campus Elementary School was an enjoyable one, but did not measure up to my experience at Bronxville. The difference was that the learning experience was narrow, in that it was confined only to elementary school-level activities. The next ten weeks went very fast, and before I knew it, my last semester on campus was over. Ahead of me lay one summer session, and I would earn my degree. As per usual, the spring of the year was when public school administrators started looking for candidates to fill teaching and coaching positions for the following fall semester. The job opportunities in 1948 for teachers and coaches were plentiful, and all graduating seniors were assured of finding meaningful employment. Job offers were forwarded to the University Placement Office, and the staff made them available to the graduating seniors. Oddly enough, a position for a physical education teacher/coach and science teacher was posted for the town of Amenia, N.Y. in Dutchess County, just twenty-five miles from my childhood high school in Pawling. It was the school from which my good friend Ralph Whitney graduated, and the school I had competed against many times in basketball and baseball during my four years at Pawling High School. Actually, when I first told Ralph about the opening, he was more excited about me applying for the job than I was."

Ralph Whitney recalls his reaction to the job opening at Amenia, N.Y.

"When Dee told me about the Amenia job, I think I was more excited about it than he was. We debated the subject and I pointed out all the pluses. First of all, I told him, that he was already well-known in Amenia for his great athletic ability from his playing days at Pawling High, and the fact that he was an All-American Soccer Player could only enhance his status. Secondly, I mentioned that he would be working for my old principal, Howard Lonsdale, who was highly respected by his teaching staff, the kids and the community as well. My arguments were convincing and Dee applied for the job."

"Along with the persuasive arguments that Ralph made, there were other extenuating circumstances that helped to convince me that this would be a good decision," said Dee. "I liked the idea of being close to home. My mother was not in the best of health at the time, and my father was in his late sixties. All in all, the familiarity with my surroundings and the closeness to my family and friends made the prospects of the job feel enticingly comfortable. I confided in Celeste, and she agreed that the prospects sounded good and that I had nothing to lose by going for an interview. I contacted Mr. Lonsdale and made an appointment for an interview.

"When I arrived at Howard Lonsdale's office in Amenia, he greeted me like an old friend. We reminisced about my high school days as an athlete and my career at Cortland, all of which made me feel very comfortable and relaxed. I began to get a sense of the man, and what my friend Ralph Whitney had told me about him turned out to be true. About half-way through the interview I was convinced that I could work for the man. The interview ended with Mr. Lonsdale making me an offer on the spot.

"Look," he said, "you're the perfect guy for this job. I am offering you the job right now."

"Before I could utter a word in response, he pre-empted me."

"Now, don't worry about looking any further for a job, because as of right now, you have a job," he said.

"Never having interviewed for a teaching position before, I was somewhat taken aback with his sudden offer and couldn't think of anything else to say, so I accepted his offer. We shook hands on it, and the deal was done. Starting in the fall, I would be the physical education teacher, varsity coach for football, basketball and baseball, and a teacher of biology and general science. The starting salary was $2,500 dollars for the year."

"Before returning to the Cortland campus, I visited with my parents in Stone House and told them of my good fortune. As expected, they were proud and delighted with the situation, especially with the fact that I would be close to home. I did not tell them of my possible marriage to Celeste, mainly because she and I had not yet approached her parents with the idea. We were fairly certain that her parents would not receive the idea with great enthusiasm.

"I returned to the Cortland campus, and Celeste, Ralph Whitney, and my other friends and classmates congratulated me on my successful interview, and we had a celebration to commemorate the occasion.

"During my last spring semester, I was surprised by the return of my old roommate, Nick Nicolato, who had been discharged from the Navy and had enrolled at Cortland. Needless to say, I and many of his other friends, were glad to have him back, only this time he was not a seventeen-year-old kid, but a Navy veteran receiving G.I. Bill benefits."

Nick Nicolato tells of his return to Cortland State.

"In the spring of 1948, I matriculated at Cortland for one semester, and then transferred to Ithaca College, located in Ithaca, N.Y. about 20 miles south of Cortland. I graduated from Ithaca College in 1951 and went on to Cornell Law School and graduated in June 1954. Dee and I stayed in touch, even though we did not see much of each other during my years at Ithaca and Cornell. I was later employed by the legal department of General Foods in White Plains, N.Y. and we renewed our friendship."

"The students in the accelerated program, I, being one of them, would not have completed all our course work until the end of the summer session," said Dee. In spite of this fact, the administration invited us to attend the May graduation ceremony with the Class of 1948. The ceremony was to take place out-of-doors in front of Old Main for the graduating class of about 100 seniors, along with several hundred family and friends in attendance. As fate would have it though, I came as close to missing it as anyone could come.

"The evening before the great day, I was playing softball and collided with another player and injured my ankle bad enough that I could not stand up. Everyone was concerned, and it was decided that I should go to the hospital. At the hospital I was diagnosed with a broken ankle, and it had to be set by an orthopedic surgeon and placed in a plaster cast. I was ordered to remain overnight in the hospital for further observation before the doctor would release me. Celeste, of course, visited me at the hospital and we had a good laugh. The next day I begged the doctor to release me so that I could attend the graduation ceremony. After a lengthy discussion and a solemn promise on my part, to observe the greatest precaution, he issued me a set of crutches and released me into the custody of Celeste and some of my friends. When I arrived at the ceremony, I limped to my place in the procession, to the jeers and humorous comments from my classmates. I am still reminded of that occasion fifty or more years later. Celeste was there to share this wonderful occasion with me. My family did not attend the ceremony because of my mother's ill health.

"By the end of August 1948, I completed all the requirements for my bachelor's degree in Physical Education and my license to teach. My mission to become a gym teacher was accomplished. An impossible dream had come true, not only for me, but for my parents as well, and all because my mother had contacted my high school Principal, Mr. Earle Norton, in September of 1945 and told him, 'my-a-son has become a bum. Can you help him?'

Emilio "Dee" DaBramo's Graduation Picture of 1948.
(Courtesy of Dee DaBramo)

"After a three-year hiatus at Cortland State Teachers College, where a great healing took place for a battered Airman of World War II, it was now time to return to the real world. I have always looked back at those days as the most wonderful time of my life. And, on the day I left Cortland to take my first teaching job at Amenia, I knew that this wonderful time was over forever. I felt a sense of melancholy and wondered to myself if all this hadn't just been a glorious dream."

CHAPTER 7

Back to the Real World

CHAPTER 7
Back to the Real World

"By the end of the spring semester of 1948, Celeste and I had made the decision to get married, and now we had the awkward task of confronting her parents with the idea. Celeste turned twenty-years-old on May 22, 1948, and had completed her sophomore year at Cortland. Like my parents, her folks also had strong convictions about the need for a good education. Knowing this, I knew the task of telling them was not going to be easy or pleasant. The judgment day came that summer and, as expected, her parents were not happy with our decision. Her father, Ralph, was adamant in his protest, stressing the fact that they had made the sacrifices to send Celeste to college, and they wanted her to finish school and get her degree. Her mother, Angelina, wasn't happy about it either, and she echoed Ralph's sentiments. I tried to handle each of their objections as best I could, emphasizing the fact that I had a good job waiting for me in Amenia where I felt I had a good chance to succeed and provide a home and financial security for Celeste and myself. During the ordeal I am sure that they were aware of the fact that Celeste was of age, and in spite of all their objections, she would make the final decision. Finally, they very reluctantly gave in to the inevitable. The wedding date was set for Thursday, Thanksgiving Day, November 25, 1948.

Celeste's mother, Angelina, at age ninety recalls her first impression of Dee.

"When we met Dee for the first time we thought he was a very fresh guy," said Angelina in her Sicilian accent. He was always joking around and was very funny, but we liked him," was Angelina's assessment of Dee, as she recalled the occasion.

Celeste Cannizzo Weds Teacher

MRS. EMILIO DA BRAMO

AUBURN—Miss Celeste Cannizzo, daughter of Mr. and Mrs. Ralph Cannizzo, 2 Orchard av., and Emilio da Bramo, son of Mr. and Mrs. Michael da Bramo of Pawling, were married Nov. 25 in St. Francis Church by the Rt. Rev. Msgr. Adolpt Gabbani, pastor.

Attendents were Edna E. Backus, Sarah da Bramo, sister of the bridegroom; Elizabeth Sidello, and Douglas Clarke.

After a trip to Canada Mr. and Mrs. Da Bramo will reside in Amenia where Dr Bramo is a teacher in the Amenia High School.

Newspaper Announcement of the wedding of Celeste Cannizzo and Emilio "Dee" DaBramo. (Courtesy of Dee DaBramo)

"During the summer of 1948, when I was attending my last summer session at Cortland College, Celeste was living at home in Auburn. On most weekends I commuted the forty miles to Auburn to visit with her, and on occasion, stayed at her family's home."

Amenia High School.

"Arriving in Amenia to start my first teaching job in late August 1948 was like going home. My parents and old friends lived a mere twenty-five miles south of Amenia, in and around Pawling. Upon arrival I met with principal, Howard Lonsdale, at the Amenia High School building that was built in 1929 on the site of the old seminary building. After welcoming me, he told me of a place he had found in town that might be ideal for me to live. He gave me the name of the owners and the address of the house, and I took off in my car, loaded with my worldly belongings, to find it. When I arrived at the house, I discovered that it was completely furnished. An elderly woman, who had owned it, had passed away and her heirs were willing to rent it as it stood. Realizing how lucky I was, I rented it immediately for about sixty dollars a month. I was quite certain that Celeste would like it too."

Amenia, in 1948, was a small Victorian village in Dutchess County with a population of about 3,000 people. A major portion of the population was of Irish origin and Catholic. In those days it was not what one would call a cultural center, but rather a typical town, as depicted by Life Magazine in their feature Typical Town USA in the late 1930s or 1940s. Amenia was picked for one of these articles which gave the residents a sense of great pride.

Amenia Lake was a major tourist attraction for many years. In the summer, folks from New York City would arrive by train to occupy their rented cottages on the lake and stay for the summer. Dairy farming was one of the main occupations in the surrounding area which was encouraged by the invention of condensed milk by Gail Borden in 1861. He opened the world's first factory for producing milk that did not need refrigeration. It is known today as Borden's Eagle Brand Condensed Milk.

"The largest single employer in Amenia was the Wassaic State School for the mentally handicapped and was operated by the New York State Department of Mental Hygiene. The institution employed a staff of over 800. Little did I know at the time that this institution, in a very profound way, would influence the direction of my future career," Dee remarked.

"My friend Ralph Whitney's father was the financial and facilities manager of this institution.

"The students at Amenia High School came from two elementary schools, a Catholic school located in the basement of the Catholic Church and the Amenia Elementary School that was housed on the first floor of the high school building. The graduating class of 1948 numbered sixteen students. Amenia was, indeed, a small rural community. It had none of the amenities of the Bronxville school system where I had done my student teaching.

"Principal Lonsdale gave me the responsibility for the entire physical education program, from the elementary level through high school. This was an opportunity of a lifetime. For most kids it would be the first time to have a regularly scheduled physical education class since 1941, when their last physical education teacher left for service in the Navy during WWII and didn't return."

Evelyn Tompkins, a former student of Amenia High School, tells of the community's acceptance of Dee.

"The school faculty and children's parents reacted very positively to Dee's arrival. I was a senior when Dee first arrived at the high school, and I know that all the girls would have signed up for physical education every day if that option was available, because Dee was young and very good-looking."

Marion Reynolds, former teacher at Amenia High School, tells of Dee's arrival.

"The faculty at the school had no trouble accepting Dee. His outgoing and friendly personality won the friendship of all of us, and the kids all liked him too."

"In addition to my physical education program," said Dee, "I taught biology and general science. Believe me, it was a full schedule and I was not alone in this. All the teachers in those days had a very full load, and never complained about it. We all felt that it was our duty and responsibility to do as much as we could for the kids.

"My extra-curricular activities included coaching. That fall I gathered the high school boys together to allow them to choose between two fall varsity sports--six-man football or soccer. Of course, I was prejudiced toward soccer, but the boys wanted football. So, football it would be. The only contact I had with football was playing halfback with a Cortland town team one season, and a football-coaching course that I had taken at Cortland. To get started, I sought the advice and help from Ben Bedini, a very successful coach at a neighboring school. Ben was a graduate from Springfield College with a major in physical education. He took time to come to my first practice to get me started. On several occasions he would come by to help when I called him for assistance. Sometimes he would stop by to see how I was doing and would pitch in and help. I have never forgotten how wonderful a friend he was. The season was a challenge, and I learned football along with the team. We finished the season with a record of five wins and two losses."

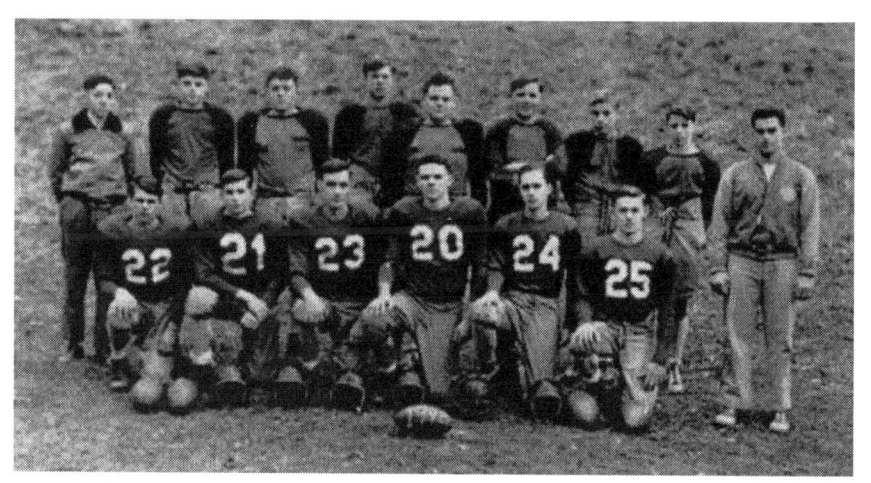

Dee, far right, with his Amenia High School six-man football team of 1948, his first team as a coaching professional. (Courtesy of Dee DaBramo)

Leo McEnroe, a former player on Dee's first team, describes the kind of coach he was.

"All the players liked him very much. He was a great motivator and morale builder. He gave us a lot of encouragement to do our best. He and our principal, Mr. Lonsdale, got along well with each other, and because of that Dee was able to talk him into buying new football equipment, which was a blessing for the team."

"Celeste and I spoke frequently on the telephone during the fall months. Getting time off to drive to Auburn for a visit was difficult. With teaching and coaching, it was a rare occasion when I could get away for a weekend.

"With my job going well and the wedding coming up, I decided it was time to trade my faithful 1931 DeSoto coupe for a new 1948 Pontiac coupe. Having made friends with a local car dealer, financial arrangements were made to pay for the car over a period of time.

"The time for the wedding was drawing near and Celeste and her mother Angelina were busy making plans. The wedding would take place in Auburn. My sister Sadie was one of the bridesmaids, and my old high school friend and basketball teammate, Douglas Clarke, was to be my best man. The two of them had to be in Auburn a few days early, so they and several of my other high school chums, Dennis Clum, Leon Tanner, and Vernon Lynch all drove to Auburn together. A day or so later my sister Aida, who was a senior at Albany State, arrived by car with my mother Josephine and father Michael.

Angelina, Celeste's ninety-year old mother, recalls her first meeting with Michael and Josephine DaBramo.

"I remember when I first met Josephine and Michael. It was a few days before the wedding. Josephine was a farm girl from Italy and I was from Sicily. We had difficulty talking with each other because we spoke different dialects, but we got along just fine. Michael was a very nice old man."

"As a wedding gift," explained Dee, "Mr. Lonsdale allowed me to take Wednesday off from my teaching duties. This gave me a whole day to travel the 300 miles to Auburn. The drive in those days took at least eight hours. Since I had Wednesday off, I left Amenia Tuesday afternoon after school let out. I arrived in Auburn, Wednesday morning at about one o'clock the day before Thanksgiving. In spite of the late hour, I met with my friends from Pawling and celebrated until the wee hours of the morning.

"All the wedding arrangements had been made, and all I had to do was to relax on Wednesday and then show up at the church on Thursday. It was a typically wonderful Italian wedding and reception, which seemed to go on forever."

Sadie, Dee's youngest sister, described the wedding.

"The wedding took place at 9 a.m. at the St. Francis Catholic Church in Auburn. The church was filled to capacity with hundreds of Celeste's friends and neighbors and some of Dee's buddies from his hometown of Pawling and some from college. The ceremony was conducted by Reverend Msgr. Adolph Gabbani. In those days a Catholic wedding ceremony had to be conducted before noon. Why that was so, I am not sure. I was one of the bridesmaids and participated in the ceremony with Edna Backus, Elizabeth Sidello and the best man, Douglas Clarke. After Dee and Celeste were declared husband and wife, the wedding party and family members were invited to a breakfast at a local club hall. This was followed later in the early afternoon by a special sit-down Thanksgiving dinner at an Auburn restaurant for family and wedding party members. The actual wedding reception was held late in the afternoon at the same hall where we had breakfast. Hundreds of people attended the reception that sported a live band that played traditional Italian love songs and dance music of the time."

The official wedding picture of Celeste and Emilio DaBramo, November 25, 1948. (Courtesy of Dee DaBramo)

"I had hidden my new Pontiac coupe where I thought no one could find it," said Dee. "Somehow my trusted friends from Pawling and Cortland College found it and removed all the wheels. After considerable teasing and delay, I finally got the car back together, and Celeste and I ran the rice gauntlet and drove twenty-five miles to a hotel in Syracuse for our wedding night. It was reported that the party continued on well into early Friday morning.

"The next morning, after a hardy breakfast at the hotel restaurant, we took off driving to Montreal, Canada. We had three days left before I had to report back to work on Monday. We arrived in Montreal late Friday and honeymooned in this beautiful French Canadian city until Sunday morning, when we set off for Amenia where we would share our first two years together.

"The 250-mile drive from Montreal to Amenia took about eight hours. We stopped for lunch on the way south and arrived in Amenia at about seven o'clock Sunday evening, and were rather exhausted from the long ride. Celeste would get her first look at her new home. She was pleased with what she saw. I am sure the euphoria of the last few days was still omnipresent in her mind, and she did not give serious thought to her environs. At that time she was not aware of the impact of moving from a vibrant city of 35,000 inhabitants to a farm community of 3,000 would have on her psyche. One thing was certain though, none of the things in her new home was ours and that was bound to change.

"On Monday morning, we were awakened abruptly by the ringing of the telephone next to the bed. I jumped up and answered it, and to my astonishment it was Mr. Lonsdale.

"Hello," I muttered.

"Dee, is that you?" the voice on the other end of the line replied.

"Yes," I said. "Oh, my gosh! Is that you Mr. Lonsdale? What time is it?"

"It's work time," he laughed.

"Yes sir, I'm sorry, I guess I overslept. I'll be right there."

"I can understand that," he laughed again. "See you in a short while then?"

"Yes sir, I'll be there in a few minutes."

"I hung up the telephone and rushed around, showered and shaved, got dressed, kissed my new bride goodbye and ran from the house. When

I arrived at school I was met by Mr. Lonsdale who sported a huge smile on his face to greet my sheepish look. All was forgiven.

"The people of Amenia made a concerted effort to make Celeste feel wanted and comfortable with her social surroundings. This was especially true of the women teachers of the school. They knew that Celeste had studied elementary education at Cortland, so they had something in common. She was given an informal tour of the town and surrounding areas and information on the best places to shop in town and surrounding communities. Celeste was an accomplished golfer and tennis player, and as a result of that she made many friends. She even played tennis in the wintertime whenever the courts were free of snow. Soon after her arrival, the Wassaic State School hired her as a counselor's aid. She was kept quite busy.

"That winter I coached varsity basketball and we had a break-even season, winning eight games and losing eight. Part way through the season some of our fans seemed frustrated with our performance. One of these fans was a local merchant in town. On two occasions he came up to me at the games to give me advice on how I should coach the team. At first I just listened, not wanting to offend or embarrass him. After the third or forth time listening to him, I realized he didn't know what he was talking about. I finally took him aside in private and told him in a soft and unthreatening voice, 'Sir, you run your store and I'll run the basketball team. Do we have a deal?' I never heard from him again, although he remained a loyal fan. In those days the local high school teams, in small towns like Amenia, were the center of the universe for the towns' people. They took great pride in their school and community.

"Spring at Amenia High School meant baseball. In past years they always did well in baseball, and because of this, all eyes were on me, the new coach. My good friend Ralph Whitney used to joke about how easy it was to coach the baseball team at Amenia High School. He would tell me, 'Dee, as coach, all you have to do is see to it that the balls and bats arrive at the field and the kids will win another championship.' My luck held out, and we won the 1949 sectional championship.

"One of the interesting events that occurred was an incident with a fourth grade student that I had in my elementary school physical education program. The young man was seventeen-years old, and seemingly mentally challenged. He was an excellent baseball player, but had no school team to play on. I thought this was very unfair for him and was rather adamant about it. I gave him a tryout with the high school team, and he made the team. Then, I wrote to the New York State High School Athletic Department in Albany to get special permission for him, as an elementary pupil, to play on our high school team. Permission was granted, and he played second base that year and we won the sectional championship. Later in life, he went on to establish his own electrical business with two employees. He got married and owned his own home. I often wondered if the young man's condition was misdiagnosed. From this experience, the notion of mainstreaming the mentally and physically challenged in the public schools began to ferment in my mind.

Dee's 1949 Amenia High School basketball team. Front L to R: Tom McEnroe, Tom Murphy, Don Herring, Ray Foley. Back L to R: Dee DaBramo Coach, John Lesee, Leo McEnroe, Fred Gobilot. (Courtesy of Dee DaBramo)

"Another event of monumental proportion occurred in April of 1949. Celeste announced that she was pregnant with our first child. Of course, unlike today with ultrasound equipment available, we had no idea if the baby would be a boy or a girl. We did know, however, that the baby would most likely be born in late December of 1949 or early January 1950. We were both in a state of euphoria, and decided to find a new home for our expanding family. We notified the parents on both sides of the family and they were as euphoric as we were. The newborn would be the first grandchild in each family.

"This time it would be a house that Celeste could make into a home of her own liking. We found a house in the countryside about three miles north of Amenia. The house was an unfurnished, white-shingled vacation bungalow with three bedrooms, a large living room, a kitchen and a bath. We began collecting new and used furnishings, mostly used since my $2,500 salary limited our purchasing power. The cottage had one drawback, it was not insulated. In the winter, I had to close off some of the rooms to save on our heating expenses and make the house more comfortable.

"In the spring, soon after we had moved into the cottage, I drove to Auburn to pick up Celeste's mother, Angelina, and brought her to Amenia for her first visit. When we approached Amenia, I played a clever joke on her, knowing full well how she would react. To play out my ruse, I had picked out an old shack located in the countryside near the edge of town. I drove up to the shack, stopped the car, got out and removed Angelina's luggage from the trunk of the car and placed them on the ground. Then, I said to her in a most convincing voice, 'Angelina, we're home.' As I approached the passenger side door to help her out, there she sat with the most stunned look on her face. Her face was white with horror and disbelief. She couldn't move. 'Come on now, Angelina, we're home,' I repeated. I can only guess at what she was thinking and I am sure it wasn't publishable. Just as she was about to say something, I started laughing. It was then that she realized I was joking. At first she admonished me and then we both broke out in hardy laughter.

"Of primary importance to Celeste was to decorate and furnish one of the rooms for our new arrival. Celeste and her mother took on the project with gusto. Within a month or so after Angelina's visit Celeste had the room ready for our first baby. The project gave Celeste a great sense of worth.

"The school year of 1948/49 ended in June, and I felt a sense of accomplishment, both as a teacher in the classroom and a coach on the field. My contract was renewed for the next year and I received a $250 raise.

"In June of 1949, my sister Aida graduated with honors from Albany State Teachers College with a B.S. Degree in mathematics and Latin. At about the same time, my sister Sadie had borrowed $1,500 from our father, Michael, and opened up her own beauty shop that was very successful.

"Prior to the end of the school year, encouraged by my friend Ralph Whitney, I applied for a summer job at the Wassaic State School as an instructor with the recreation department."

Ralph Whitney describes the situation at Wassaic from the perspective of a person who grew up living on the campus of the institution with his family.

"My father was hired as the facilities and financial manager when the institution opened in 1931. It was a very responsible position. The facility resembled a small college with forty buildings and 800 staff members to care for 3,000 on-campus patients. The mental illness treated at the school was described in those days as mental retardation. The mental retardation of the patients ranged from mild to severe. Most of them came from the eastern part of New York State, with the majority from metropolitan New York City. Their ages ranged from school-aged kids to middle-aged adults, with most of the population being Caucasian.

"Some of the patients were interned at the school because their parents could not deal with the severity of their mental illness. Some came from broken homes, and, unfortunately for many others, they were sent there by the courts. During the depression days, homelessness, truancy, and vagrancy were not looked upon too kindly. The institution was unlike any other of its kind. There were no bars on the windows or doors. There were no walls or fences surrounding the campus to imprison the patients, or uniformed guards patrolling the grounds at Wassaic. If a person approaching the facility for the first time, and didn't know it was a school for the mentally challenged, they would have thought it was a small Ivy League college campus.

"The patients were closely supervised by a dedicated professional staff and other employees from the surrounding area, 800 in all, which made Wassaic the largest single employer in the area. Life for the patients was so unlike the horror stories told in Mary Jane Ward's book, The Snake Pit, published in 1946 and the subsequent movie of the same name in 1948, starring Olivia de Havilland and Mark Stevens, in which the horrors of the treatment of the mentally ill in an insane asylum were graphically depicted. The book and the movie were instrumental in bringing about the re-examination of our nation's mental institutions.

"The medical and administrative staffs were provided housing on the campus. This was where I grew up as a child. The facility operated a dairy farm that boasted to having the largest herd of Holstein milk cows in Dutchess County. The farm provided many of the dairy products for the inhabitants of the facilities. The farm also produced most of the seasonal produce which was shared with the patients and the staff who lived on the campus. Life for our family was very good during the depression, and we often reminded ourselves of this good fortune.

"During the day, most of the male patients were engaged in light work on the farm, assisting employees in the maintenance shops, and in work groups caring for the beautiful grounds. The female patients were trained to work in the dining halls, laundry and to work as domestics in staff houses. The wide range of work activities for the patients allowed them to be productive and useful human beings, which, I am sure, raised their self-esteem and confidence.

"As a young boy, the campus grounds were often my playground, and I was very comfortable with the patients that worked in our home and on the neighboring farms and in the shops. Many evenings in the summer after supper, I would hop on my bike and join in the evening softball game with the men's group.

"Patients of school age attended the two training schools provided for them. There was one school for the boys and the other for the girls. In January 1949, I graduated from Cortland State Teachers College with a B.S. degree in physical education and was hired as the school's physical education teacher, which turned out to be a very rewarding experience. The students had never had gym before, and they loved it. In the spring of the same year, I, together with the staff music teacher, directed the kids in a gym show that show-cased their special talents in dance and gymnastics. The show highlighted the wonderful results that could be attained from individual training. Dee, who was teaching in nearby Amenia, attended the show and was greatly impressed with what he saw.

"In the summer of 1949, Dee and I were hired by the director of the newly formed recreation department to start a summer recreation program for the male patients. Dee, with his outgoing personality, had a great way of relating to the patients. They liked him and his enthusiastic way of getting them to try new activities. It really didn't surprise me that he would become a pioneer in the Special Olympics and be one who would devote so much time to the mentally and physically challenged.

"For me, working at Wassaic was an interesting and rewarding eight months of my career in education, but I was under contract to work at a school on Long Island the following fall, and I left the facility.

"I often look back at my experience at Wassaic, and believe that it served the mentally challenged of the 1930s and 1940s well. One has to remember that special education programs in the public schools, as well as the excellent programs of the Association for Retarded Children, were decades away. However, for the times, Wassaic was a landmark idea by the State of New York as a way of caring for the mentally challenged."

"In late spring of 1949," said Dee, "I was asked by my dear friend, Ralph Whitney, if I would like to work with him in the recreation department to help run a summer program for the male patients at Wassaic. Since Celeste had been working at the school for most of the year, she and I had had many discussions regarding the work being done at the school with the mentally challenged. In addition to the discussions with Celeste, I had also had the occasional opportunity to observe Ralph at work with the school-age kids at the training school on the campus, and I was impressed with what he had accomplished in his physical education program. I was also intrigued with the idea that much more could be done, so I accepted his offer to join him that summer.

"In 1949, the population at Wassaic included a wide range of age groups of males and females, from infants to adults. Some were fifty years old. The campus facility was divided into two wings, the men's wing and the women's wing. The grounds resembled an Ivy League campus. Ralph and I worked together in the men's wing. Constructive physical education and recreation programs for the patients were not highly developed at that time. When I look at the Special Olympic events of today, the programs in 1949 at Wassaic were primitive at best. Without a prepared recreation program in hand, Ralph and I were given the latitude and the opportunity to invent one. This was an opportunity for us to chart new territory.

"I discovered that once you realize that a mentally challenged person has the same basic needs as any other human being-- affection, recognition, and a need to express themselves. Once this is realized, you can begin to deal with the situation. It became our job to try and fulfill these needs, at least in the time that we had to spend with them. As we began to work with our assigned groups, it quickly became clear that we had a wide range of physical and mental abilities to deal with. Falling back on Ralph's experience with the kids at the training school, our decision was to keep the program simple, and work with individuals one-on-one as much as we could. At first, the recreation activities included camping and swimming. On the campus was a fine camp facility with small group cabins and a kitchen. We took the groups on short hikes and picnics, and at night we saw to it that they were fed well and bedded them down in the cabins. On many occasions, Ralph and I would take a busload of boys to a remote stretch of the nearby *Ten Mile River* for a picnic and swim party. This was one activity where they got a chance to interact freely and informally with each other and with their counselors. Teaching them to swim was an important life sport activity that they could enjoy throughout their lifetime. At the time, I was amazed how they attached themselves to their counselors, seeking the affection and recognition that they so craved.

"Later on we began to experiment with many simple activities like running, jumping, skipping, throwing a ball, bouncing a ball, batting a ball, rope skipping and jumping, playing kick ball and other simple group sports. These activities were incorporated into the recreation program by the Director, and were used from that summer on.

"As I look back at my experience at Wassaic, I have often wondered who it was in the New York State government that was so far-reaching in his or her thinking, to provide the funding to build, operate and maintain the Wassaic facility during the Great Depression. Not surprisingly, it turned out to be Governor Franklin Delano Roosevelt, an individual that had been stricken with polio early in his life and had great empathy for the less fortunate. He was governor of New York from 1929 through 1932, prior to winning the Presidency of the United States in 1933.

"My summer at Wassaic was one of the most enlightened experiences of my young professional life, out of which I began to develop an insight into the problems of the mentally and physically challenged.

"The summer of 1949 went quickly. Celeste was now about five months pregnant and life was becoming a bit more uncomfortable for her. She worked a month or two more at Wassaic before resigning. By early September, I was back in the classroom, teaching science, conducting physical education classes and coaching six-man football for my second year. The football team had good success, winning the larger percent of their games.

"By the end of November it was basketball season again, and it was our goal to improve our play and win a few more games than the previous year, and we succeeded.

"The most important event of our newly married life came on Monday, January 9, 1950, when our first son was born. When the time came, I drove Celeste to the hospital in Sharon, Connecticut, a small town about seven miles northeast of Amenia. We named our son Michael in honor of my father. Angelina traveled to Amenia to assist Celeste with the newborn after she returned home from the hospital. It wasn't long after Celeste came home with Michael that my parents and sisters came to visit the

Celeste and Dee with their first born son Michael in 1950. (Courtesy of Dee DaBramo)

new arrival. They were in a state of total euphoria with their first grandchild and nephew.

In the spring of 1950, I fielded my second baseball team at Amenia High School, and we won the sectional title for the second year in a row.

"A few months later after Michael was born, it became obvious that the loss of Celeste's income from her job at Wassaic, put us in an economic bind. In spite of the fact that I enjoyed working for Mr. Lonsdale and teaching/coaching the kids at Amenia, I had to make an important decision concerning my family's welfare.

Coach DaBramo's 1950 League Championship Baseball Team at Amenia High School. (Courtesy of Dee DaBramo)

"As life would have it with me, things just seem to happen, and finding my next job was no exception. One day in May 1950, I got a call from a Mr. Morton Snyder, the Headmaster of the Rye Country Day School, a private school in the affluent city of Rye, New York, inquiring as to my interest in taking a position as Physical Education Director for Boys at the school. I was completely taken by surprise.

"The chain of events that led him to call me went something like this. The wife of my supervising teacher at Bronxville, Dan Mattiel, was the

Elementary School Principal at Rye Country Day. A position opened up at the school for a Physical Education Director for boys and coach for football, basketball, soccer and baseball. Mrs. Mattiel told her husband Dan about the opening, and Dan recommended me immediately. She, in turn, notified Mr. Snyder, who respected Dan Mattiel's work at the Bronxville schools.

"Mr. Snyder called me to inquire if I might be interested in the position. I told him I was willing to entertain his offer. After receiving permission from my Principal, Mr. Lonsdale, Mr. Snyder and other administrators from Rye, traveled to Amenia to observe me teaching. They not only wanted to meet and interview me, but also meet my wife Celeste. The objective of interviewing Celeste was to see if she would fit into the social environs of Rye. Apparently she passed the test, and I was offered the job. I often credited Celeste for nailing down that position for me with her poise, intelligence, beauty and charm. The financial package they offered me was $3600 salary and provided a $400 cash supplement for our rent in this affluent community of Rye. Being a private school, they could offer perks to attract good teachers that a public school could not.

"Leaving Amenia was not easy for me personally. I just loved working for Howard Lonsdale and I loved the kids. Howard gave me free reign with the physical education program. Besides coaching three varsity sports, I was able to institute many of the lifelong sports and activities I was exposed to when practice teaching at Bronxville. Some of these included tennis, volleyball and badminton.

"Philosophically, the underlying things I took with me from the experience in Amenia were that I knew I liked kids and the teaching profession. I was thankful that my high school Principal, Earle Norton, steered me into teaching on the day we met in September 1945, after I was discharged from the Army Air Corps. I liked the idea that I was able to help kids develop, not only academically and physically, but also socially. This was particularly evident with the street kids that were growing up in poor families, like I did. I understood them probably better than I did some of the other kids. Because of the fact that I liked my job and enjoyed teaching, coaching and helping kids, I gained a greater respect for myself. I began to realize that, in spite of the fact that I was raised in a poor family, I had something to offer to others, and I felt good about that.

"So it was with sadness we bid farewell to Howard Lonsdale, the faculty, our friends and kids in Amenia, and headed south, about seventy-five miles to the city of Rye and the Rye Country Day School, located on the north shore of Long Island Sound and a stone's throw west of the Connecticut border.

"In the summer of 1950, just prior to moving to Rye, I decided to start my masters degree program at Cortland State Teachers College. Celeste, Michael and I moved to Cortland for the summer session. I took nine credit hours related to physical education curriculum development and supervision."

Rye Country Day School, Rye, New York.

"At the time Celeste, our son Michael and I arrived in late summer 1950, Rye had a population of about 8,000. It was then, and still is today, a very affluent community, much like Bronxville. Its origin goes as far back as the year 1660, when it was established as the first permanent settlement in Westchester County. It became the county's smallest incorporated city in 1942. The contrast between Amenia and Rye was stark in terms of their socio-economic status. Rye had all the amenities of the good life, which were alien to my upbringing. At first, I felt somewhat uncomfortable in the situation, much like I did when I was a kid and moved from Pansy Baker's one-room schoolhouse in Poughquag to Pawling High School, and was thrown in with the rich kids from Pawling. It was Celeste, with her charm and city upbringing that smoothed the way for me.

"I did know one of the faculty members at the school, Mrs. Dan Mattiel, the wife of Dan Mattiel, who was my master teacher at Bronxville. She was the elementary school principal at the time. I was thankful to Dan for recommending me for the job, and we renewed our friendship which lasted a lifetime.

"Rye Country Day School had a long and rich history going as far back as 1869. It was formed by a group of parents that wanted a quality education for their children, and that philosophy has sustained itself to today. Mr. Morton Snyder, who hired me, became Head Master in 1928 and was responsible for the school's growth and expansion over a period of twenty-five years. The school accommodated students from K-12 and was coed. Although it was coed, the girls and boys were taught in separate classes. Its main academic thrust was college preparatory.

"The physical education facilities included a boy's gymnasium that was contiguous with the main building, a girls athletic field and an outdoor cage (jungle gym) plus playing fields for baseball, football and soccer, all of which I was to coach.

"The faculty embraced my family and me with open arms, and Celeste became active once again in playing tennis and golf. The recreation facilities in Rye were outstanding, and we all benefited from them socially. In the summer the Rye City Beach was available on Long Island Sound, and Celeste and I enjoyed taking Michael there to swim and frolic on the sandy beach. Life was very good, and we felt fortunate.

"The kids at Rye Country Day were great. They were very interested in learning and in physical education. These attitudes were due, in large measure, to the fact that their parents were well-educated and were dedicated to seeing to it that their children got the best education possible, as they had had. For a teacher at Rye, this prevailing attitude could not have been more rewarding. To top it all off, the parents were very appreciative of the teachers. At Christmas time, for example, we were showered with gifts, ranging from gift certificates for suits and airline tickets to trips and cruises. The sum total of these gifts often rivaled the amount of our total salaries. As a result, my first year at Rye Country Day was an enormous financial and professional success. I was able to institute many of the extra curricular programs and lifelong sports that I had learned at Bronxville from Dan Mattiel and Art Lynch.

"During the summer of 1951, I attended New Paltz State Teachers College to continue my studies toward my masters degree. New Paltz College is located about fifty-five miles north of Rye and was a fairly easy commute. I completed thirteen course hours in the two summer sessions that year.

"My second year at Rye Country Day was similar to the first- - very rewarding, both professionally and financially. Although my two years at Rye Country Day School were productive and enjoyable, to say nothing of the financial rewards for my efforts, I longed for the environs of the public school system. Why? The article I wrote in the 1951 Rye Country Day yearbook The Echo, outlining the philosophy of the physical education program for boys, will help to explain this longing.

The Echo
by Emilio DaBramo

We believe the stressing of fundamentals is extremely important in the development of basic skills. We encourage our students to grow and develop a wide variety of techniques that will result in the feeling of personal growth and successful achievement. Our athletic program not only builds good physical health, but makes an important contribution to a good working morale and intelligent citizenship.

The athletic environment is such as to liberate and organize their capacities through activities that are dynamic and purposeful. Our athletic program makes an important contribution to the all-around development of personality and the fullness of life which are the results of a sane physical regime that keeps the students' minds eager and alert and their bodies glowing with health. Our students find that the acquirement of new athletic skills leads to a wide range of interests and capacities. Finally, the development of initiative, resourcefulness, and poise leads to self-mastery, social adjustment, and new friendships.

End of article

"When the article is examined closely, there is no mention of programs for the socio/economic disadvantaged, the mentally or physically challenged or at-risk students, as there might have been in a public school. This in no way was a discredit to the school, since it was set up to provide specific educational services and not be all inclusive as public schools are, and this is what I missed. The fact of the matter is that there was no other place I can think of where a dedicated teacher would gain more satisfaction out of pure teaching than at Rye Country Day. They were teaching better than average students whose parents were genuinely interested in their children's education and an administration that bent over backwards to be sure they provided the best programs and teachers they could find. For me, the job was almost too easy.

"The students attending Rye Country Day and their parents were homogeneous, in the sense that they were all from well-to-do families with advanced educations and with few if any material needs or wants. Most were well adjusted and, if they were not, their parents could afford to get them help. I felt a little uncomfortable in that social environment, since I came from poor beginnings. I could not identify with them as well as I could identify with the kids that I taught and coached in Amenia. I wanted to be able to help the more unfortunate kids. The other reason for leaving had to do with financial security. From the time my father landed at Ellis

Island in 1899 at 17 years of age, he started working for the Newburg & Dutchess & Connecticut Railroad, and held that job for over 50 years until his retirement. Those years included the *Great Depression* of the 1930s. He was always concerned about security for his family, and this was drummed into my head all during my childhood. Working at Rye Country Day School in the 1950s did not provide for a retirement and the public schools did, so I used this as part of my rationale for making up my mind to leave. What my father would not have advised me to do, however, was to leave one job without a sure prospect in hand. That was my failure, not his.

"In fairness to Head Master Morton Snyder, who I admired, I tendered my resignation in January 1952, giving him six months to find a replacement for my position. The first question Mr. Snyder asked me was, 'Dee, do you have another job lined up for next fall.' Of course, my answer was no. This gave him hope that I would change my mind, which he kindly expressed in his letter to me accepting my resignation, and in a letter of recommendation to the Director of Placement at Cortland State Teachers College.

> *Mr. Emilio DaBramo*
> *Rye Country Day School*
> *Rye, New York*
>
> *Dear Mr. DaBramo,*
> *As I have told you, I am sorry to have your resignation as Physical Director for Boys. I hoped when you were appointed in 1950 that you would stay for five years. As you know, it has been my intention to offer you reappointment for next year, with the expectation that you would carry on for at least two more years. However, I understand your interest in older boys and your preference for public high school work. With regret, therefore, I accept your resignation, to take effect at the end of the present school year. I have only commendation for the work which you have done for the school and with the boys. With this good opinion in my mind, I have confidence that you would make further desirable growth and I am sorry that I shall not have the pleasure of observing your continued development.*
>
>
> *With all good wishes,*
> *Cordially Yours,*
> *Morton Snyder*
>

Letter to Director of Placement at Cortland State Teachers College.

Miss Blanche B. Bates
Director of Placement
State Teachers College
Cortland, New York

My Dear Miss Bates:
   Emilio DaBramo has, as you know, resigned his position here, very much to our regret. As a matter of fact, he has been offered reappointment and I still hope to persuade him that his best interest will be served to staying here two more years. This is another way of saying that Emilio has given good service and has won a place for himself in the school. He is a good coach, works well with boys and with his colleagues, is enthusiastic and hard-working and spares no pains to make things come out satisfactorily. I recommend him cordially and should be glad to answer any questions concerning him.

   Sincerely yours,
   Morton Snyder, Headmaster

"When the summer of 1952 rolled around, six months after I tendered my resignation, I did not have a job offer in hand. This was a bit worrisome, but I was still confident and perhaps even cocky that I would find employment soon.

"Celeste, who was now pregnant with our second child, our son Michael and I moved to Cortland where I would spend a summer session at Cortland State Teachers College to continue work on my masters' degree and be close to the placement office at the college.

"June and July passed and we were in the first week of August 1952, and I still had not found employment. Morton Snyder had called me several times during the summer offering to rehire me for the next school year, but I kept refusing him in hopes I would find a job. Part of this stubborn refusal was based on false pride and not wanting to admit that the logic of my original decision was flawed. During the last call he made to me he told me that time was running out for him as well and he needed to make a decision on applicants he had interviewed. With my refusal, he hired Allen Hall, who was a wonderful gentleman whom I later befriended, and we became working colleagues in several physical education projects over the years. But now, I was really out in the cold and my confidence was waning.

"Around the middle of August, Blanche Bates, Director of the Placement Office, called me to her office. When I arrived at her office she had an application for a job in Brockport, N.Y. for a junior high school physical education teacher and varsity basketball coach.

"Within a couple of days I was in Brockport for an interview. When I arrived I found out that there were two other candidates interviewing for the same job. I was the last to be interviewed. I sat down with the Director of Athletics, Bob Pepper, and the supervising principal, Dudley Hare.

"Mr. DaBramo, why did you leave your job at the Rye Country Day School before you had another job in hand?" was the first question Mr. Hare asked me. I handled that question by telling them the truth. I explained my rationale for leaving Rye Country Day in the same manner as I did to Morton Snyder. Then, they threw in a job requirement that I was not prepared to handle. The job also required that I teach driver education, and I was not certified. For a moment or two my heart sunk. Thinking fast, I told them that I still had time to return to summer school and earn my certification as a driver education teacher. They accepted my explanation for leaving Rye Country Day, and on the promise that I would obtain certification as a driver education teacher, they hired me on the spot. A sense of relief permeated my whole body, and I felt lucky that my poor decision did not result in a disaster for my family and me. I also told myself that I would never again leave one job without having another in hand.

"I completed my course requirements for my masters degree by the middle of August 1952, and formally received my degree in June 1953 from Cortland State Teachers College.

"At the end of August I moved my family from Rye to Brockport with the financial assistance from my sister Sadie, bless her heart, who at the time, was operating a very successful beauty salon. In fact, at the time, she was making more money than I was.

"The Village of Brockport is located on the south side of the historic Erie Barge Canal in northwest New York State. When we arrived, Brockport had a population of nearly 5,000 residents. The largest single employer at the time was General Electric's House Ware Division. With the climate tempered by the proximity of two Great Lakes, Erie and Ontario, the surrounding area was a center of productive agriculture, with farms raising a variety of crops -- apples, cherries, corn, cabbage, onions and other produce. It was also in the center of the wine country.

"For Celeste, moving to Brockport was like going home. Auburn, her hometown, was only 70 miles south and east of the village. Rye, where we resided previously, was nearly 300 miles from Auburn. She was now able to visit with her family and old friends more frequently. With the new baby scheduled to arrive sometime in February of 1953, her mother would be close by to assist her after arriving home from the hospital with the new baby. Another thing that pleased Celeste was the proximity of the shops in the large metropolis of Rochester, which was only twelve miles to the east of Brockport. In essence, we were living in a small town with the amenities of a large city nearby.

"We rented a large old house at 2 Utica Street, a block off Main Street near the center of the village, and within walking distance to the high school and Brockport State Teachers College whose grounds were contiguous. The house we rented had five or six bedrooms, so we decided we would rent some of the rooms to students to help subsidize our rent.

"Brockport State Teachers College, at the time, had a very small enrollment of about one thousand students, which was less than that of the local junior/senior high school. In spite of its size, it lent a great deal to the social and cultural environment of the community, and in that respect it was a lot like Cortland. Celeste and I made many friends with the faculty of the college and chidingly perpetuated the rivalry between the two state schools, Cortland and Brockport.

"The Brockport Junior/ Senior High Schools were housed in the same building, so I got to know most of the faculty and students from both schools. The student population was diverse, as one would expect in a typical high school in a small rural town like Brockport. I felt very comfortable with them, as I knew I would, which was one of the reasons why I left Rye Country Day School in the first place.

"With the proximity of the Teachers College, we had many students on campus participating in their student teaching program. I often teased them about attending Brockport Normal School which never failed to rile them up a bit. I was delighted to have them, and as a result, I learned the fundamentals of being a mentor that would serve me well later in my career.

"With basketball season on the horizon, there was great anticipation among the students and town's folk as to how the team would fare under the new coach. Like at Amenia, the game of basketball in the small towns of upstate New York was the centerpiece of their winter entertainment and there was great rivalry among the neighboring towns in Monroe County. Prior to my arrival, the Brockport varsity hadn't done very well the past few years, so I was on the spot to perform. As best as I can remember, we had a winning season and everyone was pleased.

The basketball write-up in the 1953 Brockport High School Yearbook described the team's season.

"The team won all of their non-league games and a high percentage of the Monroe County league games. The team scored big victories over Brighton, Fairport and Webster."

Ed Banker, a first-year teacher at Brockport High School when Dee arrived, recalled a very interesting incident involving Dee at a home high school basketball game.

"The team Dee was coaching one evening in the Brockport High School Gym was engaged in a very tight game. A controversial foul call by an official could give the game to either team. That's how close the game was. A foul call was made by one of the officials, and it went against the Brockport team. The crowd was furious and started booing and shouting at the official unmercifully. Dee recognized the fact that the situation was close to getting out of hand and took quick action. He ran out onto center court waving his arms and stopped the game. This raised the curiosity of the crowd and they stopped booing and shouting and the place went silent. At that point Dee addressed the crowd in a calm and charismatic manner.

"ladies and gentleman, we here at Brockport do not behave in this manner in this gym. If this behavior continues, I will forfeit the game."

"The crowd was stunned and silenced as he walked back to the bench, and the game resumed. That act won him the respect of everyone, and the rule held for many years after Dee left Brockport," said Ed Banker.

"On February 18, 1953, Celeste gave birth to our second child, our daughter Debbie, at the Brookside Hospital in Brockport. Celeste's mother Angelina came to Brockport to assist Celeste with the new baby and care for three-year-old Michael, while I was at work.

"My first year at Brockport was a successful one. Celeste and I liked our life in this small college town, and were making plans to buy a home and settle there. On June 24, 1953, I signed my second-year contract, which included a $300 dollar increase in my salary for a total of $4,800. With a fourth member in our family now, the salary increase was appreciated.

"Within a day or two after signing the contract, I received a call from Mr. James B. Jackson, principal of Quaker Ridge Public School in Scarsdale, New York. I had known Mr. Jackson when I was employed at Rye Country Day School. His son was one of my students. The ensuing telephone conversation went something like this:

"Dee, we are in the process of trying to locate a physical education teacher here at Quaker Ridge and your name came to mind almost immediately. I remember the great job you did with my son and the other boys at Rye Country Day, and I want to offer you a position here at Quaker Ridge. The starting salary is $6,000 and we will pay half of your moving expenses."

Wow! I couldn't believe the offer. I thanked him for the offer and told him that I would have to discuss the opportunity with Celeste before making a decision, and would contact him in a day or so. The offer really put me in a dilemma. As Celeste and I had done before, we sat down and weighed the pros and cons of the offer.

"On the negative side of leaving, to begin with, Celeste and I were enjoying our life in Brockport and were seriously thinking of buying a house and had been actively searching for one. In addition, Celeste enjoyed being near her family and hometown friends in Auburn, and I was very happy with my job and the people I work with. A move would also mean displacing the family for the second time in one year. Then there was the feeling of guilt about leaving, since I felt I had an obligation to the administration, and especially Principal Hare, for saving me from my disastrous decision to resign from Rye Country Day School before having another job in hand.

"On the positive side of our discussion, we reasoned that if we moved we would be moving to an area that we liked and knew very well. Scarsdale was located less than ten miles west and north of Rye, where we had lived a year earlier. We had a lot of friends in the area, and were very familiar with the make-up of the community. For us to make the social adjustment would be relatively easy. The starting salary was $1,200 more than what I would be earning at Brockport, and the future earning potential would be much greater. Of course, the state teachers' retirement would follow me to Scarsdale, which was a public school. In addition, the Scarsdale schools were well-financed, the facilities were excellent, and the potential for initiating innovative programs and having the money to institute them was very good. Thrown into the mix was our desire to have more children in the future.

"Our decision, however painful, was to opt for the future and take the offer. With a great sense of guilt and my tail between my legs, I sheepishly went to see my principal, Dudley Hare, to break the news to him of my resignation. Dudley was shocked when I told him.

"What are you doing?" he said with surprised anger. "You just got here, and we were counting on you to be here for several years."

"His reaction was what I had expected, and should have been able to handle it but I couldn't because I liked and respected him a lot, and the fact was he was deeply hurt.

"He went on to tell me of the wonderful future I had ahead of me at Brockport and finally got me to delay my decision another day. I agreed to give more thought to my decision and left his office. Celeste and I deliberated our decision once again, and we decided to stick with it. On June 30, 1952, I painfully tendered my resignation, made my best apologies to Mr. Hare, and we parted friends."

CHAPTER 8

Scarsdale, a Time of Stability

CHAPTER 8
Scarsdale, a Time of Stability

The history of the Village of Scarsdale, New York, goes as far back as before the American Revolution. Two of its past residents have distinguished themselves: In 1826 James Fennimore Cooper published his most famous novel <u>The Last of the Mohicans.</u>

Daniel D. Thompkins was twice elected as governor of New York State, first in 1812 and again in 1816. In 1817, while serving as governor, he was elected Vice President of the United States under President James Monroe (1817– 1825).

"In August of 1953, when Celeste and I arrived in Scarsdale, the village had a population of about 17,000. It was known by New Yorkers as one of the richest suburban communities in the U.S., serving professionals that commuted to New York City."

The article <u>This is Scarsdale</u>, published by the League of Women Voters of Scarsdale, N.Y., 1998, Page 3, explains how the residents valued their community.

> *In 1922 the Village Board adopted a Village-wide zoning plan, the first zoning law passed in New York State by a suburban community. Court challenges to the code have been met successfully, and Scarsdale has remained primarily a residential community of single-family detached houses.*

"With housing costs in the hundreds of thousands of dollars, needless to say, Celeste and I, with our two children Michael three and Debbie less than six months old, could not afford to take up residency in this affluent neighborhood, so we found housing in neighboring Mamaroneck, which had a more diversified socio-economic population.

"The Quaker Ridge Elementary School, where I was assigned as physical education teacher, was built in 1947, and was a well-equipped facility. But what impressed me more was that the Village provided a lot of open spaces dedicated to parks, playgrounds, playing fields and other facilities, many of which were set aside for life-long sports activities, such as tennis courts, paddle tennis courts, municipal swimming pool and golf courses. It reminded me of my first practice teaching experience at Bronxville under my mentor Dan Mattiel, who was the first person to introduce me to the concept of life-long or life-time sports and their importance to the health and welfare of a community.

"All in all, Celeste and I were pleased with what we saw. Reflecting back at this decision, I must admit that the position was much like that at Rye Country Day School with one exception, as a public school it offered a teachers' retirement program which Rye did not. The salary was a factor as well. It's interesting how one's attitude changes regarding money and idealism when you have a growing family. Survival seems to prevail.

"My assignment was as physical education teacher for grades kindergarten through eighth grade and I coached soccer, baseball and basketball at the seventh and eighth grade levels. Most of our competition was with private schools. In addition, I taught Physical Education to the special education classes. As mentioned earlier, Scarsdale was a community of the rich and famous. It was here that I had as students Kyle Rote Jr., son of the famous New York Giants football great Kyle Rote Sr.(1951-1961), and Liza Minnelli, daughter of the famous actress Judy Garland. Kyle Rote Jr. later became a professional soccer star and was the first American-born player to become the leading scorer in the North American Soccer League in his second year as a player for the Dallas Tornado team. Liza Minnelli, of course, became a superstar on stage and in the movies. Because of the affluence of the community, as teachers we received generous gifts at Christmas for us and our families.

"The downside to my job at Scarsdale was that the community services for special groups were already well-organized, and the opportunity to get involved was considerably less than I would experience in later years working in Mamaroneck.

"Looking back at my eight years at Scarsdale, I can point to several highlights of my career and my life in general. From the point of view of our family life, the highlights were the birth of our third and fourth children, Shelly, born on October 10, 1954, and Jim, born on January 24, 1958. Celeste was now the mother of four small children, the oldest being Michael who was eight years old.

"In May of 1954, less than ten months on the job, I was stricken with rheumatic fever, and to make things worse Celeste was four months pregnant with our third child, Shelly. I spent six weeks in a hospital in Bronxville. When I returned home, I was unable to walk for ten weeks. The upside to this whole affair was the reaction of the Scarsdale community. They rallied to our side and collected donations of about $1500 dollars to help cover my medical expenses. This was an act of kindness I will never forget, and it was instrumental in influencing me to stay on at Scarsdale for eight years. In 1959, however, I did interview for a job in Schenectady, New York more out of curiosity than anything else. The call I received was from the Assistant Superintendent, Mr. Bernie Haake. I went to the interview, but during the interview he realized that he could not match the salary that I was receiving at Scarsdale, so nothing came of it."

When I interviewed Bernie Haake's wife, Grace, I discovered that Bernie had passed away. She, however, remembered the substance of the interview her husband had with Dee in 1959 and related it to me.

"One day Bernie came home and told me about the interview with Dee." 'Grace,' he said, 'today I interviewed an extraordinary physical education teacher. His name is Dee DaBramo who is employed at Scarsdale. Unfortunately, I could not match his Scarsdale salary; otherwise I would have hired him on the spot.'

"From a professional point of view, there were two important highlights to my career at Scarsdale. I was instrumental in starting a gymnastic program which served as a catalyst for other schools in the area to get involved in the sport.

"The second professional highlight of my career at Scarsdale occurred on January 18, 1958, seven days before Celeste gave birth to Shelly, our third child. My good friend and former roommate at Cortland State Teachers College, Ralph Whitney, from Lloyd Harbor School in Huntington, New York, and I teamed up to present a two-hour program for the annual conference of New York State Association for Health, Physical Education and Recreation. With a combined group of 70 kids from our schools, we demonstrated selected physical education activities, as conducted at our schools, to 1500 conference participants. The activities included gymnastics, life-time activity skills and sport skills, and the methods for teaching these skills. The program was very successful and provided both of us with professional exposure we could not have gotten in any other forum."

The following are excerpts of a letter written by the Director of the N.Y. State Division of Health, Physical Education and Recreation, George H. Grover addressed to Ralph Whitney's Principal, Mr. George F. Zimmerman, at Lloyd Harbor School, Huntington, N.Y. dated January 28, 1958.

As a member of the Executive Committee of this Association and as Director of this Division, it is a sincere pleasure for me to report that, in my opinion and in the opinion of the many persons with whom I conferred, Mr. Whitney and Mr. DaBramo provided an outstanding program – one which was undoubtedly a highlight if not the highlight of the conference. An overflow audience and much note-taking by the attendees attest to the tremendous interest manifested in this program. I believe these men are deserving of the highest praise, not merely for the demonstration but also for the quality of program in physical education which they must be providing their respective schools and which was so clearly reflected in this demonstration. A special word of commendation is also due the seventy-plus pupils from the two schools who participated in the program. Their deportment and effort left nothing to be desired. Furthermore they gave every evidence that they are learning more than physical skills and developing more than physical fitness – they are also learning how to live through the development of those social qualities so necessary for personal success and survival of our democracy."

"I continued working at Scarsdale, until I resigned in 1960 to take the position as Director of Health, Physical Education and Safety in the neighboring town of Mamaroneck, N.Y.

CHAPTER 9

Mamaroneck

CHAPTER 9
Mamaroneck

"In the summer of 1960 I received a call from none other than Dr. Bernie Haake, who had interviewed me for a position in the Schenectady School System in 1959," said Dee. This time Bernie was not calling me from Schenectady, but from Mamaroneck as its Superintendent of Schools. His Assistant Superintendent at the time was Earl Hobbs. The conversation went something like this:

"Dee, I want to open up a position here in Mamaroneck for a Director of Physical Education, Health and Safety, but I want to know who I am going to get before I do it," he said.

"I want to hire you for the job, and I will not open up the job unless you promise to apply for it. Now, there are several people in the system who I know will be applying for the job, and they are politically well-connected, but the board will not hire anyone without my recommendation. What do you say?"

"Needless to say, I was stunned and flattered. The best answer I could give him at that moment was that I would need some time to discuss the offer with Celeste, and I would get back to him in a day or so. Celeste and I agreed that the career move would be challenging and rewarding, and she encouraged me to accept the offer. I called Dr. Haake back in a few days, and promised to apply for the position. He was delighted with my response and assured me that I had the job, and he was true to his word. But not all was rosy over his decision. Skepticism of his decision was voiced by many, 'Why in the world did Haake hire an elementary school physical education teacher to supervise a huge program like Mamaroneck's?'

"Soon after I was hired, Dr. Haake called a meeting of the Physical

Education Department staff and introduced me to them. One could feel the tension in the air, but he did not waver. His last private remarks to me after the meeting were, 'Dee, you're on your own. I'll help you as much as I can, but I have to lay low for a while.'

"Being on my own was exactly what I wanted, but looking back at our conversation, I'm not sure *being on your own* meant the same to him as it did to me. With this auspicious beginning, I began my nearly eighteen-year career at Mamaroneck."

For Dee, accepting this position was the highlight of his career, although he didn't realize it at the time-- no one did. No one could have predicted his accomplishments in the nearly eighteen years of his tenure at Mamaroneck, not only in the school system, but in the Community of Mamaroneck, nationally and internationally, with the Special Olympics and the President's Council for Physical Fitness and Sports.

As the author of this book, it has been very difficult to get a grasp on this part of Dee's life. For some time I struggled with trying to organize it in some form of chronological order which proved to be impossible. Impossible, because he was involved in so many projects that overlapped each other. I have been amazed at how many balls he juggled at one time, and seemingly managed not to drop a single one.

The first key to his success was his personality. He loved everyone, and everyone with whom he worked felt it. And, most of all, he had a genuine love for the kids he was paid to serve, and everyone around him felt it. His energy and enthusiasm were contagious and rubbed off on his staff, his students, and his supervisors.

The second key to his success was his vision of what a comprehensive physical education program should be like, that would totally involve the students, teachers, parents and community.

Third, was his leadership style. More than once he told me, "The key to my success has been that, first, I hired a staff that was smarter than me. Second, I gave them some direction, and then got the hell out of their way and let them do their job. That's how I was able to juggle so many balls without dropping them."

To present this phase of Dee's life, I have divided this chapter into three parts:

Part I - Dee's Philosophy of Physical Education. Part II - Developing Educational Programs that meet the needs of all the socio-economic, cultural and ethnic groups in a community. Part III - Education and Community Politics.

Part I - Dee's Philosophy of Physical Education.

In the March 1968 issue of School Management Magazine, there is an article which outlines Dee's philosophy in great detail, told to the author of the article by Dee himself. In the following pages I am going to quote verbatim from this article.

DaBramo:

"Mamaroneck instructors have largely abandoned the deadly dull calisthenics routine currently in vogue in many districts – in favor of emphasizing life-time skills: Golf, tennis, fly-casting, archery, and bowling – sports that are carried over into adult life.

"Mamaroneck physical education teachers also hold special classes for the system's physical underachievers, for the mentally retarded and for emotionally disturbed children. They've even managed to get administrators and other faculty members into the act: principals doing figure eights at ice skating parties, and classroom teachers playing games at in-service meetings.

"But let one thing be understood: Mamaroneck is not the kind of *sports-minded* community that puts high school football on a pedestal. Far from it. Last fall, for example, the high school football team would have had a *perfect season* – had it not been for that one victory. Nobody lost any sleep over it either."

Reporter:

"Just the best, that's all."

DaBramo:

"Mamaroneck's physical education program has three things going for it: drive, enthusiasm and innovation."

Reporter:

"Chief driver, enthusiast and innovator is Emilio DaBramo, Physical Education Director. For a man who has as many irons in the fire as a politician at election time, DaBramo has a remarkably uncluttered idea of what he's aiming for.

"All he wants, he says, is for Mamaroneck's program to be the best in the country and for the physical education department to be put on an equal footing with every other department in the school system. No more ...no less."

DaBramo:

"For too many years now, physical education has been the stepchild of education," he says. "A classroom teacher can ask for - and get – a special in-service course. But a physical education teacher can't. The science department can usually get money for a new laboratory. But let the physical education department ask for a tennis court, and the Board talks about priorities and frills.

"We've changed all this in Mamaroneck. In-service courses? We have 60 meetings a year now. Money for a new swimming pool? Last year, when the school board was readying a $9.5 million bond proposal, we put in a request for a swimming pool, an enlargement of one of our gymnasiums and a number of other things besides – and got everything we asked for."

Reporter:
Starting from ground zero.

"Things haven't always run as smoothly. When DaBramo arrived eight years ago, he found a physical education program that was working independently at each school: No systematic approach to sports instruction, no special classes, no curriculum innovation, lukewarm student interest and so-so staff morale.

"But, shortly, the wheels began to turn and they've been turning ever since: New courses and equipment, special classes, co-educational instruction, life-time sports and skyrocketing morale.

"Guiding principle for this physical education program with pizzazz can be summed up this way:"

DaBramo:

De-emphasize the physical: "Body-building exercises are important," says DaBramo, "but don't base your whole program on them. Exercise should develop coordination and agility for a variety of sports, rather than just build an imposing physique."

Emphasize the academic: "We try to relate physical education to the classroom. For example, what geometric principles are involved in swinging a golf club? What do laws of physics have to do with a back flip?"

Reach them while they're young: "If the most formative years of a student's life are from kindergarten to fourth grade, that's the time to expose them to as many sports as possible."

Teach all of the students: "Too often, physical education is for the gifted few, while the great mass of students merely go through the motions. We're concerned with the physically and mentally retarded, as well as with normal students and outstanding athletes."

Reporter:

"But DaBramo and his staff are more than just problem-solvers. They're problem *seekers*. The following problems and solutions are some of the major ones they have taken on."

Problem: Building up staff esprit de corps.
Solution: Improve the physical education image.

Reporter:

"How do you whip up enthusiasm for a physical education program that had been lying fallow for so many years? DaBramo zeroed in on his staff. He went to the administration and asked for an in-service program. His argument: Physical education deserves the same academic treatment as math or science.

"He made his point. Today the department offers 60 meetings a year for professional credit. Among the topics offered: Teaching progression in all sports, mental health, safety, teaching retarded children, folk dancing, modern dance and gymnastics.

"Two things distinguish the courses: (1) Everyone takes part in them. The staff doesn't just sit by while an expert explains how to hit a golf ball. Everyone gets in a few swings. (2) Outside experts are brought in. If there's a subject that can't be taught by a physical education teacher, or by someone from within the school system, DaBramo imports outside expertise.

"A recent meeting brought both of these distinguishing features into play. DaBramo decided that, since body mechanics in dancing are very basically related to sports movements, he'd give his staff a class in modern dance. Accordingly, he got a modern dancer and a pianist to donate their time for one evening. It was a notable first on two counts: For the physical education instructors, who found themselves doing mass arabesques--for the dancer, who found herself telling a large football coach to express himself with a little more sincerity.

Mr. Vincent "Vinny" D'Autorio, member of U.S. Olympic gymnastics team (1948 and 1952) putting on a gymnastic demonstration at the Mamaroneck High School. (Courtesy of Dee DaBramo)

"The total in-service program did far more than just increase the staff's competence, it improved the instructors' self-concept. By treating physical education professionally, they began to think of themselves as professionals involved in a serious academic job.

"It's one thing, however, to uplift the morale of a physical education staff, and another thing entirely to get classroom teachers to sit up and take notice.

"Again, DaBramo turned to the in-service program. He opened up the courses to classroom teachers, and urged them to take part for professional credit."

"We hoped to have the classroom teachers appreciate and understand that physical education is as much a discipline as any other subject," he says.

"Since DaBramo put out his first call, many classroom teachers have signed up for courses in mass games, mental health, safety, even for the more technical courses in sports and gymnastics. The rules aren't softened one iota for them: Classroom teachers are expected to take just as active a part as the physical education teachers. (As a result, one junior high school Spanish teacher can now do back flips on the trampoline.)

"The participation of classroom teachers isn't just limited to taking in-service training. The welcome mat is always out for teachers who wish to visit the gymnasiums. More than that, teachers are urged to join with the students in extracurricular sporting activities. One science teacher, for example, is the guiding hand behind a sixth-grade skiing club.

"Winning the professional esteem of the Administration and School Board was a tougher nut. DaBramo has done it over a span of two years, at least partly by utilizing all facilities to the utmost. Equipment is transported from one school to another (usually by DaBramo and his staff), and every inch of available space is used (a 12 by 16-foot room adjacent to the high school gymnasium was turned into a weight room, at a cost of $75). When DaBramo didn't have equipment, he improvised (students slammed whiffle balls against the side of a building for two years before indoor golf facilities were set up). Says DaBramo: 'I think the Board and the Administration looked at it this way: If those physical education boys are that serious about it, we might as well give them what they need.'

"Winning over the community was the easiest part of all. DaBramo relied on word-of-mouth: Students telling parents about their physical education course, parents telling other parents, and those parents telling friends. The upshot of it all: Physical education requests were virtually unscathed in last year's $9.5 million bond proposal."

Problem: Making Phys Ed part of the regular curriculum.
Solution: Give classroom teachers portfolios of games.

DaBramo:

"Every elementary school teacher has at least one ace-in-the-hole when children need exercise," says DaBramo. "We collected 25 of the best games, wrote them up and distributed them to all classroom teachers."

Reporter:

"To make sure the games were thoroughly understood, DaBramo encouraged classroom teachers to actually play them with physical education instructors in in-service courses."

DaBramo:

"Many of the *aces* are outdoor games - *kick the can and capture the flag*, for example. But some can be played in the classroom: Relay races from one end of the room to the other or shoestring races, which require pupils to remove one shoe and hop to the finish line."

Reporter:

"A variation on this aces-in-the-hole theme: Mamaroneck's red-white-and-blue tests, so named because three different sets of classroom calisthenics are mimeographed on red, white and blue paper for the patriotic color scheme. Teachers can see, at a glance, whether all students are doing the same exercise."

"A quick run-through of one test for the whole class," says DaBramo, "and you've wrung a lot of fidgets and giggles out of a lot of kids."

Problem: Helping the physical underachiever to achieve.
Solution: You have to start from scratch.

DaBramo:

"One of our biggest challenges is the kid who's always playing in right field because he can't catch the ball," says DaBramo.

"About 5% of any school's enrollment falls into this not-so-good-enough category. These are children who, although physically and mentally sound, can't compete in sports. It's more serious than it sounds: They're the after thought in choosing up sides, the uninvited when other children go on skating parties, the butt-end of jokes in the fiercely athletic world of youngsters."

Reporter:

"In Mamaroneck elementary schools, these underachievers get an extra physical education class every week. Each class begins with a brief run-through of exercises designed to increase strength and coordination, then follows practice in basic athletic skills – running, jumping, starting and stopping quickly, catching and throwing a ball.

"Instructors start from scratch with the 15 or so students in each class. For example, underachievers learn to catch a ball, first by bouncing a basketball on the ground, then against a wall, then tossing it back and forth to one another. When they've got the hang of the basketball, they learn to catch a tennis ball – by lining up in front of the tennis practice machine, which lobs ball after ball at them until they develop the coordination of other youngsters their age.

"When the underachiever gets competent enough to join other children in sports, on a more or less equal basis, he "graduates" out of the special classes and back to four physical education classes a week. Average stay: one year.

"Approval to get into a special class is necessary from the phys ed instructor, the school nurse, the teacher, the principal, the parents and child himself. To date, no parent or child has turned down the opportunity."

Problem: Making physical education make sense.
Solution: Base the curriculum on teaching progressions.

Reporter:

"No one would ever think of using a set of basic facts for sixth-grade algebra, and then substituting another set for seventh grade. Yet, this unsystematic approach is accepted in physical education – and shrugged off – in many school districts.

"Does it really matter, though, whether you insist that a student hold a softball bat one way in elementary school, another way in junior high school, and still another way in high school? The answer is, Yes – if you're serious, in the first place, about *physical education*.

"In Mamaroneck schools, all physical education teachers approach the fundamentals of various sports in basically the same way – thanks to a curriculum of sequential teaching progressions. Take tennis, for example:

"The staff decides to start teaching tennis in the fourth grade, and to continue it every year through high school. One of the high school instructors is a better-than-average tennis player. DaBramo gives him the assignment of drawing up a sequential teaching progression.

"The instructor sits down and writes a step-by-step account of how tennis should be taught: First, the forehand and backhand grips, then the service, then the volley strokes, the follow-through, the fact that you must keep your eye on the ball at all times – up to and including the scoring and strategy of the game.

"Once the draft is written, it is hashed over by the other instructors. Is this the best way to teach a small child the backhand grip? Shouldn't return of service be introduced earlier in the sequence? Isn't the scoring of tennis too complicated for a fourth grader to grasp?

"Out of each question comes a final draft – written by one expert, polished and honed to a fine edge by other experts.

"The next step is to teach the progressions to all physical education instructors in an in-service course.

"Then, the progressions are used with students, starting in the first grade. Basic progressions have been developed for almost all the life-time sports taught in the Mamaroneck program."

Problem: Teaching mentally and emotionally handicapped children.
Solution: There's no pat answer for this one.

Reporter:

"Children with mental or emotional problems desperately need more physical education. But they seldom get it.

"Not so at Mamaroneck. There, all of the district's trainable, educable and emotionally disturbed children get regular physical education classes. Trainable and educable students - 20 of them attend the same elementary school – take daily physical education together, under the supervision of their own classroom teachers and the school's two physical education instructors.

"For the most part, the children are allowed to set their own pace. They jump rope, throw basketballs, bounce on the trampoline and swing on gymnastic rings. Physical exercise is the prime purpose of these classes – not physical prowess.

"There is a curriculum of sort, however – an oversimplified, underplayed, adapted-to-each child's abilities curriculum. For example, instructors try to teach retarded children how to do a handstand, just as they do with normal children. They even use a sequential teaching progression. The main difference is that, with a normal child, 10 steps will be needed before he masters the trick; with a retarded child, 20 or more teaching steps may be needed – and even then he may not get it.

"Recently, a physical education instructor and classroom teacher, working as a team, spent the better part of one period teaching a trainable student to skip rope once. His reward--a few minutes on the trampoline.

"Emotionally disturbed children present a different sort of problem. These are children, whose emotional problems are so severe that they must be isolated from the other children, (at Mamaroneck, they're taught by teams of teachers and mothers in what amounts to a constant one-to-one relationship). There are 14 such students and they receive phys ed once a week, in groups of seven. DaBramo himself – often accompanied by members of his staff and *always* accompanied by the teachers of the disturbed children – takes charge of instruction.

"The curriculum for this class resembles the curriculum for the class of mentally retarded students. It's geared to the individual child, rather than to the class as a whole. With children so emotionally maladjusted that one chance remark may send them into a tantrum, you play it largely by ear.

"Generally speaking, this course has four main objectives: *Exercise.* Emotionally disturbed children are encouraged to be as active as they desire; often, this proves to be a therapeutic release.

Self-confidence. "DaBramo and the other instructors don't give up easily on a child; they stay with him until he's mastered that flip on the trampoline – if not that day, then another day.

A sense of relationship with others. "Because these students often live in an isolated world of their own making, it's important to involve them in team sports. Last spring, DaBramo had them playing kickball (a progression to baseball) and softball against a teacher/mother team. They were also taught to play tennis and golf.

Success. "Here's one example: One little girl used to run away in terror each time a ball was rolled across the floor toward her. It took time and patience, but now she's able to catch a ball.

Problem: Fighting senior physical education slump.
Solution: Teach life-time sports – co-educationally.

Reporter:

"By the time most students get to be juniors and seniors they're sick and tired of the whole physical education grind. And who can blame them? For the past four or five years, it's been twice around the track and mass soccer (35 to a team) for the boys, sitting-up exercises and basketball (women's rules) for girls.

"It's a different story at Mamaroneck. Here, standard high school sports have had to move over and make room for archery, fly casting, bowling, canoeing, tennis, golf, badminton and a host of other activities – *adult* activities that will be carried *beyond* high school by the students.

"There's more to it, though, than just offering these life-time sports activities. At Mamaroneck, they're taught co-educationally. 'After all,' argues DaBramo, 'if you're stressing the fact that these are sports people will play throughout their lives, let's teach them the *way* they'll be played – boys and girls (or, men and women) *together*. For that matter, why stop at life-time sports? Why not drop the old Victorian segregation of boys and girls and make all physical education co-educational?'

"That's just what Mamaroneck has done. Boys and girls play volleyball together, work out on the parallel bars together and line up together for their turn on the tumbling mats.

"Diehards, who are convinced that co-educational physical education will never catch on, usually come up with two objections:

"First, boys play harder than girls – therefore, it's unfair to both sexes to have them play softball together.

"Second, the situation is loaded with dynamite because of the sex angle."

"DaBramo makes short shrift to both objections. 'In the first place,' he says, 'boys and girls learn a lot more if they take physical education together. They learn to be considerate of each other. It's not uncommon to see one of our boys helping a girl learn a gymnastics stunt, or to see a girl helping one of the boys. That's far better training than having the chance to hit a softball harder.'

DaBramo:

"As for the sex angle, it's the same old story: Sex is here to stay. It's something most of us are interested in, so let's not pretend it doesn't exist. And let's not let Victorian notions about sex get in the way of good education. Some of our girls walk around the gym in tights, and it's the most natural thing in the world. Usually, they don't get a second glance from the boys, because they're all too busy. And if they do get a second glance once in a while, so what?"

Problem: Teaching life-time sports – indoors.
Solution: Transform your gym into the great outdoors.

DaBramo:

"The trouble with teaching sports like golf, archery and fly casting is that the weatherman must cooperate. How, for example, do you polish up the old mashie shot when the local golf course is under three feet of snow?"

Reporter:

"Simple, the way Mamaroneck handles it. String up some heavy netting in your gymnasium - string it up on a pulley arrangement, so it can be drawn back like a curtain when you're not using it – lay down some rubber doormats, provide golf balls, clubs and tees. And let the students swing away.

"Archery and fly casting are even easier propositions. All you need here – aside from rods, reels, bows, arrows, etc. are plenty of space and protective netting and/or padding.

"Although bowling hardly depends upon the weatherman, it fits into the general category of non-gymnasium sports. After all, you *do* have alleys and gutters and big, heavy bowling balls. Or do you? Mamaroneck thinks otherwise: Gymnasiums are supplied with light plastic bowling balls and pins, which serve to teach students the fundamentals."

Problem: Facilitating independent study.
Solution: Set up video tape projector in your gym.

Reporter:

"There's nothing startling about using video tapes to perfect various body movements. Professional athletes use them all the time.

"What is unique, though, is installing projectors in gymnasiums and encouraging students to make free use of them. That's what the physical education staff of one Mamaroneck elementary school has done.

"Also available: A small library of films, showing experts performing gymnastics. Recently, one sixth-grader watched silently as the projector repeated, over and over again, a complicated flip on the trampoline. When he had seen enough, he switched off the projector and walked over to the trampoline. He stood there for a few moments, then did an about face and returned to the projector. He ran the film two more times, went back to the trampoline, climbed on ....and he did the flip perfectly on the first try. An exceptional example, perhaps. But that's the general idea."

End of article.

Part II - Developing Educational Programs that meet the needs of all socio-economic, cultural and ethnic groups in a community.

The Development of the Community School.

"The situation in the Mamaroneck Avenue School neighborhood was rather dire," Dee remarked. "It was made up of under-privileged African American and Italian families. In December 1968, *The Community School Project* was developed out of our desire to provide the kids in this neighborhood with some of the extra educational and cultural amenities enjoyed by the privileged kids in the more affluent neighborhoods, which the kids in the Mamaroneck Avenue School neighborhoods could not privately afford. To accomplish this goal, money was added to the community recreation budget. At the time, I was a member of the Mamaroneck Village Parks and Recreation Commission."

The following article by Paul Byrne in the Mamaroneck, N.Y. Newspaper, The Daily Times, March 26, 1969, titled, Community School is Designed for Everyone, best describes the program.

Parents Join Children. A new kind of school is in session each Tuesday evening at the Avenue School – it's called the Community School, because its purpose is to serve the entire community – the children, the parents, the neighborhood of Mamaroneck Avenue.

"The outgrowth of a pilot carol-singing project just before Christmas (1968), the Community School draws from 150 to 300 youngsters each week, along with 50 or more adults who watch, or help, or take part in the varied activities.

"The staff, headed by Emilio (Dee) DaBramo, Director of Physical Education, Health and Safety for the school system, consists of teachers and volunteers. Some of the teachers are paid out of the funds obtained under Title I, Elementary and Secondary Education Act, and some are participants in an in-service course.

"There are also 10 volunteers working with Mr. DaBramo, who is a member of the Mamaroneck Village Parks and Recreation Commission.

"The ESEA, Title I grant is $4,000 for staff, equipment and supplies. Volunteers help stretch these funds to accommodate the growing school enrollment."

End of Article.

"Activities included art, ceramics, music, gymnastics, ping pong, golf and other organized recreational activities," said Dee.

The Summer Co-Op Program.

Prior to initiating this summer program in 1966, Dee had an interesting and instructive experience putting together and directing a similar summer program in New York City. He was organizer of Governor Rockefeller's Program for Disadvantaged Youth that was headed up by its Director, Major League's first African-American Baseball Star, Jackie Robinson, who played for the Brooklyn Dodgers from 1947 through 1956. The details of this program and Dee's relationship with Jackie Robinson are revealed later in this chapter.

"As a follow-up to the Community School in the Summer of 1968, I initiated the summer Co-Op Camp for the same disadvantaged kids in the neighborhood serviced by the Mamaroneck Avenue School," said Dee. "Besides being under-privileged, the majority of the kids had nothing to do during the summer months, so they sometimes resorted to vandalism and other questionable activities that were destroying the neighborhood -- to say nothing about how the situation was destroying the kids. To the police, this was a hot spot in the community where they were spending an inordinate amount of time and resources, to the neglect of the rest of the community. As a result, resentment had built up between the people of the neighborhood and the Police Department. Something had to be done, now. My overall goal was to overcome their resentment to the police, and encourage cooperation and trust. But, first, I had to do something to raise their self-esteem and pride in the kids themselves.

"As a teacher and administrator, I had contact with most of these kids in the schools, and over the years had gained the trust of many. My solution to the problem was to give the younger kids something constructive to do during the summer, and provide the older high school kids with responsibility through the creation of paying jobs.

"I proposed to the Town Board of Trustees that we set up a summer Co-Op Camp that would provide recreation activities for the younger kids, such as swimming, tennis, golf, gymnastics and field trips to places they have never been. On the academic side, we would provide courses in math and reading. The program would be offered five days a week, from nine in the morning to three o'clock in the afternoon, with a free lunch every day. For the older high school kids, I proposed providing them with paying jobs as counselors.

"It was at this point in my proposal that I threw them a *curve ball*. I told them that I intended to hire the toughest underprivileged neighborhood guys and gals from the high school as senior counselors. My rationale, I explained to them, was two-fold. First, to provide them with a paying job that would put money in their pockets that they had earned from honest work, and second, to help raise their self-esteem and pride in themselves by providing them with an opportunity to help others, namely the younger kids in their neighborhood. My intention, I told them, was also to hire senior counselors from the privileged group of kids at the high school and team them up. In most cases, these were caucasians from privileged families. The reason for this was quite obvious. I wanted the two socio-economic groups to work together, and while doing so they would gain some insight and appreciation for each other. I recalled from my childhood how uncomfortable and embarrassed I felt when I first encountered the rich kids at Pawling High School, after graduating from a very poor one-room schoolhouse in Poughquag, New York. It took me many years to get over that feeling.

"I also told them that I wanted the men and women of the police force to play an active role in the program. Then, I revealed to them my expected outcomes. One - the Title I money I expected to get in the amount of 30 to 40 thousand dollars, would go a long way to provide a lot of kids jobs as counselors, and this would work to reduce the vandalism and juvenile delinquency rate in the community. Two - to change the attitude of the neighborhood toward the police and the attitude of the police toward the neighborhood, to one of respect and trust. Three - to change the attitude of the kids toward their schools from that of vandalism to respect for public property and the welfare of their fellow classmates.

"When I first made the proposal to the town trustees, they thought I was crazy."

"Come on, Dee, how are you going to get this done?" they asked.

"I told them that getting it done was my job and all I wanted from them was their blessing to pursue the idea. At the end of the meeting they agreed, although somewhat pessimistically.

"My first order of business was to obtain the cooperation of the schools, which was not a problem since the purpose of the program had the potential for solving many of the discipline problems in the schools. Then, I approached the White Plains County Board for Disadvantaged Kids and got Title I money. Then I convinced the Trustees of the Town of Mamaroneck to provide additional funding. The idea was well accepted by all, and I hired a staff of people I knew could do the job, and we were off and running.

"As director of the program, I made it clear at the beginning that I did not want any remuneration, and for good reason. I did not want anyone to say, or even think, that I came up with the idea so I could feather my own nest. This, I think, helped sell the idea to all parties involved.

"With my professional staff, we put together an organizational structure designed to maximize the use of neighborhood kids as counselors. As mentioned earlier, we identified the toughest high school kids from the neighborhood and hired them as senior counselors, and matched them up with kids from privileged families. The mix was multi-ethnic, multi-cultural and multi-socio-economic. The next layer of paid counselors in the organizational scheme, were junior counselors. They, too, were high school students. In our planning for the future, we recruited junior high school student volunteers to be Junior-Junior counselors. The incentive for these kids was, if they did a good job and kept their noses clean, they were in line for a paid Co-Op Camp counselor job when they were in high school. The objective for us was to make leaders out of them before they became problems in the high school.

"We divided the kids into groups by grade level, with about twenty in a group. We assigned four senior counselors to a group, a boy and a girl from the under-privileged neighborhood and a boy and a girl from the privileged neighborhood. We never had all senior counselors together from the under-privileged neighborhood. They were always mixed with the privileged neighborhood kids. One senior counselor was in charge, and that was always the under- privileged neighborhood kid. The point being, we wanted to make leaders out of them. The same system held true for the junior counselors.

"To be sure that our objective of making these kids into leaders, the staff prepared a leadership program for them. The instructors included me, the Chief of Police and several of his officers, the principal of the high school, high school coaches and other key teachers as well. The theme was, *who is a leader and who is not a leader?* We emphasized the fact that a leader was not a boss, but a person that commanded respect and led by example. This was a three-day program.

"The counselors reacted to the program with great enthusiasm. Perhaps for the first time in their lives they were the focus of attention from people that genuinely wanted them to succeed. Perhaps for the first time in their lives, police officers were focused on helping and encouraging them to succeed, instead of harassing them and arresting them.

"The program attracted about 300 elementary school-age students from Mamaroneck Avenue Elementary School. It was interesting to note that the first time we took the kids to the pool, none of them could swim. By the end of the first summer we had kids swimming, and by the end of the fourth summer, we had a competitive swim team. The highlight of each summer was the trip to the famous Jones Beach on the south shore of Long Island. We would hire as many buses as we needed and made the trip to the beach. Upon arrival at the beach, we staked out a sanctuary for our group, using posts with orange flags. To keep track of the 300 kids when they left the sanctuary area, we required them to wear an orange Tee-shirt that had the name CO-OP CAMP stenciled on it in big letters.

"A conscious effort was made to have the Chief of Police and many of the department patrolmen visit the campsite every day to help the kids, participate in their games, sit and chat with them and hug them. Arrangements were made to take the counselors and their kids on boat rides and fishing trips on police boats in Long Island Sound, which further solidified the growing bond between them.

"We arranged to have photos taken and a story written about the Co-Op Camp in the local newspaper, which was a huge confidence builder for the counselors and the campers. The stories and pictures depicted police officers engaged in activities with the kids, playing tennis, golf, baseball, and laughing and having a good time with each other.

"As the days progressed, the counselors discovered that the elementary school kids were looking up to them as leaders, and genuinely enjoyed being with them. Suddenly these *tough dudes* (guys and gals) were being looked up to by their peers and the younger kids. We would reinforce the notion that if they were being looked up to, then they had to continue to be a shining example, and they were.

"The Co-Op program had a positive ripple effect throughout the community. This was especially evident in the relationship between the police officers and the families in the under-privileged neighborhoods. The police patrolling the neighborhood now knew many of the kids, because they met them during the summer Co-Op program, and visa-a-versa. When they met on the street they would greet each other with a genuine friendly 'Hi Sergeant, how ya doin.' The patrolmen would stop and talk and inquire how the kids were doing in school, and reminisce about the summer Co-Op Camp happenings. The Co-Op counselor leaders continued their leadership roles at the high school and were instrumental in controlling the discipline in the high school.

"The Co-Op program also had an effect on the high school teaching staff and the school system administration. When we invited the high school teachers, the principal, the superintendent and the assistant superintendent to participate in the program, they met many kids that they had not met during the regular school year, much like the experience that the police had. This had a way of creating an *esprit de corps* between the students and teachers.

"In 1970, I was elected to the position of Trustee in Mamaroneck and became the Police Commissioner. My position as Police Commissioner allowed me to further expand the Summer Co-Op program to where it became one of the main activities of the Police Department, that paid great social dividends back to the community as a whole. My political career as Trustee and Police Commissioner lasted through three two-year terms. This six-year period afforded me the opportunity to really cement the relationship between the police force and the community, and especially with the families in the underprivileged neighborhoods."

TEAM Project.

"Four years later in 1971, we changed the name and the concept of the *Community School*. The program name was changed to TEAM (Tuesday Evening At Mamaroneck Avenue School). The concept now was to accommodate only 7th through 12th grade students and adults. The focus of the program was to give teens and adults an opportunity to work together and relate to one another.

"The younger elementary and junior high-aged students, who had participated in previous years, were scheduled for two hours of supervised after-school recreation each week.

"The offerings to the TEAM participants included basketball, modern dance, drama, art, guitar, auto mechanics, home repair and homemaking which included sewing, cooking, knitting and needlework, basic education, English as a second language, Black Culture, Italian Culture, and media which included videotaping, film and photography.

"The staff for this new program was all paid, which was a good indication of the success the program had in the eyes of the community. At this time in the program I relinquished the Directorship and became chief advisor to the new coordinator, George Sands."

The APPLE Program.

Having been a teacher myself for a short while, and very interested in education, I was particularly interested in what Dee had to tell me about the APPLE program, when I interviewed him at his log cabin hide-a-way in Conesville. The following are excerpts from that interview.

"What does the acronym APPLE mean," I asked Dee.

"The name APPLE stands for - *A Place People Learn Excellence*. We wanted a name that was simple to remember and had an educational connotation. The word APPLE seemed appropriate," he responded.

"Why and when did this APPLE program get its start," was my next question.

"Dr. Calvert Schlick, who replaced Earl Hobbs as our Assistant Superintendent, came up with the idea, and asked me to organize the program. The problem was that some of the kids, especially those from the underprivileged neighborhoods, were falling through the academic cracks, and as a result, they were disrupting the classes and thwarting the efforts of the teachers to teach and the other kids to learn. Something had to be done to stop it, and expelling them from school was not an option.

What I wanted to do was to turn them around by changing their attitude toward school and learning."

"Did you ever feel threatened by these kids?"

"No," was his unhesitating reply.

"Why not?"

"Because, in some ways I grew up like some of them and I understood why they were like they were, and they could not intimidate me. No, I would rather they beat the shit out of me than back down from them, and they knew it.

"At this time the Superintendent at Mamaroneck was Dr. Otty R. Norwood. Dr. Haake had resigned from Mamaroneck to take the position of Assistant Commissioner of Education for the State of New York. So, Cal Schlick and I went to our boss, Dr. Otty R. Norwood, and presented our proposal to start an alternative school with the philosophy that *the kids always win,* and see if we couldn't solve the problem in a positive way. Dr. Norwood agreed. The process now was to convince the high school principal that this was a good idea, and then go to the Board of Education with a convincing argument to get their approval and funding for the project. With the Principal and Superintendent behind us, the Board of Education approved the project, and steps were taken to implement the plan in September of 1977.

"The next step in the process was to sell the program to the high school faculty, and, if possible, find teachers that would be willing to be teachers in the program. My concern in hiring teachers for the program was to find those that were not prejudiced toward the kids they would be teaching. As with any new idea or project, there are always skeptics and doomsday-sayers. I did not want to have teachers on my staff that had negative attitudes toward the students they were to teach. To avoid this from happening, there was one thing I insisted upon, and that was that I would hire the teachers of my choice from within the Mamaroneck system or from outside the system. There was no way the program would work if I did not have dedicated teachers that believed in the philosophy of NEVER GIVING UP ON A KID. My idea was to hire *street smart teachers* who understood the mentality of the kids they were going to teach. The dynamics behind this approach was to establish our faculty as the strong force, and not the kids. Years ago when I was a kid, I was stronger-willed than some of my teachers, and I remembered that. I remembered how, as a kid, I took advantage of this for my own satisfaction. I wanted to be sure the teachers I hired were going to be able to stand up to these kids. During the interviews, I tested their resolve by asking them intimidating questions. In one interview, a perspective candidate came back at me quite strongly.

"Shove-it," he told me. " I don't need your bullshit. Do you want me as a teacher or not," he said. I settled him down by telling him, 'Look, if you can't take my bullshit, those kids are going to eat you alive. I'm a piece of cake compared to them.' He smiled and settled down after he realized what I had been up to."

Frank Pia describes his interview with Dee.

"Prior to the interview with Dee, I had worked at Morris High School in the South Bronx. For two years, I was employed as a classroom teacher for emotionally disturbed non-English-speaking students, and then worked as a full-time coordinator of student affairs who was the ombudsman for the students and the intermediary between the students, faculty, administration, and community. During this time, I also served as a member of the city-wide Crisis Prevention Team for the Office of High Schools for the New York City Board of Education.

"Dee, did test our resolve during the interview. Jerry Trezza, Mike Sudano and I were raised in the tough areas of the South Bronx. Dee's questions and strategies, while provocative, were not intimidating. To the male staff members being interviewed, some of his questions were a source of amusement. We lived in the tough sections of the Bronx, but also endured twelve years of elementary and high school parochial education. Nuns, Irish Christian Brothers, Jesuits, and Vincentia Missionaries were intimidating. At age 54, Dee had become an enjoyable benign person. During my interview, Dee asked me to explain why I had come so highly recommended for the English teacher position. After hearing my work history answers, he informed me that he felt school psychologists were worthless, and that my lifeguard supervision and administration work at Orchard Beach, Bronx, New York for nearly twenty years was a job for screw-ups. My experience living in the Bronx, working at Orchard Beach, teaching at Morris High School, and working as a city-wide crisis prevention and intervention team member, caused me to smile at Dee. When he asked me, 'what I was thinking,' I replied, "I was wondering how much I want this job versus when I'm going to tell you to take this job and shove it. The net result was, he hired me."

"My original five staff members," said Dee, "were Frank Pia, English teacher and school psychologist; Jerry Trezza, head football coach and social studies teacher; Michael Sudano, assistant football coach and career education teacher and acting coordinator; Lorna Greenhouse, was my math teacher; and Terry Johnson, science teacher. I had five teachers whom I was sure could not be out-smarted by our potential street-smart students. For me, this was the key to the success of the program. Our very competent secretary was Mary Chiodo.

"Our facilities were located on the third floor of the Post Road High School, which we shared with six regular school teachers. We had six rooms in close proximity to each other. We had four classrooms, a small cafeteria and a larger room for assemblies. The idea of having all our facilities on the third floor was two-fold. First, I wanted to isolate our facilities and students from the other students as much as we could. Second, I wanted to insure that the faculty and students were always together like a family. This could not be accomplished if the students and faculty were spread out from one end of the building to the other end. It would have been impossible, under those conditions, to build an *espirit de corps* within the group. The APPLE program became a school within a school. It was a family school so to speak.

"One of the first tasks we undertook, as a group, was to prepare an APPLE Handbook that: (1) Outlined the policies and procedures for conducting the program, (2) Described the curriculum outline for each of the five curriculum areas, (3) Outlined the student tracking, evaluation and conference schedule information, and (4) Outlined the APPLE Career Internship Program procedures and rules and regulations. Nothing was left to chance. Precise organization was part of the key to success.

"The system for enrolling in the APPLE program was designed to be difficult in the sense that we did not want the potential students, their parents and the high school faculty to think that this was the dumping ground for the students they couldn't control. We especially did not want to give the kids the idea that it was going to be easy to get in. If it was perceived that it was easy, then it would have had no meaning to them. It was sort of like wanting to join the Marine Corps. It's tough, and everyone knows it. We wanted them to believe that this was their last chance to be a success in life.

"The key to our success in getting the kids to be believers in our system was in how we choreographed our selection and interview process. Prior to the interview, we all reviewed the candidate's school records as far back as elementary school. We also consulted with their high school teachers and counselors. With this preparation and background knowledge of the candidate, we had a good idea of who we were dealing with, and could formulate questions that would be useful to us in evaluating his or her motivations and sincerity.

"We set up an interview system that included the student, the parent or legal guardian, our five faculty members and me. If a student came to the interview without his parent or guardian, he or she was dismissed and told to reschedule the interview when their parent or guardian was available. With a parent or guardian on hand, we could, to some degree, assess the home environment in which the kid was living. It was a group interview designed to be a bit intimidating. It was intimidating insofar as to show to all concerned that this was serious business and their future was at stake. Throughout the interviewing process, however, we reinforced our stated goal of making each student a success in his or her life by attending this school. The final decision of whether a student should be accepted into the program was made by the five facility members, and not by me. The understanding was that if I didn't trust them in the first place, I wouldn't have hired them."

I asked Dee to give me a typical scenario of how an interview would be conducted. The following scenario served as an example.

"Okay, let me set the scene for you," he said. "First of all, the entire staff participated in the interview with the student and the student's parent or guardian. We had the kid's records in front of us which we had all studied beforehand. We would confront the student with the facts in a tone of voice that was non-threatening.

"Joanne, I see from your record that you failed English, math and science last semester. Also, you got kicked out of school three times for cursing at your teachers, and ran away from home twice. Is that correct?" We would wait patiently for Joanne to respond.

"Yet, I look back at your elementary school records and I see that you were an "A" student. That tells me you're smart, but now you're a loser. Why has this changed?"

"Again, we would wait patiently for Joanne to respond and listen patiently as she tells us her story. Then we would inform Joanne of the basic rules of the program.

"Joanne, if you come into our program, our goal will be to get you back to when you were an "A" student. To accomplish this, you must do your part. Here are three basic rules you must follow: One, get to all your classes on time. Do you understand what that means? It means that if your class starts at 8 a.m., then you are to be there by 8 a.m., or before, and not 8:01 a.m. Two, be a good citizen. Do you understand what this means? It means to just be a nice person. There is no need to be nasty to anyone. When a person asks you a question, you answer nicely, and you never talk back to your teachers. If you need something, you ask for it. If you don't agree with a teacher, you say, 'I don't agree with that Mr./Ms. Jones because ....' The teacher's response will be, 'Well, you may be right. Let's talk about it.' "Three, do the best you are capable of doing. Your teachers will decide what you are capable of doing, not you. If you are potentially an "A" student, and you think you only need to do "B" work to get by, then we don't want you. If you have student potential of "C", then we will not expect "B" work. We expect "C" work. Of course, if you do better than "C," it is to your benefit. So, whatever you are capable of doing, then that is what we want. We do not want you to be doing the minimum. You don't come into this program with a potential of an "A" student, and say to yourself, 'I can do "C" work with little effort,' and spend the rest of your time cutting up and wasting other people's time. If that's what you are thinking, we don't want you. Do you understand that?

"If a student had the potential as an athlete, we would make it a condition that he or she tries out for a team or individual sport. With two coaches on the staff, we could make this happen. The purpose of imposing a sport on them was to get them involved in the school environment and learn teamwork from organized sports. If they refused, then the interview was terminated. If a student did not have the potential as a competitor, then he or she had to (no refusal accepted) get involved in a sports program as a team manager, ball boy, water girl, etc. We also pointed out to the candidates that we would not tolerate them trying to *outsmart* us. To bring this home to them, I would tell them this, 'If you outsmart us THEN YOU LOSE.'

"After all staff members and students had an opportunity to ask and answer questions, we would ask the student and the parent/guardian if they will agree to these conditions. If all parties agreed, then we would dismiss the student and his/her parent or guardian from the room, so that the final decision could be made by the staff. As director, I left the decision up to the staff that would be responsible for guiding and teaching the candidate student. After the decision was made, we called the student and parent back to the interview room and gave them our decision. It was rare that we did not accept a student.

"We rarely, if ever, had a parent who would not agree to the conditions we set down for the behavior we expected from their child. At the beginning, some students would not accept some of these conditions the first time around. But invariably almost all of them, who refused the first time around, came back to ask for another chance. This was especially true once success of the program was demonstrated by the behavior change in the kids already participating in the program. It got to the point where APPLE students were confiding in us about their friends who were all screwed up, and asking us to help them. Our APPLE students became our best recruiters.

"An interesting phenomenon resulted from this. Students recruited by our APPLE students rarely became a problem, because they feared that their friends, who recommended them for the program, would gang up on them. In essence, a self-disciplinary system emerged."

"At the beginning, what was the reaction of the regular high school teachers to the program as they saw it unfolding?" I asked Dee.

"Well, as we were going through the process of recruiting students, the toughest part was when we were opening up the school," said Dee. "The regular school teachers were saying, 'Well, they have five teachers, a director, and a full-time secretary and they only have a very few kids in the program. Hell, we could do as well in regular school if we had all that support.'

"What they failed to realize at the time," said Dee was that when you start a program, you have to go through the process of recruiting. If you don't do it properly, especially with this special program, you might just as well keep the kids in regular school. As a result of this disgruntled attitude, not by all I might add, I had to go to the regular school staff meetings to tell them not to beat up on us yet. Give us a few months to get the kids in the program that are disrupting your classes. If we just take them without screening them and indoctrinating them to our way of thinking, the result would be just another regular class. In addition, I spoke with some of the teachers who were personal friends of mine, and explained the situation to them on a one-on-one basis. This helped quell the dissention and gave us some breathing room. I have found, over my many years in education, that teachers, as a group, can be impatient and trying at times, especially when new ideas are introduced. After a few months, and the program was rolling along, our enrollment increased. Soon our program was accommodating about forty or so kids, and the school attitude began to change. Many of the troubled kids were out of the regular school classrooms, and this made the teachers happy."

Frank Pia, Alternative School teacher recalls the circumstances that prevailed when the APPLE program was getting started.

"I do not recall a time at the beginning of the program when we only had just a few kids in the program. We had to incorporate into the APPLE program the youngsters who were enrolled in the KICK program, which was the predecessor to the APPLE program. During the first weeks of the program, the relationship between the student and teacher and the student/teacher/and curriculum changed greatly for the former KICK students. The students in the KICK program called teachers by their first name and selected the curriculum they wished to study. There were adjustment problems on the part of the students when they attempted to call us by our first names, and when they wanted to determine the material that they were to study. Concurrently to working with these students, we were also interviewing students for placement in the APPLE program."

"Within two weeks after the APPLE program started, the regular teachers on the third floor adjacent to the APPLE student's classrooms came to us and thanked us for restoring order to the third floor of the Post Road building," said Dee.

"The APPLE kids were beginning to succeed as students and human beings, bringing about a change in their attitude toward school and life for that matter. There is nothing like success to breed more success.

"Academic success of the program could be attributed to several key factors. First, each grade level had a maximum of 15 to 20 students. Second, we used a team approach to teaching, and the classroom instruction was individualized. Third, in addition to the core courses, we added a Career Internship Component to the program, as described in the overview of the APPLE Handbook."

Career Internship Program.

"Our Career Internship Program was designed to allow qualified juniors and seniors in the APPLE program to explore a field in which they were interested," Dee informed me. "Testing their career perceptions against reality, interns gained first-hand knowledge concerning a specific occupation, as well as to further clarify their own interests, attitudes and preferences. In addition, it was expected that students would begin to acquire good work habits and develop interpersonal relationship skills, which are key components to successful job performance. The ultimate objective is for the students to make as well-informed career decisions as possible, utilizing first-hand experiences, in addition to practical and theoretical knowledge.

Parent/Student/Teacher Conferences.

"Parent/student/teacher conferences were scheduled four times a year during school hours. Classes met during the conferences, and were staffed by substitute teachers and teachers' aides. Staff members would periodically leave the conferences to check their classes to ensure the students were completing their assignments. There were some days when we taught classes in the morning and held conferences in the afternoon. Both the parent and the student were to be present at these conferences. If the student came without his parent, the conference was rescheduled.

"These conferences served three purposes. First, it kept the lines of communication open between our teachers, parents and students. Second, it allowed our instructors time with the parents to gain their trust. Third, the conference provided our staff with an opportunity to make adjustments in the student's program, to air grievances and overcome problems, enhance the learning process and promote maximum cooperation from the students and parents alike. Additional conferences were scheduled, as requested by a parent or staff member.

"Major problems were handled in a special way, which could not have occurred in a normal school environment. As soon as a major problem occurred, the APPLE school was shut down and everyone reported to the assembly room. For example: One day someone accidentally set a fire in a waste paper basket on the third floor. After the fire was put out, I shut the school down and we all met in the assembly room. 'Okay,' I said, 'what's the story?' Unlike most school situations like this, every kid would clam up, not wanting to be a snitch. But, once trust had been established between the students and the staff, the APPLE students, in this situation, came forth with the truth, regardless of where the chips fell, and the situation was resolved quickly. In this particular case, someone had been smoking a cigarette and accidentally dropped a snuffed-out cigarette in a trash basket. This goes back to what I said earlier, the APPLE students took it upon themselves to discipline themselves. The program meant success to them and they did not want this process interrupted.

"As teachers, when we think of discipline in the classroom, we all know that the best kind of discipline is self-discipline. In a regular school situation, a classroom encounter is handled on the spot by the classroom teacher. Disciplining an APPLE student for a major offense was a staff function. The staff, and not me as director, had the authority to remove or retain a student in the program for a major offense. The student was given a hearing, with his or her parents present, and a final decision to keep or dismiss a pupil from the program was made by the staff. Deliberations were made in private, with the student and parent absent. More than 99% of the time, the student was given a second chance, under strict conditions that were clearly defined. This was especially true if the incident was a first offense. The purpose of the formal meeting was to maximize the seriousness of the offense in the minds of the student and his or her parents, and to bring the student to the brink of the possibility that he or she could be expelled from the program. In addition, the staff wanted to observe the reaction of the student to the proceedings, to see if he or she was, to use a religious term, repentant, or showed remorse for his or her behavior. The staff also wanted to observe the parent's reaction to the proceedings. The overall effect was to show the student and parent that this was a no-nonsense program. The student was required to apologize to all the staff members for his or her behavior, and promise that he or she would not repeat the offense. If the offense was repeated, the student was dropped from the program following a specific procedure laid out in the handbook. I might add here that any student, at any time, could withdraw from the program.

"After the program got rolling, we provided the kids with special treats like rides in the police boats on Long Island Sound. Since most of these students were from tough neighborhoods, this kind of activity helped to develop mutual trust between the kids and the police.

"On occasions, I would get some extra funding to buy tickets to a Broadway show in New York City. This was something that their families could never have afforded. The down-side to providing these extra field trips was that the non-APPLE students would complain, 'Boy, the only way you can get extra things in this school is to be a screw-up.' And, on the surface, they were right. How I handled this situation was to go to these kids and tell them, 'Look, these kids have had it tough, let's not spoil a good deal.' We had to explain to them that these kids had never experienced anything good. Then, they would back off. We didn't go to these kids and say, 'Who do you think you are criticizing this program?' This would only have exacerbated the situation. Bringing logic and reason to the problem helped a great deal. Eventually, some of the best kids in the school would come in to talk and have lunch with our kids, and we encouraged this."

Then I asked Dee, "How many of your APPLE students graduated from high school?"

"About 98%, was his quick response. We tracked them all the way through college. The majority (60 to 70 percent) of these students went on to college, and about 98% of them graduated from college. Many went into the teaching profession. Some became social workers and business people. Others studied law. In fact, many times our staff would take a weekend and visit the kids at their college campus. Since most of them attended colleges in New York State it was easy for us to jump in our cars and take off for one of these campus visits."

The following article written by staff writers Melissa Klein and Robert Viagas in the Mamaroneck, N.Y. Newspaper, *The Daily Times*, **February 14, 1979, titled, <u>Apple Students Praise DaBramo</u>,** best describes the breadth of success that the Apple program had.

Although it occurred a day early, perhaps the greatest outpouring of love for a single person this Valentine's Day was by 85 members of the MHS APPLE (A Place People Learn Excellence) program, for their "fearless leader" Emilio "Dee" DaBramo.

DaBramo and company attended the Mamaroneck School Board meeting to make a presentation on the function of APPLE, but most of those teachers, parents and students, who rose to detail the program, devoted a large portion of their speeches to praise DaBramo.

APPLE not to be confused with PERFECT (Physical Education Reaching For Every Child Today), a program for the handicapped which DaBramo also heads, is an alternative high school program geared to the needs of those students who have been turned off from the regular classroom environment for a variety of reasons.

"The APPLE staff loves Dee," stated teacher Michael Sudano. "Some talk about doing things for kids, but Dee does them."

"Dee has been a second father to my son," added Nancy Davis, who also proclaimed, "If I had my life to live over, I would like to be a teacher on the APPLE staff."

Charles Albert, an APPLE parent, said, "Like most parents, I came to him in desperation. The first thing I saw was that it's obvious that this (the staff) is not just a bunch of professionals, it's a family." He went on to cite the, "patience, love and tenderness" that APPLE lavishes upon its members – words not usually associated with education.

According to the nearly two dozen speakers, APPLE is working to "turn on" students to education. "From this child, all of a sudden he realized it isn't cool to be dumb," said Mrs. Davis, who said the only reason her son wanted to go to high school was to play football."

She said that when she saw Warren's latest report card, "I was never so proud in my life. My son owes his life to this staff and Mr. DaBramo."

According to DaBramo, who brushed aside the avalanche of praise, the program was designed for 60 students, but served 85, with more on the waiting list.

But what does APPLE have that evokes such rapture from its members? It is a combination of academics, career counseling, physical fitness, and the glue holding them together (and holding formerly wayward students in the program), is the one-on-one counseling that motivates students to learn.

"I hung out in the halls, cut classes and got into trouble," said freshman Dom Forti, "but since coming to APPLE, I've become an A-1 student. They make you work whether you like it or not, and they don't take any garbage from you. They demand that you treat them with respect."

"Before I came, I was a total shambles," added Robert Baldera, "but I learned to respect myself."

End of Article

The following article was written eight years after Dee resigned from the Mamaroneck School System. Michael Sudano was the APPLE Coordinator at this time. Dee was invited to the tenth anniversary celebration.

The article written by staff writer Melissa Klein of the Mamaroneck, N.Y. Newspaper, *The Daily Times*, 1979 issue, titled, <u>Mamaroneck High School's APPLE program celebrates 10th anniversary</u>, tells of the success of the program over the first ten years.

Six years ago Nadine Ferrari cut classes at Mamaroneck High School and never considered going to college. Today, she is preparing to enter law school. "If it wasn't for APPLE, I would have never gone to college," said Miss Ferrari, who was a graduate this month from Pace University, and is filling out applications for law school.

APPLE – A Place People Learn Excellence – celebrated its 10th anniversary Thursday night as the alternative high school program at Mamaroneck High School.

More than 270 students, alumni, parents and staff members attended an anniversary party at Rye Golf Club – a celebration that occasionally resembled the gathering of a large family. "I feel like the father of the bride," said Michael Sudano, APPLE Coordinator for the past seven years, as he embraced former students.

APPLE was the brainchild of Dee DaBramo, former coordinator of the program, who said he used to walk through the halls of the high school and see "all these great kids who were falling down through the cracks."

Although the school already had an alternative program, DaBramo, who was curriculum supervisor at the school, said he wanted to start one with a different philosophy. His goal, he said, "was to have every student reach his potential."

"The first years of the program were tough," he said, "as five teachers struggled to build a sense of trust with the students. You can't kid a kid. They know if you care," said DaBramo, who retired in 1979.

Frank Pia, an English teacher who has been with APPLE since its inception said, "I have watched the program grow from one, where just getting students to class was an accomplishment, into a curriculum where learning is just as important as in regular high school.

"Students go through a tough interview process to be admitted to APPLE" Pia said. "The program's staff must feel there is a commitment on the part of the student to do well. Most Apple students were underachievers in the regular high school program and had poor self- images because of academic problems," Pia said. "Using a team approach, small classes and instant discipline, APPLE helps students become successful," he said. "Although students can leave the APPLE program at any time, most opt to stay," Pia said. He added that the majority of APPLE graduates go on to college.

Jerry Trezza, the program's social studies teacher, said "APPLE students are a pleasure to teach because they really want to succeed. They give you back everything you gave to them."

Jodi Stern, who graduated from the school in 1982, and now works as a real estate appraiser, said, "The APPLE program was like a family. It's not a dumb place. We just needed discipline," she said.

Lisa Fail Lance, who graduated in 1981, said she cried when her mother suggested that she enter APPLE because there was "nothing wrong with me." But after having gone through the program, she said, "It was the best thing that ever happened to me."

End of article.

"If I was to summarize the APPLE program," Dee proclaimed, "I would say this. The first year was a bit rough on all of us. Our major struggle was to gain the trust of the kids and parents and the respect of the regular high school teachers for the program. The former was easier than the latter. The second year was a good bit easier because we had some experience behind us. By the time we went through a complete four-year cycle we had the situation well in hand. It was funny because, by now, our reputation for success preceded us, and we even had parents and kids coming to our interviews in their *Sunday go-to-church clothes*," Dee proudly told me.

The appreciation of Dee's work with the APPLE program by the Mamaroneck community is summarized in an editorial, written in the Mamaroneck, N.Y., newspaper, *The Daily Times* in 1979, titled, <u>200 Attend Surprise Party for DaBramo.</u>

More than 200 family members, friends and school and village officials crowded into Alex and Henry's Restaurant in Scarsdale Thursday night to throw a surprise retirement party for Mamaroneck educator Emilio "Dee" DaBramo.

DaBramo, who heads the APPLE (A Place People Learn Excellence) program at MHS, officially retires from the Mamaroneck Union Free

School District at the end of this school year. He is expected, however, to take on a part-time consultant's position for a similar APPLE program at the Hommocks School. In the summer, he is the coordinator of the Co-Op Camp and the Special Olympics.

For 15 years, DaBramo's energies have carried him into virtually every aspect of school life, a characteristic which won him the "Super Emilio" theme at his party. The Superman concept was carried over musically and poetically in the spirit of good fun.

"They are super people," said DaBramo, returning the compliment today. "I didn't know anything about it. There were many close friends there." Master of Ceremonies for the event was Calvert E. Schlick, Jr., Assistant Superintendent of Schools. Perry Martin and his orchestra entertained with original music and lyrics.

A book of letters and photographs were presented to the 56-year-old administrator, but one of the evening's highlights was a singing telegram sent from the family of Gloria Landes, the renowned Larchmont dance instructor.

Among the party's guests were School Superintendent Dr. Otty Norwood, School Board President Jane Orans, Mayor Suzi Oppenheimer, Mamaroneck Village Manager Armand Gianunzio and Mamaroneck Police Chief Louis LiFrieri. Assemblyman John M. Perone, R-Mamaroneck also made an appearance. Rep. Richard Otinger, D-Mamaroneck, could not attend, but expressed his regrets and good wishes to DaBramo in a letter.

End of article

The Project PERFECT Program.

The PERFECT program, *Physical Education Reaching For Every Child Today* was designed to implement a system of athletic competitions for the handicapped in the area of interscholastic sports. Dee initiated the program in the Mamaroneck school system in 1977. It was the first of its kind in the United States. The prelude leading up to this program, however, began many years before its introduction at Mamaroneck. His first encounter with the mentally challenged and Down's syndrome individuals came in 1948 in Amenia, New York at the Wassaic Mental Institute, as described in Chapter 7. The experience with these individuals made an indelible impression on his mind. Then, of course, his experience with the Special Olympics beginning in 1968, as described in Chapter

10, had a profound influence on his decision to launch the PERFECT program as well.

"It wasn't until I arrived in Mamaroneck that the opportunity arose to do something for the intellectually and physically challenged children of a school system on a grand scale," Dee said. "The educational environment under Superintendent Dr. Norwood, and Assistant Superintendent Cal Schlick, Jr. was conducive to new innovations, so I seized the opportunity.

"I always felt the handicapped kids in the public schools were getting short-changed when it came to physical education and sports. The schools were spending hundreds of thousands of dollars for sports programs for kids that were physically fit, and nothing for kids that needed it the most. It just didn't seem fair to me. So, Cal Schlick and I went to Dr. Norwood with our proposal. Knowing of my eight years of experience with the Special Olympics, he listened intently to my rationale, asked a few poignant questions as he always did, and without hesitation, gave Cal and me the go-ahead. I just loved that man. He was one of the most intelligent guys I had ever met. He was quick at evaluating a situation and decisive in his decision-making. Our long-standing relationship of mutual trust helped a great deal.

"Now my job was to convince the special education teachers, the kids' parents and the Board of Education that what we were proposing was worthwhile.

"Prior to instituting project PERFECT, I and the physical education staff, had been working to improve the physical education programs for the special education students in all the Mamaroneck schools. (Described in Part I of this chapter.)

"In addition to improving the physical education program for these kids, we also worked hard to change the perception of how the administration, teachers and the community viewed special education. Traditionally, the special education program was treated as the stepchild of the system. After a while we were able to elevate the status of the program where they got the best facilities and a budget that would support innovative teaching programs, audio visual equipment and money for an outdoor education program.

"One of our first outdoor education programs took place at a remote location in Pawling, New York. We would take a group of about twenty special education kids and ten high school student volunteers to the Holiday Hills YMCA Conference Center in Pawling, for a week."

Holiday Hills YMCA Conference Center was part of the same facility used by the Army Air Corps during and after WWII as a rehabilitation center for combat fatigued airmen. Dee spent six months rehabilitating at this facility from February 1945 to the day of his discharge on September 4, 1945, after flying more than thirty missions as a radio operator on a B-24 bomber over German occupied Europe. (Reference Chapter 5)

"We would arrive on Monday morning and return to Mamaroneck on Friday night," Dee continued. "The program was highly structured. The outdoor activities depended on the season of the year. The activities included hiking, outdoor education experiences requiring social interaction and working together. Art and music were very important parts of the program as well. I would always have a music teacher and an art teacher spend a few days with the kids. The kids loved to draw and sing, and these activities became a very important part of the program. When the kids returned to school, we would organize a parent night for them to exhibit and share their camping experience with their parents and friends.

"Before we started this outdoor camping program, we had skeptics from both teachers and parents. Most parents of these children are overprotective. 'Oh, I don't know about this. My kid wets the bed at night, and it could be very embarrassing for him, etc. etc.' Our job was to meet with the parents, and listen to their objections/suggestions, and involve them in the decision-making process. To solve the bed wetting problem, for example, we brought rubber mats for the beds, but if we hadn't listened to the parents, we would not have been prepared to handle the situation. Ninety nine percent of the time we were successful in handling the parents' and teachers' objections to their satisfaction, and we did this by carefully listening to them.

"Some of the ideas incorporated in this program did not avoid criticism. We were criticized by the State Education Department for a lot of things we were doing. Their objections ranged from, 'This wasn't done with the regular kids, and all of a sudden you're doing these things with Down's syndrome kids. What about if a kid gets hurt, who's responsible? What about the possibility of getting sued? etc. etc.'

"I got so sick of listening to these objections and getting little encouragement. My attitude to this kind of pessimism was that you have to be a little bit gutsy in this world if you are going to create change, but we prevailed," said Dee.

"With our physical education program for the special education kids in place, project PERFECT was a natural progression in the scheme of things. We had no problem convincing the special education teachers to buy into project PERFECT. They were amazed at the fact that there was a nut out there willing to work with their kids. The parents were equally as enthusiastic.

"Project PERFECT was instituted in Mamaroneck schools first. We organized our first sports festival involving only the schools within the Mamaroneck school system. For this to be a success, we had to plan every detail before a single event was staged.

"We put together a three-tier training program. First, our physical education instructors were already working with the kids in their physical education classes. (Described in Part I of this chapter.) Second, we conducted in-service training for the special education classroom teachers in all the physical fitness and sporting activities. Third, we had to train many volunteers. The volunteers included parents of the special education students, high school students who were sisters or brothers of special education students, or other parents and high school students that were very interested in working with these kids.

"Sensitivity training for the volunteers was an important component of the training program. We wanted them to be familiar with the behavior and mannerisms they might expect from these children. Of course, we couldn't cover every behavioral pattern they might encounter, but we succeeded in making them feel comfortable in what they were about to be confronted with.

"Then there were the nuts and bolts training required to run the festival events. This had to be precise and detailed, as was practiced at the Special Olympic Games. Every competitor was linked up with a volunteer counselor. The counselors were provided with an event schedule, and their responsibility was to stick with that competitor from the time he or she arrived on the scene until the events of the day were over. Their job was also to make them feel welcome, comfortable, and at home. They were required to take them to the locker room and locate their locker, know where and when they had to go to compete, when and where to go for lunch, and escort them to the bathroom, and so on. All the competitors had to do was to follow their counselors. This took a great deal of time, but without this training the competition would not have succeeded.

"The competition was held in Mamaroneck during the regular school schedule. This was done by design. We wanted the regular school kids to be able to observe the special education students in action. We even had the special education kids and the regular school students eat lunch together in the same cafeteria. We felt that this would be a good way to expose and sensitize them to special education students, and perhaps change their attitude toward the way they perceived them. In other words, we were not hiding them away from society, which had been the practice in the past.

"Thankfully, our first interscholastic competition for physically and mentally-challenged and socially-maladjusted students went very well. The event was witnessed by many skeptics whom we successfully converted into believers.

"The natural progression of events was to have a Section One Interscholastic Sports Competition for the mentally and physically challenged. Section One included schools in Dutchess, Putnam, Rockland and Westchester counties.

"By 1979, Project PERFECT became a New York state-wide program under Title VI-B and funded by the Division for the Handicapped."

The Article, What is Project PERFECT?, published in Volume 1, Number 1, November 17, 1977 Newsletter, *PERFECT-LY Speaking,* written by the Mamaroneck Project PERFECT staff, under the direction of Dee DaBramo, best tells about the inner workings of the program.

Project PERFECT, which is being developed as a portable method to be disseminated to other communities in New York State, involves physically and mentally-handicapped and socially-maladjusted students in our schools, providing daily physical education experiences. In addition, the project coordinators are initiating interscholastic programs for all handicapped students in Section I, a first in New York State, and possibly in the entire nation.

Additional objectives and goals include the involvement of administrators, physical educators and parents through the development of workshops and in-service sessions to make educators more capable of meeting the specific needs of the handicapped. A course given at the College of New Rochelle, as part of the project for classroom teachers, as well as physical educators, further creates the chance to expand additional awareness and techniques of adapted physical education.

The program employs a staff of five: Emilio "Dee" DaBramo, curriculum supervisor, three full-time physical educators who coordinate the project, and a stenographer. Students are scheduled, in supplement to their regular physical education classes, in groups or as individuals. Long-term goals are for all handicapped students to have the opportunity to experience all that any other student can and does.

STUDENTS INVOLVED.

The PERFECT staff is involved with approximately fifty-five students throughout the Mamaroneck system. Classroom teachers work directly with the PERFECT staff on a regular basis. Individual students are involved with the project coordinators at each of the schools, for additional experiences. All students have been, or are in the process of being tested, to determine capabilities and necessary areas of improvement.

PHYSICAL EDUCATION ACTIVITIES.

The project PERFECT staff provides supplemental physical education classes to handicapped children's usual gym period. The PERFECT staff tries to be as consistent with the usual physical education curriculum as possible. There are activities which bring the children out of the physical educators' learning laboratory –the gym. For example: Every Monday morning children from Mamaroneck are bused to the Fox Hills Stable in Pleasantville as part of the Pegasus Riding Therapy Program. Safety is the utmost concern. Children are given riding helmets, and each child is spotted by two side walkers and a third person leading the horse. An instructor leads the children through an obstacle course, therapeutic exercises to gain confidence on the horse and improve balance as well. Children also receive instructions on proper grooming, bridling and saddling.

A group of students also goes to the Loyal Inn Bowling Alley. There, they improve their bowling averages. On Fridays, the children go swimming in the indoor pool at the Hommocks School. These activities help to aid the children's social development as well as their physical development.

INTERSCHOLASTICS FITNESS FESTIVAL.

As part of Project PERFECT, we are, for the first time in New York and probably nationwide, initiating the opportunity for the handicapped students in Mamaroneck schools to participate in the newly formed Section I Handicapped Interscholastic Program.

Tournaments will be held throughout the school year in various activities and skills between students from many districts in the Section. At least six school districts are already participating in the Fitness Festival. All training and preparation will take place within the normal activity periods allotted during the school day.

Our first tournament has already been organized and is scheduled for Thursday, November 17, 1977 from 4:00 to 7:00 p.m., at the Hommocks School. Inaugural competition will be a Fitness Festival including strength and agility exercises, which all of our students are familiar with. We are excited with the prospect of offering such an opportunity to our students. The Project PERFECT staff, along with the additional Mamaroneck staff will be in charge of supervision of all participating Mamaroneck students.

End of Article.

"The first Section One Interscholastic Tournament for the Handicapped occurred on November 17, 1977 at the Hommocks Middle School in Mamaroneck," Dee recalled. "I chose Hammocks because I had complete control over the facilities and had good working relations with the administration and faculty. The first competition was a Fitness Festival made up of twelve fitness test items that all competitors were trained in, prior to their participation. Ten schools sent representatives – Arlington, Blind Brook, BOCES – Dutchess County, Kingston, Mamaroneck, Pawling, Port Chester, Sleepy Hollow, White Plains and Yonkers. Sixty-two students participated. It was a great success. Organizing this event was a major operation. At this time, however, I was President of South East Zone of the New York State Association for Health, Physical Education, Recreation and Dance, and knew or had befriended all the key administrators in Section One. I wrote a letter to each school administrator, inviting them to have their Special Education students participate. Ten schools responded, along with some of my staff, and about 40 other volunteers.

"To get the Section One physical education instructors and special education teachers up to speed on the program, I held in-service training two to three evenings a week, at the Westchester County Center. Some of these teachers were skeptical and made remarks, such as 'those kids shouldn't be doing that. People are going to laugh at them.' In addition to training them, I felt it was my job to motivate them by always being upbeat and enthusiastic about everything I taught them. And, it worked.

"For the school year of 1977-1978, seven other interscholastic tournaments were scheduled for the special education students. They included indoor soccer, bowling, volleyball, gymnastics, swimming, Frisbee-tennis and track and field.

"With each tournament the number of schools participating increased. The soccer tournament attracted sixteen schools. By the end of the 1977-1978 school year, twenty-five Section One Schools had participated in one or more tournaments.

"In 1980, my staff of J. Kenneth Hafner, Sandy Morley and Mae Timer prepared the final draft of the Rules and Regulations for interscholastic meets for the handicapped for the New York State Public High School Athletic Association, Inc.

"As the years went by, Project PERFECT was recognized by every school in New York State, and each of the eleven sections had a program in place.

"Since I was familiar with the facilities of the University of Rochester, I decided to contact the Chancellor to obtain his permission to use their facilities to hold the first State Interscholastic Meet for the Handicapped. He generously agreed to my proposal. The first task of the planning committee was to survey the facilities at the university, and select dates that would fall between the end of the spring semester and the beginning of the summer session so that we could take advantage of the campus housing to house the athletes and our staff of volunteers. The volunteers for the meet came from the students and faculty of the University of Rochester and the participating school districts. To recruit these volunteers, we visited the classes on campus and asked for volunteers to sign up. Our recruiting campaign was successful. This meant that we had to train these volunteers in the system, as we had previously done with the parents and kids at Mamaroneck. The planning and training took almost a year. The meet ran from Friday night through sometime on Sunday. It drew 800 to 900 participants from all over the state and was a great success. The meet generated a lot of publicity throughout the state, and at the next convention of the New York State Association of Health, Physical Education, Recreation and Dance, the place was buzzing about the PERFECT Interscholastic Meet for the Handicapped held at the University of Rochester. To reinforce the concept at the convention, we had people who participated in the program-- teachers, volunteers and participants, including Down's syndrome kids, give testimonials to our convention audiences. With the success of the meet, the controversy over the idea had ended and everyone wanted to climb on board. This was exactly what we wanted and expected to happen. Successive meets were even bigger until the attendance leveled off at about 1000 to 1200 participants."

Part III Education and Community Politics.

"Until 1970, I had no idea of ever getting involved in public politics. One day, several months before the March 17, 1970 elections for the Mamaroneck Village Board of Trustees, a representative from the Democratic Party, I don't remember specifically who it was, approached me to run as a candidate for Village Trustee. The representative argued the point that since I have been an administrator in the Mamaroneck Schools for twelve years and active in the community, Games Director for the New York State Special Olympics, etc., that I had good name recognition and was well-liked in the community, and that the party thought I would be an ideal candidate for the position of Trustee. My first reaction was, I was flattered and shocked at the same time. I asked the representative for a few days to deliberate the offer and that I would get back in touch in with him. During the deliberation process, I thought of how being in the position of Trustee could enhance my ability to advance the school and community programs for kids. I accepted the offer, not knowing what getting into public politics was all about. It turned out to be a rude awakening. Having spent twenty-four years as an educator, I had learned the art of persuasion, using logic and reason dealing with like-minded people. I quickly found out that politics with some people was a belief system that is closely aligned to a religious theology, which can be impenetrable to logic and reason.

"I went through a brief training session in the art of door-to-door campaigning, passing out leaflets and introducing myself. On the whole, I had an easy time of it since I knew many of the people I was approaching. Early in the campaign, in fact on the first day of knocking on doors, I ran into a guy who was aligned with one of the two opposition parties running against me. When he came to the door to respond to my knock, and found out that I was running on the Democratic ticket, he began chewing me up one side and down the other for no other reason, except that I was a Democrat. For one of the few times in my life I didn't know what to say, so I just walked away, embarrassed and furious over his lack of respect for his fellow man. I remember thinking that man had never learned the importance of respecting his fellow man like my father, Michael, had taught me as a kid.

"Well, I had the last laugh over that guy. I was the top vote-getter and won the Trustee Seat on March 17, 1970. I took office as one of the Village Trustees and as Police Commissioner on April 1, 1970."

Two years later Dee ran again. He ran on his record of accomplishments with the youth programs he had helped to initiate with the other village trustees in the community.

The following article in the Mamaroneck, N.Y. newspaper, *The Daily Times*, March 15, 1972, titled, DaBramo Cites Youth Programs, best describes these accomplishments.

"Since my life's work has been devoted to the growth and development of young people, I take particular pride in the youth programs that Trustees John Porter, Dan Natchez and I have instituted during the past two years," Trustee DaBramo told a meeting of voters at the home of Mac Cohen, 705 Palmer Court.

"Our young people represent our greatest resource," he continued, "and our youth programs are our most important investment."

DaBramo said: "Our youth programs have three main goals. First, to make our youth a part of our community life; second, to help those youths who are in trouble; and, third, to provide a broad range of recreational and cultural activities in which our youngsters can participate. In each of these areas, our efforts have been successful. I hope we will be able to continue this work."

"The Youth Who Care program," DaBramo said, "has made young people a positive force in community life. The participants in this program have undertaken successful projects to clean up the village and river, lessen harbor pollution, and measure Village streets. The participants have had the valuable experience of seeing how community needs can be met by community effort, and the village has had the benefit of their cooperative endeavors."

DaBramo also discussed, "one of the gravest problems facing our youth today is drugs." He discussed the creation and purpose of the Narcotics

Guidance Council which has recently been established, "and is actively working with young people who have narcotic problems." He noted that, "in recognition of the fact that narcotics and other youth problems exist seven days a week and 24 hours a day, an around the clock 'hot line' has been set up, making immediate counseling available to any youth in need."

On the subject of recreational and cultural activities for youth, DaBramo suggested that the voters ask their children and their neighbors' children what is going on for them, indoors or outdoors, summer or winter. I don't think you can find another community with so much to offer," he said.

End of Article.

Dee won a second term as Village of Mamaroneck Trustee and for a second time garnered the most votes of any of the candidates. In 1974, Dee ran for a third term as Village Trustee.

The following article in the Mamaroneck, N.Y. newspaper, *The Daily Times*, March, 1974, titled, DaBramo, describes his philosophy of leadership and his accomplishments in the community of Mamaroneck.

Emilio DaBramo, seeking re-election to a third term as Trustee, feels that he has done a great deal to develop mutual trust in his four years on the village board. "Without mutual trust, nothing happens," says DaBramo, adding, "I'm easy to talk to and have always honestly told residents how I feel about projects and programs, rather than tell them what they want to hear.

"Because of this, I think I have developed a great deal of respect and trust from residents. And, in times like these, that's important," DaBramo says.

DaBramo, who served on the Village Parks and Recreation Commission from 1967 until his election as Trustee in 1970, has been a teacher since 1948, and is presently Director for Health, Physical Education and Safety in the Mamaroneck Schools.

"I'm honest and have never promised anything, but have tried to help people. Anyone can check my record as to the time I have devoted to the village. My record of accomplishments for the village, I feel, speaks for itself," DaBramo says.

DaBramo is active in the New York State Special Olympics and other programs for retarded children, including Camp Smith for Retarded Children, and is a clinician for the President's Council on Physical Fitness. Himself, a member of the All American Soccer Team in 1947, DaBramo is a member of and has served in official roles with the Soccer Coaches and Officials Association, the Gymnastics Coaches and Officials Association, and the New York State Association for Health, Physical Education and Recreation.

DaBramo recently received the Pace Award for Citizenship given to him by the Italian-American Democratic Organization.

End of Article.

Dee handily won a third term as a Village Trustee, and for the third time garnered more votes than any other candidate from all political parties.

Dee's original assumption for running for office in 1970 was, "During my deliberation process, I made the assumption that becoming a Village Trustee had the potential for enhancing my ability to advance the goals of the school and programs for kids in the community." This turned out to be a valid assumption.

Dee Resigns from the Mamaroneck Union Free School System.

At the end of the school year in 1979, Dee resigned from his position with the Mamaroneck School System, and contracted to be the Acting Principal at the Pleasantville High School in Pleasantville, New York. This decision to resign had a personal side and a political side. From the personal side of his life, Dee and his wife, Celeste, were divorced in 1976, and he moved to an apartment in White Plains.

As the author of this book, I can not definitively state the political reasons for his resignation, since I was not a witness to the everyday happenings in the Village of Mamaroneck. The best I can offer is excerpts from the writings of others in the Mamaroneck newspaper, and allow you, the reader, to come to your own conclusions. In addition, the names of the individuals involved in the debate have been dropped.

Excerpts from the interview with Dee written by Mary Bauer of the Mamaroneck, N.Y. newspaper, *The Daily Times* on August 22, 1980, titled: <u>DaBramo bids Mamaroneck Farewell</u>, provides some insights into the reasons for his resignation.

Emilio "Dee" DaBramo, a feverish force in the Mamaroneck School District for 18 years, looked back recently on the final dispute that led to his departure from the system and concluded. "You always pay a wicked price for being yourself."

After three years with APPLE, which he helped to start, DaBramo bowed out this year, following a decision by the school board to cut his time and compensation from four to two days a week.

The compromise decision, reached between trustees who wanted to retain DaBramo and those who wanted to drop him, goes deeper than the effort to save $13,500, the difference between four-and two-days a week remuneration. DaBramo insists the friction between him and the board was not over his undisputed ability to do the job, but over his no-holds-barred personality, which he admits can be abrasive. "Some Trustee," DaBramo said, "couldn't wait to see me leave."

Privately, top school officials say, without hesitation, that DaBramo's irreverence for the polished dignity and euphemistic language of the board rooms –counterbalanced by his fierce devotion to kids – irritated the starch out of several policy-makers.

...... Former board president XXXX XXXXX championed DaBramo through the public and private budget debates over his compensation (which accounts for a thimble's worth of the $22.6 million ocean of the budget).

Mrs. XXXXX frequently said she was driven to tears of anger by her colleagues' insistence that DaBramo's role could easily be taken over by regular staff members.

Ironically, DaBramo agrees on this point with the board members who pushed through the decision that ultimately led to his departure.

"Leadership," he said, "is the ability to put together a program and a team that can keep on functioning effectively, even after the originator has departed. Teamwork, a collective effort to thrash out problems and their solutions, is at the heart of the APPLE program," he said.

DaBramo said this week he is confident APPLE will thrive under the leaders and staff that carry on. He expressed similar confidence in Summer Co-Op Camp which he helped to bring from a dream to a bustling reality, beginning twelve years ago.

For DaBramo admirers (and, as he agrees, people either love him or hate him, but rarely feel neutral toward him) the question wells up: Why not stay with APPLE, even for two days a week? Why not stay with Co-Op Camp during the summers?

"Because it would never work," DaBramo replies. "The bonds between APPLE students and staff hold tight after the 3 p.m. bell rings. The concern of Co-Op counselors for campers remains firm from August to the following June.

"Both programs are designed to light a spark in children who have no use for school. Both," DaBramo said, "demand of him and all staffers a 100 percent commitment."

"On a four-day-a-week contract last year," he said, "I spent five days at the school because there was no other way I could do the job. On a two-day-a-week contract," he said, "the situation would be no different."

Similarly, DaBramo said, he could not work in Co-Op Camp only during the summers, because most counselors work with and grow with the campers throughout the year. "This attitude," DaBramo said, "is essential."

Interviewed in December, Dr. Otty Norwood, Superintendent of Schools, said, "APPLE staffers give up their weekends and evenings to go into the students' homes and talk with the families. It's almost a vocation."

DaBramo said, "I'll miss the APPLE students unbelievably, but I've learned to take the ups with the downs." He concluded, "It's a big world, and there's a lot to do."

End of Article.

On September 4, 1980, Alan Scott, former member of the Mamaroneck Board of Education, wrote the following Letter to the Editor of the Mamaroneck, N.Y. newspaper *The Daily Times*, **regarding Dee leaving the Mamaroneck Schools, titled, <u>Dee Was a Doer.</u>**

It was with a good deal of sadness that I read the article about (Emilio) Dee DaBramo leaving our school system. In my opinion, it is a great loss.

It would take a letter longer than this for me to catalogue Dee's service to this community. The Bible says, 'You are your brother's keeper.' Dee was the embodiment of this spirit. He was a one-man interracial committee. He was trusted by and could talk to all the forgotten kids in our school district. He inspired Co-Op Camp, which developed leadership in our youngsters and provided an excellent summer program. He had his own "Outward Bound" group at the Hommocks, and – just one example of its effectiveness – he taught a handicapped boy, confined in a wheelchair, how to swim. Weekend after weekend he took handicapped kids to his place in the mountains. All this barely scratched the surface of his good work.

In public meetings he was abrasive to some, but my rule of thumb with Dee was not to judge him by what he said but rather by what he did. The incredible number of kind, good things Dee accomplished puts him very high on the list of people I admire.

It's sad to lose him in our school system, and I think our community owes him a very, very large "thank you."

I'd like to be first in line to do that. ALLAN SCOTT, Larchmont.

End of Letter to the Editor.

As author, I would be remiss if I did not speak of Dee's family life during his career at Mamaroneck. He and his wife, Celeste, raised four children - Michael, Debbie, Shelly and Jim. They all graduated from Rye Neck High School in Mamaroneck. Michael, the oldest of the four children, graduated in 1968, and went on to Rochester University, graduating in 1972. Debbie graduated in 1971, and attended Southern Connecticut State University. Shelly graduated in 1972 and matriculated at Springfield College in Springfield, Massachusetts, graduating in 1976. Jim graduated in 1976 and went on to Hartwick College in Oneonta, N.Y., graduating in 1980.

Dee's life in Mamaroneck was not free of disappointment and tragedy. On May 21, 1968, Dee's mother, Josephine, whom he cherished dearly, had a stroke and passed away.

Julie Czerenda, Dee's niece, tells of her grandmother's last days. "My Grandmother, Josephine, died May 21, 1968 when I was nine years old. She had suffered a second stroke and was in a coma for eleven days and died in the hospital. My mother, Aida, and my Aunt Sadie were with her daily during that time."

In 1976, Michael, Dee's father, died at age 94 while living with

Dee's sister Sadie since age 90. Julie Czerenda speaks of her love for her grandfather and of his love for his wife Josephine.

"During my junior year of high school, my family and I spent all of our Christmas vacation with Grandpa and Sadie's family. I remember the ride home in the car talking with my parents about how much Grandpa was forgetting and how sad it made me.

" I remember feeling so strange when my father told me Grandpa had passed away. I was at school that day and my trigonometry teacher told me go to the office to take a phone call. The call was from my Daddy who told me that Grandpa had died, and he was coming to pick me up and bring me home. I remember Grandpa fondly. When he was visiting with us, or I was with him in Pawling at Aunt Sadie's house, at night I used to help him into bed and cover him up. When I would bend over to kiss him good night, he would always say, 'You be a good girl now.' Mom used to say, 'You'll always know what that means!'

"Grandpa prayed in Italian every night. After Grandma died, he used to talk with her during his prayers. I asked Mommy what he was saying, and she and I listened one night. Grandpa was speaking to God saying he had tried to live a good life and do what was right and that he was ready whenever he wanted to take him. He missed his "Pippenelle" (his name of endearment for grandma) and that he wanted to be with her, but he would wait until God was ready to take him."

In the same year Dee and Celeste were divorced. 1976 was a very traumatic year for all members of the DaBramo family.

Summary of Dee's contribution to the Mamaroneck Union Free School District, the Mamaroneck Community, the State of New York, and Nationally and Internationally during his 18-year Career in Mamaroneck.

Contributions to the Mamaroneck Union Free School District
- Director of Health and Physical Education and Safety.
- Curriculum Supervisor (K-12).
- House Principal – Mamaroneck High School.
- APPLE Program.
- PERFECT Program.
- YETP Youth Employment Training Program.

- Career Internship Program.
- Mamaroneck Avenue School's – Neighborhood Community School and TEAM Program.
- Promoted Gymnastics in Westchester County with two-time Olympian (1948 /1952) Vincent D'Autorio who, along with Mamaroneck High School gymnasts went from school to school presenting gymnastic shows and encouraged schools to purchase equipment. He helped to train coaches and establish teams.
- Promoted tennis as a life-long sport with tennis great Arthur Ashe holding tennis clinics.

Contributions to the Mamaroneck Community
- Village of Mamaroneck Trustee (6 years).
- Village of Mamaroneck Police Commissioner (6 years).
- Member - County of Westchester Criminal Justice Coordinating Commission.
- Member - Westchester County Mental Health Services.
- Founder/Coordinator Summer CO-OP Program.
- Member - Project Ageless Committee.
- Member - Project Aging Committee.
- Member - Mamaroneck Village Parks and Recreation Commission.
- Member - Mamaroneck Village Group Housing Committee.
- Member of the Advisory Commission for the Westchester Office for the Handicapped.
- Member - County of Westchester Youth Board.
- Consultant for Community Drug Publications.

Contributions to the State of New York
- 1966 - President, New York State Association for Health, Physical Education, Recreation and Dance.
- 1966 – Organizer of Governor Rockefeller's Program for Disadvantaged Youth under Director, Major League Baseball great, Jackie Robinson.
- 1967 - Initiated "Project Opportunity" at SUNY College at Cortland.
- 1968-1980 - Games Director for the New York State Special Olympics.

- 1971 - Organized the Jean Ann Kennedy Smith Summer Co-Op Camp for mentally and physically challenged individuals in Pawling, New York.

Contributions to National and International Organizations.
- 1968 –1980 Member - National Advisory Committee, Joseph P. Kennedy Jr. Foundation for the Mentally Retarded.
- 1971-1985 - Advisor and Clinician, President's Council on Physical Fitness and Sports.
- 1976- U.S. Representative to Portugal for The President's Council on Physical Fitness and Sports.
- 1978 - Representative to Italy for Eunice Kennedy Shriver to promote the Special Olympics in that country.

University Degrees and Professional Certifications
- SUNY Cortland, BS 1948, MS 1953.
- New York State Chief School Officer.
- New York State School Administrator and Supervisor.
- Certified as teacher of Health and Physical Education.

Honors and Special Awards up to 1979.
- 1969 - Recipient of the Cortland College Alumni Association Distinguished Alumni Service Award.
- 1971 - Inducted into the "C" club Hall of Fame at SUNY Cortland. As an undergraduate he was the first All-American Soccer Player from Cortland to be selected for the honor.
- 1971 – Received the 1971 Annual Award for the Most Valuable Person to the Special Olympics in the Atlantic and Northeastern Region.
- 1974 - Awarded the William Pace Award for Outstanding Service to the Community of Mamaroneck by the Federation of Italian-American Democratic Organizations of the State of New York. The award is named for the only signer of the Declaration of Independence who was of Italian Ancestry. William Pace was a member of the Continental Congress from the state of Maryland.

There are three programs, listed under New York State, that Dee developed during his tenure at Mamaroneck that deserve to be singled out for their extraordinary accomplishments.

(1) Organizer of Governor Rockefeller's Program for Disadvantaged Youth with Director Jackie Robinson (1966).
(2) Project Opportunity Program at State University College at Cortland (1967).
(3) The Jean Ann Kennedy Smith Summer Co-Op camp for mentally and physically challenged individuals in the Quaker Hill neighborhood of Pawling, New York (1971).

Organizer of Governor Rockefeller's Program for Disadvantaged Youth with Director Jackie Robinson (1966).

"My boss," Dee told me, "was none other than the great baseball player Jackie Robinson, who was the first African American to play Major League Baseball as a member of the Brooklyn Dodgers during the years 1947 through 1956. I was thrilled at the opportunity to just meet the man, let alone work with him for nearly a year."

In 1964 Jackie Robinson was asked by then Governor Nelson Rockefeller to be one of six deputy directors for his Republican Presidential campaign. To take on this job, Jackie left his executive position at the Chuck-Full-of-Nuts Corporation.

When Dee met Jackie in 1966, Jackie was Governor Rockefeller's Special Assistant for Community Affairs during the Governor's third term in office.

"I don't remember exactly how I was recommended to help Jackie Robinson with this program, but I suspect it was the result of my work as President of the N.Y.S. Association for Health, Physical Education, Recreation and Dance in 1966," Dee said. "As best as I can recollect, our first meeting took place sometime in early 1966, at his office in Manhattan. I'll always remember my first meeting with Jackie Robinson. He was such a regular guy, and very articulate. I was really impressed. He told me that the mission of the program was to provide a summer recreation program for disadvantaged kids from Harlem in Manhattan and Bedford Stuyvesant in Brooklyn. He wanted to get these kids out of the ghettos for a short while to show them that there was another life out there that they might appreciate, and perhaps encourage them to strive to do better in their lives. The facility made available to Jackie was the New York State National Guard Training Center at Camp Smith.

Camp Smith is a 2000-acre training facility located in Westchester County, overlooking the east bank of the Hudson River, and northward to the border of Putnam County. Across the river, on the west bank of the Hudson, is Bear Mountain State Park.

"After accepting the assignment," said Dee, "my first suggestion to Jackie was that I should perform a facilities survey of Camp Smith to see what the facilities had to offer in terms of housing, food service, recreation and sports, to sustain a week-long camp for the kids. He agreed. We made an appointment to meet again in a few weeks to review my survey findings.

"My survey of Camp Smith was encouraging. The facilities were ideal for what Jackie wanted to accomplish with the kids. In addition, I ventured over the river to Bear Mountain State Park and surveyed the recreational facilities there as well. It was ideal for swimming and hiking, and I decided to make it part of the program.

"At the second meeting with Jackie Robinson, I outlined the program I had designed for him. I told him that the Camp Smith Facilities could accommodate up to one thousand kids per week. The thousand kids would be divided into groups of one hundred. For each group of one hundred there would be ten counselors, for a ratio of one counselor per ten kids. One chief counselor would be in charge of the other nine counselors. To be sure we covered absenteeism, and other contingencies, I suggested we hire one hundred twenty-five counselors.

"Jackie listened carefully, and then asked an important question for which I was prepared to answer.

"Who will you hire as counselors?" he asked.

"Kids from the ghetto," I replied. "We will interview teenage kids, make our selection and then provide them with leadership training. To pay them, we could use Youth Corps money," I suggested to him.

"Jackie was well aware of the availability of money from the Youth Corps program. In 1966 it was part of President Lyndon Johnson's War on Poverty. The Federal Government had appropriated money to provide summer jobs for the youth in the inner cities. Most of these jobs were manual labor jobs designed to restore pride in their neighborhoods by having them clean up and beautify their neighborhoods."

"My proposal to him was to use some of this money to train youth leaders and pay them a salary."

"Tell me more," he said encouragingly.

"I pointed out that these trained leaders could then be used to support other youth programs during the rest of the year in the same neighborhoods. One of the programs I suggested to Jackie, was the after-six-o'clock-basketball program in the neighborhood streets, using portable basketball hoops.

"What are you going to do when the kids get to Camp Smith?" was his next key question.

"I outlined my plan in detail. The kids would be transported by bus from their neighborhoods to Camp Smith on Monday morning and returned home on Saturday afternoon. The staff would have Sunday off to prepare for the next group of kids that would arrive on the following Monday. I told him that with the available barracks facilities we could handle up to 1000 kids a week. The recreational activities would be concentrated on life-long sports, such as swimming, tennis, golf, badminton, horseshoe pitching, croquet and some others. In the mix, we would add arts and crafts and music for after-supper activities. I told him that the daily routine would go something like this. "The kids would be awaken at about 6 a.m., shower and dress and have breakfast. At 8 a.m. 500 kids would board 10 buses (50 kids per bus) and travel across the Hudson River to Bear Mountain State Park for swimming. The other 500 kids would be divided into groups of 100 each. One group would be learning to pitch horseshoes, a second group golf, a third group badminton, a fourth group croquet and the fifth group tennis. After lunch, the 500 morning swimmers would be divided into groups of 100 and engage in learning and playing life-long sports, while the other 500 would board the buses and go swimming at Bear Mountain. In the evenings, after supper, the kids would be engaged in arts and crafts, storytelling, group fun games and lots of music, including a sing-a-long.

"Jackie was a man of action. He listened carefully, and asked me some pointed questions, which I answered to his satisfaction. It didn't take long for him to make a decision, and he gave me the go-ahead.

"The great thing about this program was Jackie Robinson had a mandate from Governor Rockefeller, who, in turn, had the power to get the money for the program. Money was never an issue. We purchased all the equipment we needed, which included croquet kits, tennis equipment, golf equipment including drive nets, and horseshoe pitching equipment. You name it, we got it. The other great thing about this program was I had plenty of time to plan and put the program together.

"The six key elements of the program were the selection of the kids that would attend the program at the neighborhood level, transportation, food service, the purchase of equipment, the organization/execution of the recreation program at Camp Smith, and the coordination with the neighborhood leaders and the police. What I did was, I hired key people to head up each one of these program elements, and acted as a clearing house to direct and coordinate their activities. As I developed the details, I kept Jackie informed of my needs and wants, to which he was quick to respond.

"Transportation was one of the very important elements of the program. We had to get the kids from their neighborhoods to and from Camp Smith. We hired buses from New York City to accomplish this task. In addition, we had to have transportation to and from Bear Mountain State Park. To accomplish this, we managed to commandeer military buses from Camp Smith and from nearby West Point Military Academy. Everyone was eager to assist us.

"Soon after the first group arrived on the first day at Camp Smith, we discovered several interesting things about these kids. Of the group we took swimming on the first morning, we quickly found out after they jumped into the pool that not many of them could swim. Most of them had never been to a swimming pool. For the first few minutes the lifeguards and the counselors were busy hauling them out of the pool before they drowned. Immediately upon experiencing this, the counselors set up a screening program to test their ability to swim. Each kid was required to demonstrate his or her ability to swim by swimming across the shallow end of the pool. Those who couldn't swim were singled out and given swimming lessons.

"The other very important thing we discovered was, that in spite of the fact that these kids came from poor neighborhoods and lived under less than ideal conditions, many of them became homesick, and, on the first day, about 100 of them ran away from Camp Smith and took off hitch-hiking for home. The police were busy picking them up as they were hitchhiking home on the Taconic Parkway, heading south to the city. The critique with the counselors after the first day's experience addressed this issue. More emphasis was placed by the counselors in identifying kids that displayed homesickness and giving them special attention. In the evenings, after supper, we organized a variety of activities, some designed for individuals and some for group participation. For individuals, we had arts and crafts, and for groups we had group games, sing-a-longs and storytelling. Art and music played an important part of the evening programs. That summer we accommodated several thousand kids at Camp Smith in a very successful program.

"I will never forget how sad I felt when Jackie passed away six years later on October 24, 1972 at age 53," said Dee. I was reminded of our first meeting and how intelligent and thoughtful a person he was, and how well we got along as we worked closely together for several months to bring fun and joy to so many ghetto kids."

Author's Note:

During my research of Camp Smith on the internet (globalsecurity. org/Camp Smith) the following paragraph caught my eye. When I read it, I wondered if this was not a result of the success Jackie Robinson and Dee had using Camp Smith as a youth recreation center in 1966.

"During July 1999, over one hundred inner city youths spent a week at Camp Smith, a military camp located in the mountains of Peekskill, New York. On July 7, 1999 several FBI employees volunteered as mentors and friends, explaining and stressing drug deterrence, safety, and the importance of education, and how the law enforcement can play a positive role in their lives. "FRIDAY" at Camp Smith has become an integral part of the COP program (Community Outreach Program for Crime Prevention) in the New York Office."

Project Opportunity Program at State University College at Cortland (1967).

Remembering his humble beginnings as a student at Pawling High School, at which he barely managed to accumulate an average of a little better than 65%, yet managed to matriculate and graduate from Cortland State Teachers College in 1948 under the G.I. Bill, Dee introduced the *Project Opportunity Program* to the College Administration in 1967. The Project was designed to admit students to SUNY Cortland, who demonstrated an academic potential despite a background of economic, educational and social deprivation. The first graduate under the program was Maria Gonzalez of White Plains, N.Y. She received her baccalaureate degree in 1971. Maria was born in New York City's Harlem.

The story of how this program got started is best told by Mr. Doug DeRancy, Assistant to the Vice President of Institutional Advancement at SUNY Cortland.

"In the late 1960s Cortland's administration decided to move the college in a direction that would require much more selectivity in the admissions process. Since 1963 the college was making a "painful" transition from a teacher's college to an institution that would offer a comprehensive arts and sciences program. The mandate was to keep enrollment low, and hire a number of new faculty in the School of Arts and Sciences who had the credentials to support the development and implementation of a highly selective Arts and Science program.

"Consistent with this new direction was the hiring of an admissions director, who would be required to bring in the best and the brightest New York had to offer at that time. It was during this period that a number of students Dee had brought to the college for admission's consideration were denied. Years past, many of Dee's students were admitted. Typically, Dee's kids came from broken families or had extenuating circumstances that made it difficult for them to perform at the academic level required to get accepted to Cortland. With its new enrollment mandate, Cortland was no longer going to accept this type of student.

"Dee, being Dee, he went right to the top and met with Pete Corey (Class of '43) who, at that time, was a rising star and eventually would become the college's Vice President for Academic Affairs. Pete had a great deal of respect for Dee and Dee's generation of graduates. It was at this point that the college agreed to develop a program that would afford certain students a closer look. For the closer look, an applicant would have to have extenuating circumstances (broken home, poor health, working to help pay the family expenses, etc.). These circumstances offered one reason for the "poor" academic performance in high school. In addition, the student would be required to secure two meaningful references from alumni of Cortland, who could not be family members. Meaningful defined as an alumnus who knew the student well, and would be willing to confirm in writing why the college should take a chance on the candidate-- basically confirming in writing that the student had potential and ability to make it at Cortland. This program would be known as the Alumni Admissions Program, and would be offered jointly by the college's Admissions Office and the Alumni Association. Admissions would have the final say-- Alumni Association would only make a recommendation.

"The program still exists today, but the number of admission "slots" offered has been substantially reduced to five or six students a year. The reduction was the result of a SUNY decision, a number of years ago, to "cap" all special admissions programs. This is an effort to force the system to be more selective.

"Dee's legacy was to constantly remind his Alma Mater that it is within the Rockefeller mandate to take a chance with some students. It was the alumnus and student's responsibility to convince the folks, involved with overseeing the Alumni Admission Program, that they should take a chance.

Organized the Jean Ann Kennedy Smith Summer Day Co-Op Camp for Mentally and Physically Challenged of Pawling, N.Y. (1971).

In the winter of 1971, Dee met with Jay Sherlach, Elementary School Principal in Pawling, New York, who was one of Dee's long-time friends, going back to the days when they taught together at the Quaker Ridge School System. At that meeting, Dee suggested that the town of Pawling should sponsor a summer camp for the mentally and physically challenged kids in the area. Jay and his wife Pat were parents of an eight-year old son, Matthew, who was born with Down's syndrome, and Dee was his God parent. Jay and his wife Pat immediately reacted positively to the idea, and the concept for the establishment of a summer Co-Op Day Camp for the mentally and physically challenged was born.

The immediate challenges were to find a suitable location for the camp, financial support and a sheltering sponsor agency to administer the funds and help coordinate the plans and train the volunteer counselors.

Jay and Pat Sherlach.

"Dee came up with the idea to approach Mrs. Jean Ann Kennedy Smith, sister of the former President John F. Kennedy, who owned a 14-acre estate in the Quaker Hill area of Pawling. Since before 1968 he had worked with her sister Eunice Kennedy Shriver on her Special Olympics project as New York State's Special Olympics Games Director.

"In snowy February of 1971, Dee and I visited Mrs. Smith and laid out the details of the program and the budget. At the meeting, I marveled at Dee's ingenuity in motivating her to take on the project by challenging her Kennedy family competitive spirit. He told her that he thought she could do as good a job, if not better, than her sister, Eunice, in hosting a group of mentally and physically challenged children at her home in Quaker Hills, like Eunice did at her Maryland home in the early 1960s, where the seeds of the Special Olympics began to sprout. To insure the success of the program, he told her that he would have to get the cooperation of the Pawling community. She and her husband's cooperation was total and warmly given, including all our funding needs of $3,000," said Jay.

"The Association of Retarded Children (as it was called in those days) with Frank Pessia as President, signed on as sponsor and Walter Jenner, a school psychologist with Dutchess County BOCES, (Board of Cooperative Educational Services) became the camp director with Maureen Aiken as his assistant director and physical education instructor. Our volunteer counselors were mature college and high school students who served as mentors on a one-on-one basis with the campers. The community of Pawling embraced the project as well, providing encouragement to the volunteer counselors and eliciting a great sense of pride in us all, which led to the ultimate success of the program."

"To prepare the volunteer counselors for the camp, Dee conducted the training at his home in Conesville," said Pat Sherlach.

"But one of the most amazing volunteer efforts came from about

Jean Ann Kennedy Smith, sponsor of Camp Smith, with Dee DaBramo and John Wagner, Superintendent of Schools, Pawling N.Y., celebrating the success of the first Summer Co-Op Camp in Pawling, N.Y. (Courtesy of Dee DaBramo)

ten of Dee's experienced cadre of counselors from Mamaroneck," said Jay Sherlach. "They helped train the Pawling volunteers and remained with them all during the first summer camp. They traveled the 62 miles to and from Mamaroneck every day for the entire month the camp was in session," added Jay. Once we had trained experienced volunteer counselors in Pawling," Jay went on to say, "they helped to train the next group of volunteers for the next year and the next and the next.

"Dee, of course, was busy during the summer with his Summer Co-Op Day Camp for socially and economically deprived kids in Mamaroneck, and did not actively participate in the day-to-day operations of our camp.

"Camp Smith was held at the Smith's Estate in Quaker Hill for five consecutive years. The Program venue changed several times after that, but the Camp lasted for twenty-five consecutive years," Jay said proudly.

Jean Ann Kennedy Smith celebrating the success of the Summer Co-Op camp with parents and counselor volunteers. (Courtesy of Dee DaBramo)

"During the second summer of Camp Smith, Dee had a brilliant idea," Pat Sherlach recalled. "It had to do with his Mamaroneck summer Co-Op camp for socially and economically deprived kids and our mentally/physically challenged kids attending Camp Smith in Pawling. He wanted our kids to visit with his kids attending his Mamaroneck Summer Co-Op

Camp. The brilliance of the idea was that he wanted the socially and economically deprived kids of Mamaroneck to experience the fact that kids with mental and physical disabilities were worse off than they were. He wanted them to deduce the fact that if they applied their brain power to studying hard and learning, they had a good chance of overcoming their social and economic deprivations.

"One of the most unexpected outcomes of the camp program was the effect it had on the volunteer counselors themselves," said Pat. "From their Camp Smith experience, many of them pursued careers, not only in Special Education, but in allied fields of study --such as teaching the hearing impaired, the sight impaired and the speech impaired."

Dee's affiliation with the President's Council for Physical Fitness and Sports.

The one National/International organization, in addition to the Special Olympics, that Dee made a significant contribution to, was the President's Council for Physical Fitness and Sports.

My source of information regarding Dee's work with the President's Council for Physical Fitness and Sports was Dr. Richard Keelor, a former officer with the Council who served as Director of Federal/State Relations and Director of Program Development from 1972 through 1982. After leaving the staff, Dr. Keelor served as Special Advisor and Clinician for the organization through the year 1988.

Dr. Richard Keelor.

"Dee was never a member of the Council itself. He was a Special Advisor and clinician for the President's Council for Physical Fitness and Sports (PCPFS). He was essentially hand-picked by the Executive Director, C. Carson "Casey" Conrad, and approved by the Chairman. The Chairman at that time was Astronaut Navy Captain James Lovell. Director Conrad described Dee as 'the best teacher he had ever seen.' At that time the Chairman and the Council members were all President Nixon's appointees. Dee was selected because of his distinguished service to the Special Olympics and his reputation as a master teacher and expert in programs for the physically and mentally challenged. He was also gregarious, entertaining and a wonderful spokesman for the PCPFS mission.

"Primarily, he was a general ambassador of physical fitness with a specialty in addressing the needs of the handicapped, especially Special

Olympic kids. On occasion, he would also participate in program planning. As a clinician, he served with about every notable physical fitness and sports authority in the nation: Dr. Ken Cooper, Dr. George Sheehan, various Surgeon Generals, Jack LaLanne, Jacki Sorensen and Jim Fixx, to name a few.

Dr. Richard Keelor, front and center, Director of Federal/ State Relations for the PCPFS and clinicians (L to R) – Dr. Susan Johnson, Glen Swengros, Dee DaBramo, unidentified, unidentified and Joan Sullivan. (Courtesy of Dee DaBramo)

"The key to Dee's professional career, and what he stood for, was empathy, audacity and enthusiasm. Yes, he knew his subject and had all sorts of academic credentials, but experts are a dime a dozen. Dee's legacy will be the extent to which he changed the lives of the people and organizations he unselfishly served. They are legion.

"To the best of my knowledge, Dee served from about 1970 through 1985. However, he may have served a few years longer that I am unaware of because I left the PCPFS in 1982.

"One of the most memorable experiences I had with Dee was in the early summer of 1976. At the time I was serving as Director of Federal/State Relations for the PCPFS. Dee, Joan Sullivan, my wife Susan and I traveled together to Portugal on a very special mission for the U.S. State Department. Let me set the scene for you.

"In late June 1976, the people of Portugal were to vote in the first free presidential elections since the *Carnation Revolution*. In brief, this revolution, which started on April 25, 1974, was a military coup that ousted the Fascist and authoritarian Estado Novo (New State) regime that had ruled Portugal since 1920. The military promised that in two years they would hold free democratic elections. 1976 was that year. Four candidates took part in the election, three were democracy-leaning Independent candidates, and one was a Communist Party member with the name Actavio Rodrigues Pato. Pato was of peasant stock himself and very popular with the peasant farmers of the country. It was he that the incumbent military government and the three democratic candidates were worried about. The general atmosphere in Portugal at that time (1976) was quite politically heated, and the U.S. was very concerned that the Communist Party should not get a toe-hold, as they had done in Italy during that time. Remember, this was 1976. Having Portugal fall to the Communist Party was unthinkable.

"Since our mission was primarily international relations, Dee was perfect. Being an Italian American he spoke Italian, and apparently there were some phrases and such that the Portuguese understood, and visa versa. They also had a small, but vital Special Olympics program going, so we plugged Dee into that organization.

"Dee 's primary task, along with Joan Sullivan's, was to teach their specialty. Dee went to public schools, recreation programs, and did radio, TV and press interviews. Of course, while he was talking about the technical aspects of Special Olympics, he was his usual fun, gregarious self which was winning hearts and fans for the democratic-minded candidates. His other task was to contradict the ugly American stereotype that was being promoted by the Communist Party. Our mission was part of a highly publicized tour that hit many of the major cities, but in particular, the strongholds of the communist nominee for the presidency. Therefore, front page stories in the national newspaper and TV appearances were frequent. We also were surrounded by substantial U.S. security backup. There were pictures of Dee, working with Special Olympic kids, on the front page in the newspapers, and TV segments were common.

"Our primary contact was the Portuguese equivalent to our Secretary of State, Raldufo Begonia. He would pop in and out of our tour to talk to the press. When we were in Lisbon, he was also a very generous host, taking us out to dinner, etc. When we were traveling, we would always be greeted by local officials, given small gifts from the area we were visiting, keys to the city, certificates of appreciation, etc.

"Early in our tour, there was one very anxious moment at our hotel in Lisbon that occurred while we were eating breakfast, prior to getting ready to go out on an appearance. Our guards, all plain clothes men but well-armed, rushed to our table and escorted us back to our rooms. They explained that the Israeli ambassador to Portugal and his family had been shot at in an assassination attempt, only one or two blocks from our hotel. I don't remember the outcome of that event, but it got all our attentions. To be sure, we were not the major troops sent to buffer the cause, but our State Department was pulling out all the stops to support the independent democratic-minded candidates.

"During our visit, everything we did was very precisely orchestrated. I was the primary spokesman with the press and media, and the audience was all selected to screen out any possible objections or difficulties. However, on one occasion, I was invited to speak to the faculty at a large university in Lisbon. I was friendly with one of the professors who had visited the U.S. and the PCPFS headquarters a year or two earlier, and he asked me to talk to the faculty about the PCPFS and how we operated in the U.S. It seemed like a good idea, and being somewhat naive, I agreed. When Secretary Begonia found out I had accepted the invitation to speak to the faculty, he made a trip to our hotel to try and talk me out of it. To make a long story short, it turned out to be a large audience of about 75 people in a lecture hall. Everything went well until one of the faculty members jumped to his feet and interrupted my comments. Speaking in broken English, he ripped the U.S., calling our tour propaganda, and was getting progressively more abusive. I stood at the microphone waiting to take him on, but before I could say anything the general audience started to call him out, whistling, and several took their shoes off and pounded their desks. Following the program, dozens of people came up and apologized, explaining that this person was head of the communist party on campus.

"But the highlight story of the trip, involving Dee, was our unexpected encounter with the Communist presidential candidate himself, Octavio Rodrigues Pato and his entourage. The incident occurred one evening in a mountain village at a dinner party organized by the local officials to thank us for our work in the area that day. It was very scary. Secretary Begonia was in attendance, and we had substantial security back up.

Candidate Pato and his entourage, dressed in peasant clothes, literally crashed the dinner party. I could tell that Secretary Begonia was very upset. He came over to us and told us to be ready to evacuate the premises at a moment's notice because he did not know what might happen. He viewed Pato and his ontourage as roughnecks. In light of what happened to the Israeli ambassador in Lisbon, this was a tense situation. When Pato entered the hall, he was well-received by the people, who stood up and applauded. Pato responded to the applause with theatrical-like bows and the waving of his arms. His next move was to secure the microphone and give a political address to the audience. Of course, he spoke in Portuguese, which we could not understand, except for Dee. Having a background in Italian, he caught some of what Pato was saying. After his speech, the tension abated a bit and he and his entourage sat down for dinner with the rest of us. The dinner was very nice with lots of Portuguese wine, which I am sure helped to reduce the tension in the room. After dinner the local dignitaries had planned to provide us, their honored guests, with a demonstration of the local folk dancing, and a small orchestra took to the stage.

"Before the dancing could begin, Communist candidate Pato stepped to the microphone once again, and with the accompaniment of the orchestra, began to sing Portuguese *Fado* folk music. *Fado* folk music was very popular with the peasant population which Pato was wooing. The music is very, for lack of a better word, theatrical. It sometimes requires the artist to evoke emotions such as crying, laughing, shouting, etc. It's almost operatic and very beautiful. Pato had a great voice, which he was noted for, and had his audience spellbound. While this was going on, Dee had left our midst and was out talking with the people, trying out his Italian. Of course, by now he had had a few glasses of wine and was in a jovial mood. When Pato finished singing, Dee, with a glass of wine in each hand happily swaggered up to Pato, says something to him in Italian, shakes his hand and puts his arm around him. When Secretary Begonia saw this happening, he gave me an elbow in my ribs and in his broken English said, 'What the hell is he doing? You have to get him out of here.' Meanwhile, Dee is telling the people what a wonderful singer Pato is and how much he appreciated him coming all the way up to this mountain village to be with them. He's doing this by speaking some Italian, some English and using a lot of gestures to get his message across. For Secretary Begonia this was very embarrassing. Here was an American ambassador reversing the role he was supposed to be playing and embracing the enemy. I didn't know what to do about it. I guess I could have gone out there and tackled Dee, but that would have made things much worse. Sensing Begonia's mounting frustration, I finally got up and headed toward Dee, not knowing what I was going to say or do. Dee sighted me coming and must have realized that he was totally out of line in respect to what his mission was, said his goodbyes and retreated from the stage. As he left the stage everyone in the hall gave Dee a standing ovation, including Pato. After that, it appeared to me that everyone was relieved and relaxed. Whatever Dee said ingratiated the audience and flattered the ego of candidate Pato. The sum of Dee's action was to totally defuse the potentially nasty conflict and transformed it into an international love fest. This was pure DaBramo, 'we're just having fun, there's no problem here, it's a wonderful evening together, with brotherly love, a beautiful singer and dancing, etc., etc.'

The results of the 1976 Portuguese presidential election were that the Communist Party candidate Actavio Rodrigues Pato received about 7 percent of the vote. The winner was Antonio Ramalho Eanes with better than 60 percent of the vote.

"This is my favorite story about Dee DaBramo. When I tell this story, and especially when Dee is present, I tell my audience that this is how Dee single-handily defeated the Portuguese Communist Party Candidate in the 1976 Portuguese presidential election. In closing, let me say this, Dee's most endearing quality is his love of all people --regardless of race, religion, ethnicity or their physical or mental abilities."

On May 14, 2008, Dr. Richard Keelor received the 2008 PCPFS Lifetime Achievement Award at the President's Council's meeting in Washington, D.C. during National Physical Fitness and Sports Month.

CHAPTER 10

The Special Olympics

CHAPTER 10
The Special Olympics

Eunice Kennedy Shriver, champion of the mentally and physically challenged, and the founder of the Special Olympics, passed away on August 11, 2009. Her forty-plus years of working with the Special Olympics were instrumental in changing the attitude of the American public, and most of the rest of the western world, toward people with special needs. As a member of the most influential family in the United States, she took good advantage of her position to influence the Congress of the United States to write legislation benefiting the mentally and physically challenged people of this country.

Little did Mrs. Shriver know that in 1948 there was a young Italian immigrant teacher at Amenia, N.Y., whose mind was already formulating the same concepts regarding the welfare of the mentally and physically challenged, and whose path she would consequently cross some twenty years later. Likewise, little did Emilio "Dee" DaBramo know, in 1948, that an act of kindness and concern for a young student in one of his fourth grade gym classes in Amenia, N.Y. would garner him the attention of the highly influential Kennedy family.

An article written by Mary Jayne McKay in the Mamaroneck, N.Y. newspaper, *The Daily Times*, **Personal rewards for a public man, Saturday, November 1, 1975, best tells the story.**

Mamaroncck's Emilio (Dee) DaBramo wears many hats, but the activity that may be closest to his heart is his volunteer work with handicapped youngsters.

It does not command the headlines and prestige of his post as Mamaroneck Village Trustee, nor the security and salary of his job as curriculum supervisor for the Mamaroneck schools, but it takes him across the country, brings him into contact with interesting people and has many personal rewards of its own.

Recently appointed to an advisory committee to the Westchester Office for the Handicapped, DaBramo is games director for the state's Special Olympics Program and a member of the National Advisory Committee to the Kennedy Foundation which sponsors the Special Olympics throughout the United States.

DaBramo became involved in his work with the handicapped when he started his teaching career more than 25 years ago. In his fourth grade class at the time was a seventeen-year old mentally retarded youth who was also an excellent baseball player.

"But he didn't have a team to play on," DaBramo said. "So I gave him a tryout for the high school team and wrote to Albany getting special permission for an elementary school pupil to play on a high school team.

"He played second base that year and we were the county champs. Now, he has his own electrical business, employs two people and is married and owns his own home."

Since that time DaBramo has conducted recreation programs for the handicapped in New York State public schools and has tried to further the causes of the handicapped in every school district in which he has worked.

"I firmly believe in mainstreaming the handicapped, getting them as involved as possible in the affairs of the public schools," he said.

"It's good for the handicapped, but even better for the regular students. If they play and work with handicapped students in school, they will become used to seeing and dealing with them. And later on when they go into business, they will not be afraid to hire or work with the handicapped."

Eight years ago when the Special Olympics Program for handicapped youngsters was just getting off the ground in New York, officials in Albany, remembering DaBramo's efforts on the part of a youthful baseball player and his subsequent work with the retarded, asked him to help organize the games.

It was his work at the first state competition that brought him in contact with the Kennedy family, whose members are pictured with DaBramo in the many photographs posted on his office wall. Ethel

Kennedy attended the games and was so impressed with DaBramo's work that she and her sister-in-law, Eunice Kennedy Shriver, asked him to join the National Advisory Committee for the family's Foundation for the Handicapped. (Now known as the Joseph P. Kennedy Foundation).

Eunice Kennedy Shriver and Ethel Kennedy, wife of the late Robert F. Kennedy, and Dee, attending a Special Olympics function. (Courtesy of Dee DaBramo)

DaBramo has since traveled around the country for the Foundation, setting up Special Olympic Games and other programs for the handicapped.

"I love traveling all over and I really enjoy the people I meet," he said. "They're so good and work so hard on behalf of others.

"I wish everyone could do this type of work. Some of us complain about such insignificant things, and when you see these handicapped kids you realize that we have so much to be thankful for. But I don't mean that you have to feel sorry for these kids. You have to treat them the same as others. Once you feel sorry for them, you do more harm than good."

DaBramo plans to expand the Special Olympic Games in the state this year by adding tournaments for 10 to 22-year-olds in soccer, wrestling, gymnastics, cross country and track and field events. He also plans to add a division for 22-year-olds and older with competition in such events as fly casting, golf, badminton, bocce ball, bicycling, fencing, dancing, croquet and tennis.

DaBramo has suggested to the County Committee that each municipality be required to set aside $1,500 for every 5,000 in the population to be used for employment of the handicapped in that community. He has also advocated the organization of an All-County Band for the Blind and the inception of a "one-on-one" day for the handicapped at the County Center.

"What I have noticed in the years I have worked with Dee," said his MHS secretary, Mrs. Diana Teti, "is that no one who has ever come into or called this office has ever been refused. And many times Dee will come back here and say, Diana, I've just met this kid and we have to do something for him."

DaBramo claims that this work for the handicapped is his way of repaying all those who have helped him throughout his life.

"I firmly believe," he said, "that you can never help those who have helped you. The only way you can really pay them back is by helping someone else."

End of Article.

During my interview with Dee, he seemed to really brighten up when I broached the subject of the Special Olympics and his association with the Kennedy family, especially Eunice Kennedy Shriver. Their mutual interest in the mentally and physically challenged had obviously created a binding friendship.

For me, one of the highlights of our conversation regarding his work with Mrs. Shriver was the story he told of their first meeting.

First Meeting with Eunice Kennedy Shriver and Sargent Shriver.

"I believe it was sometime in late 1966 or early 1967 that I received a call from Mrs. Shriver regarding the Special Olympics. I'm not sure I can recall the exact conversation, but it went something like this.

"Mr. DaBramo, I have learned that you have been working with handicapped children for many years and have designed physical education and recreation programs for them that are unique."

"I acknowledged this and explained my basic philosophy regarding physical education for the Special Ed students here in the Mamaroneck schools. Apparently she was pleased with what she heard and invited me to visit with her and her husband, Sargent Shriver, at their Maryland home to talk about the Special Olympics. Of course, I was elated, if for no other reason than that I had a personal invitation to visit with her, but more importantly, that my work had been recognized as significant and important.

"She gave me directions to her home in Maryland, and a few days later I set out in my 1948 Pontiac coupe, the one I had purchased during my first year of teaching in Amenia.

"I arrived at the Shriver's property in the Maryland countryside and drove up to the house, kicked open the door on the driver's side of my car and got out. As I emerged, Mrs. Shriver walked up to meet me with a smile on her face, and we shook hands.

"Did you drive all the way down here in that?" she asked.

"Yes," I answered her, "it's the only car I own."

"Oh, my God! If I had known that I would have flown you down here."

"We both laughed at her remark, which put me at ease as we walked into the house. I don't remember much about the layout of the house, except that I remember feeling very comfortable because it appeared lived in, much like my cabin here in Conesville, only much larger. As I recall, we proceeded to the kitchen area where she introduced me to her husband, Sargent Shriver, and one other man whose name I do not recall. I found Sargent Shriver very personable and friendly, which put me at ease. As I remember, they offered up coffee and Danish.

"Our conversation began with them asking me about my family and my background. I told them a little bit about my immigrant parents and my life growing up in Stone House and going to school in a one-room school house in Poughquag. I revealed to them some of the details of my college experience at SUNY Cortland where I received my degree in physical education under the G.I. Bill and, of course, my knowledge and experience with the physically and mentally challenged kids. At this point in the conversation everyone felt quite comfortable with each other. Then a very funny thing happened. Someone asked me where I was staying for the night.

"I don't know," was my reply.

"You mean you don't have a place to stay tonight?" questioned Mrs. Shriver.

"I just drove down from New York because you wanted my help. You called me to come down here, and finding a place for me to stay is your job," I said whimsically. "At this point she turned to Sargent Shriver."

"Is anyone staying in the guest house tonight?" she asked him.

"No one," he replied.

"Mr. DaBramo, why don't you stay in the guest house tonight?" she turned to me and asked.

"Yes, thanks. That's very kind of you," I answered.

"With this behind us, we got down to the nitty-gritty of what the meeting was all about. I began by telling them of my experience with the physically and mentally challenged kids at Mamaroneck, which we discussed in detail. This included the fitness and sports activities that the kids were able to perform. When I got to gymnastics, Sargent Shriver spoke up with a questioning tone in his voice."

"Dee, are you sure that these individuals can handle gymnastics?"

"Sargent Shriver understood fitness, swimming and track and field, but had serious doubts about gymnastics. We bantered back and forth about it for a few minutes, and that's when Eunice spoke up," said Dee.

"Now, Sarge," she interrupted, "please let Dee explain the details of the program."

"At this point in the conversation, I asked if they had a roll of masking tape. They found some tape and handed it to me. I took the tape and laid a strip out on the floor and proceeded to demonstrate some of the basic exercises on the balance beam. After demonstrating some other gymnastic events, Sargent Shriver was convinced that gymnastics was worthwhile including as an event in the Special Olympic games.

"We spent all the first day, that evening at dinner, and part of the next morning discussing two important topics. One was the events that were applicable for the participants, and the second topic was the organizational structure for conducting a Special Olympics competition. They were pleased and satisfied with our meeting and thanked me for coming. I climbed into my car and I drove back to Mamaroneck.

"In 1968, Eunice Kennedy Shriver asked if I would be the Games Director of the Special Olympics for the State of New York, and I accepted.

"My first encounter with Rose Kennedy, the matriarch of the Kennedy family, came in 1969 during my first summer as the Games Director of the Special Olympics for New York State. The folks from the Special Olympics Committee in Boston, Massachusetts extended an invitation to the New

York State Committee requesting that the State of New York participate in the Northeastern Regional Special Olympics Games which were to take place that summer on the campus of Boston University. As Games Director for New York State, I was assigned the task of organizing the state's contingent. The program at Boston College went off without a hitch.

"Now, I'm not exactly sure how this happened," said Dee, "but someone came to me and said that Rose Kennedy wanted to see me. I located Mrs. Kennedy and introduced myself. She shook my hand, smiled and congratulated me on a job well-done. I told her that I was just the catalyst and the people she should really thank were the hundreds of volunteers that produced the success of the meet she had just witnessed. One word led to another, and I asked her if she would speak to the volunteer staff as a group. She said that she would be more than happy to do so. I gathered the staff together on the field, and she spoke to them for several minutes and congratulated them on the success of the games. Needless to say, the staff was delighted to meet her and hear her speak. But most importantly, they were impressed by the fact that she took the time to be with them and recognize their contribution to the Special Olympics.

"During my twelve years of working with the Special Olympics I was privileged to meet with Rafer Johnson, the 1960 Rome Olympics Champion in the Decathlon. He was a founding member of the Southern California Special Olympics Committee. As a clinician, I traveled to Southern California and held demonstrations for his group on Special Olympic events.

"From 1968 until 1980, I was the Games Director for the Special Olympics for the State of New York. In addition, during those years, I was invited by Eunice Kennedy Shriver to visit every state, including Alaska, as a Special Olympics representative to help organize Special Olympic Committees in all the states.

"In addition, I was assigned as Eunice Kennedy Shriver's special representative to Italy to assist them in organizing a Special Olympics Program in that country.

"During the time I worked with the Special Olympics, I was a volunteer, and not a paid employee of the Special Olympics Committee. I was, however, reimbursed for my travel expenses. Most of these trips occurred during the summer months after my regular school year had ended."

When I interviewed Dee about his trip to Italy to help the Italians in setting up a Special Olympics Program there, he did not offer much detail regarding the trip, except to say that he was instrumental in assisting the Italians organize a Special Olympics Committee that culminated in the formation of a nation-wide program there. It wasn't until I interviewed Naomi Yavne that the fascinating details of his visit to Italy emerged.

Rafer Johnson, the 1960 Olympic Decathlon Champion, participating in Dee's Special Olympics clinic held in Southern California. (Courtesy of Dee DaBramo)

Naomi Yavne explains the details of Dee's trip to Italy.

"In 1978, Eunice Kennedy Shriver made arrangements for Dee to visit with one of Italy's most influential politicians, Aldo Moro, his wife Eleonora and other dignitaries in the city of Rome, to discuss organizing a nation-wide Special Olympics Progam for Italy.

"Dee was a natural choice for the job," she continued. "He was fluent in Italian, he was Catholic, and there was no one more knowledgeable about the Special Olympics program, from a philosophical and practical point of view, than he was. In addition, his experience in Portugal in 1976 with Dr. Richard Keelor and the President's Council for Physical Fitness and Sports rounded out his qualifications."

Before I reveal Naomi's intriguing story, I need to provide some background information regarding the dire political situation that existed in Italy during the spring of 1978 when Dee was scheduled to arrive in Rome.

Aldo Moro's political career as leader of the Christian Democratic Party spanned over twenty years. He had held the offices of Minister of Education, Minister of Foreign Affairs, Minister of the Interior and two terms as Prime Minister, from 1963 to 1968 and 1974 to 1976. Up to that time, in the post World War II era, Aldo Moro had served longer as Prime Minister than any other Italian politician.

In early 1970, the Italian Communist Party had made deep inroads in Italian politics, and in the general election of 1976 they garnered over 30% of the popular vote. Recognizing the reality of the political situation, Moro successfully urged the Christian Democratic Party members to adopt a policy of compromise with the Communists in order to form a government of national unity. Under this arrangement, the Communist Party agreed to support the policies of the Christian Democrats in return for a voice in formulating governmental policy.

During the same period of the 1970s, the radical Marxist-Leninist left-wing Italian terrorist group, *The Red Brigade*, supported by the Soviet Union, was very active. Their main objective was to try and force Italy to abandon the NATO Alliance in order to strengthen their position in the cold war. To finance their clandestine operations, the group resorted to burglary, kidnapping and sabotage in the industrial cities of Italy. Later they resorted to murdering Italian police and magistrates, especially those who were responsible for the capture and conviction of their members.

Aldo Moro was singled out by the group for his successful efforts in neutralizing the Communist Party with his policy of *Historic Compromise*. On March 16, 1978, they kidnapped Aldo Moro, and in the process murdered his driver and his four body guards. At the time of his kidnapping, all of the founding members of the Red Brigade were in jail, and the objective of the brigade members was to use Moro as a bargaining chip to free their imprisoned members. The Italian government refused to negotiate with the terrorists, and launched a massive search for Moro which failed. The Red Brigade held Aldo Moro for about 54 days while trying to negotiate with the Italian government. On May 9, 1978 his murdered body was found in a parked car on a street in Rome. It was under these circumstances that Dee met with Aldo Moro's wife, Eleonora Moro.

"Initially when Dee arrived in Rome, he had no idea that any of this had occurred and Aldo Moro was a captive, but still alive," said Naomi. "Dee had been scheduled to have dinner with a group of Italian dignitaries, headed by former Prime Minister Aldo Moro and his wife Eleonora. In spite of the fact that her husband had not yet been found, Moro's wife held the dinner anyway. At this dinner, she was speaking with Dee about his background, education, his service in WWII, etc. She was totally unaware that he had been born in a mud hut, with no plumbing or electricity, on the side of a hill in the Apennine Mountains.

"He told her how his father had immigrated to the United States at the age of seventeen and worked as a day laborer on the railroad, living in a box car for many years and saving his money for a ship's passage to Italy to marry his mother. He then continued to explain his past and present careers. He said that she appeared to be impressed by what he had accomplished in his life, and repeatedly complimented him. He thanked her, and it was then that he said to her, that had he not left her home country, come to the U.S., become a citizen, fought in WWII, gone to college on the G.I. Bill, become an educator and worked on behalf of Special Olympics, he would NEVER have had the opportunity to be sitting and eating dinner at the same table with her! At first, she looked quite shocked at his candidness (as were most people), but he said that she did then admit that it was quite a revelation to her that one would have to leave Italy in order to raise their station in life, but that she had to agree that it would have been highly unlikely that he would ever have had the same opportunities had he stayed. The other dignitaries at the table, privy to the conversation, agreed.

"The outcome of the meeting was that Mrs. Moro did initiate a successful Special Olympics Program in Italy, in spite of the death of her husband.

"Also," said Naomi, "Dee's mom took the original monies that his father gave to her when they were first married and bought a farm, instead of bringing Dee to the U.S. The farm remained in his mother's family in Italy and was left to him in his mother's estate. Dee eventually went back to Italy, met his cousins, and gave the farm to them."

Honors and Special Awards.

Emilio "Dee" DaBramo, flanked by Rose Kennedy on his right and Eunice Kennedy Shriver on his left. The occasion Dee receiving the 1971 Annual Award as the Most Valuable Person to the Special Olympics in the Atlantic and Northeastern Region. (Courtesy of Dee DaBramo)

CHAPTER 11

Life After Mamaroneck

CHAPTER 11
Life after Mamaroneck

In an interview conducted by Mary Bauer of the Mamaroneck, N.Y. newspaper, *The Daily Times,* DaBramo Bids Mamaroneck Farewell, August 22, 1980, Dee ended the interview by saying, "It's a big world out there and there's a lot to do," and he meant it.

Upon retiring from the Mamaroneck Schools in 1979, Dee, at age 56, had no inclination to stop working. He was in good health, a bachelor, three of his four children were adults and on their own, two with university degrees and his youngest son Jim was in his senior year at Hartwick College in Oneonta, N.Y.

His success as an educator and a champion of the physically and mentally challenged extended way beyond his wildest dreams. He had worked with some of the most influential organizations and people in the country in his field of expertise, and was often instrumental in influencing them to his way of thinking, especially as to how the mentally and physically challenged should be treated as human beings. In addition, his financial needs at this time of his life were less. Although Dee mentored many of his working colleagues over his illustrious career, encouraging them to seek positions of higher responsibility, it is my belief that at this time in his life he was quite content to step aside to allow his younger peers to assume positions he held, in order to give them the opportunity to reach their potential. You will be witness to this new dimension of his life in this chapter.

This final chapter also chronicles his continued efforts, as an educator and leader, to help kids succeed in reaching their potential, and to make the community in which he resided a better place to live.

After retiring from Mamaroneck, Dee formed a company called *DaBramo Consulting Corporation*. The purpose of forming the corporation was to make him available to any school system that was in need of his experience and expertise. The response to his availability was immediate. His first assignment was as acting high school principal at Pleasantville, N.Y., a small Westchester County bedroom community with a population of about 7,000, located thirty miles north of New York City. He maintained this position from the fall of 1979 through the end of the school year in June of 1980.

His next assignment was as acting superintendent of the Gilboa Central School District, located in Gilboa, N.Y. just a few miles from his Catskill Mountain home in Conesville.

But, as Peter Fox, former teacher at Gilboa told me, "Dee almost didn't get the position as Acting Superintendent."

Peter Fox explained the situation.

"There is an irony in this," he told me. "I was chief negotiator for the teachers union in the district, and we had a bitter contract fight in the late 1970s. Because Dee and I were friends, he almost didn't get the position. When I found out, I was so angry that I went to Dee's house in Conesville and told him that I was going to quit my job if that was how they felt. Dee and I spent the afternoon (sober, mind you) sitting on his back porch and figuratively crying about the situation. It was heart-wrenching because I loved Dee like a brother, and it really hurt me to have them do this to him. At any rate, I took a leave-of-absence for a year and they hired Dee. When my year was up, I still did not want to return to Gilboa. Dee and I spent another evening crying on his back porch, and this time we were drinking. Dee talked me into coming back to Gilboa and working for him. It was one of the best career decisions I have ever made. All my important learning about school and leadership came during this experience. Dee taught me how to complete myself as a man."

Peter Fox went on to tell how Dee sacrificed his own position as superintendent to allow a younger peer to take the job.

"Dee could have stayed on as superintendent. However, he had a great friendship with Bert Wisse, who was the longtime high school principal at Gilboa. Dee wanted Bert to really challenge himself, so he talked Bert into taking his place as superintendent. Then, Dee stepped down to become high school principal for a year or two. It was typical Dee. He was a mentor to so many people, and he gave Bert the opportunity to move ahead --at Dee's expense.

"Then, as principal," Peter went on, "there was a math teacher, John

Stewart, who wanted to become an administrator. John had done his administrator's internship under Dee's supervision. When he wanted to find an administrator's job, Dee gave him his job as principal at Gilboa. Dee once again, sacrificed himself for someone else to move ahead. It was only after this that Dee went to Andes (Andes Central School District) as interim superintendent. I will tell you that I was really impressed with Dee's unselfishness at this time. He was just so caring and giving to others.

"There is one very personal story about Dee that I would like to pass along," Peter requested. "One day my seven-year old son, Tom, called his sister, Maureen, a "retard." Knowing of Dee's work with the physically and mentally challenged kids in the Special Olympics, I told Dee of the incident. At the time Dee was Games Director of the Special Olympics for the State of New York, and he came up with an object lesson for Tom. It was summer and the games were about to begin. Dee invited our family to the games. When we arrived, Dee matched Tom up with a girl competitor that had Down's syndrome. He told Tom to count how many times she could jump up and down. Tom spent the whole day as a counselor for the Special Olympics. There was a point in the day when Tom got separated from everyone he knew, and he got scared that he had been left behind. He walked to the loudspeaker table and had Dee paged. Well, by this time, I was frantically looking for Tom. When I heard the page, I went to the table, and there he was with Dee. I asked Tom, 'Why didn't you page me.' His answer was, 'You only know Dee, but Dee knows everybody.' The experience changed my son's view of the mentally and physically challenged."

In 1985, Dee became interim superintendent of the Andes Central School District and remained in that position until the end of the 1987 school year. It was during this assignment that Dee initiated Project PERFECT, an inter-scholastic sports competition program for the handicapped. This program, of course, was modeled after the first PERFECT program he started in Mamaroneck in 1977, which, in 1997, became a state-wide program.

"The state approved inter-scholastic sports for the handicapped several years ago and similar programs have been kicked off in other areas," Dee told reporter Patsy Nicosia of the Stamford, N.Y. newspaper, the *Mirror Recorder* in January 1986. "It's something that's long overdue here. It's wrong that school sports are given for the rest of the students, but the minute you're handicapped there is no inter-scholastic competition," he went on to inform her.

In 1987 Dee was hired by District Superintendent Austin Leahy and his assistant William Nagle of Otsego Northern Catskills to be principal of the alternative school for ten participating central school systems: Andes, Charlotte Valley, Gilboa –Conesville, Hunter-Tannersville, Jefferson, Margaretville, Roxbury, Stamford, South Kortright and the Windham-Ashland-Jewett School. These gentlemen were well aware of the success Dee had with the APPLE program in Mamaroneck. Dee jumped at the opportunity, for this was what he enjoyed the most --helping kids with potential that were in distress and were underachieving. Besides, he knew almost everyone in the area from his years as acting superintendent and principal in the Gilboa Central School District, and it was within a few miles of his retirement home.

The alternative school had been in existence for several years prior to Dee's arrival. During that time it was never given the full attention and resources that were required to be a success. During that time period it had two different part-time directors, both of whom felt that it was too much for them to handle along with their normal duties.

With the knowledge of Dee's successful experience with the APPLE program in Mamaroneck, Superintendent Leahy and his assistant William Nagle gave Dee their full backing for the program.

"I liked the established location of the school at the old Gilboa Schoolhouse for three reasons," said Dee. "First of all, it was isolated from all the kids' home schools which, for a host of reasons, they readily admit that they hated. Secondly, I felt that the kids would ultimately identify it as *their school* and the one that they liked. Third, the facility was ideal for the school because it offered a cafeteria, a gymnasium and two classrooms. The only problem with the location, that I could see, was that about half of the building had already been converted into apartments for senior citizens.

"I realized that the location had the potential for conflict between the students and the senior citizens housed in close proximity to each other. To insure that this would not happen, the first thing the staff and I did was to introduce the twenty-six students to the resident senior citizens. Then we set up a program in which the students were made available to help the seniors in whatever reasonable way they felt appropriate. The students would read to them, walk and talk with them, help them carry things to and from their cars, and on some occasions they even put on skits for their entertainment."

"During Dee's first Christmas at the school, he organized a Christmas dinner for the seniors, in which all the students and faculty served the dinner," remembered teacher Julie Lazina. "Santa came and distributed little gifts to all the seniors. Santa was played by one of my neighbors," she said.

"This was one way that Dee established good relations between the senior citizens, the students and the community in general," said Steve Farleigh, a former student at the school. "As a result the seniors and we students became great friends. They loved us and we loved them. When they needed some help, they came to us," Steve recalled with a sense of reverence in his voice.

"Dee was a believer in project learning," explained former teacher Peter Fox. "He wanted the kids to see their value, but more importantly, he wanted them to see their value in the context of the community. Prior to coming to Dee's alternative school, most of the kids did not feel a part of a school community. He made them part of the larger community. He taught them that giving was as important as taking. He was way ahead of his time in terms of service learning."

Dee's second major task was to select the right teachers for the job. The criteria for selecting his staff was similar to that which he used for selecting teachers for the APPLE program he had organized in Mamaroneck. The first, and most important criteria, was that the candidates must have a passion for kids and for teaching. They must be willing to spend an inordinate amount of time with the students and exhibit great patience. They must be proficient in their chosen disciplines, and must be able to challenge their students to learn. Most importantly, to Dee though, was to NEVER GIVE UP ON A KID.

When Dee arrived as principal, Jim Adair and Mike Rosa were already on the faculty and they both fit the criteria. Jim taught all math, science and health courses, and in addition, he taught two business courses -- The Introduction to Occupations and Business Law. Mike Rosa taught English. Dee hired two new staff members, Judy Lazina and Helen Davis. Dee met Judy Lazina when he was interim superintendent at Andes Central School District.

Teacher, Judy Lazina.

"I was working in Andes when Dee was the interim superintendent there," said Judy. "He asked me to come to the alternative school, and I took a leave of absence to try it out. I liked it and stayed. I taught English and social studies there," she said.

"As for Helen Davis," said Dee, "she wore several hats. She was a teaching assistant, keyboard instructor, and my secretary/office manager. Helen was sixty-years-old at the time and was known to everyone at the school as "grandma" and she loved the title.

Like the APPLE students at Mamaroneck, the students of the Northern Catskill Alternative School had the same problem of overcoming the stigma of being associated with an alternative school program. Unlike in Mamaroneck, where the students were housed in the same building with the regular students, the students at the Gilboa location were isolated from the regular students, which tended to lessen the stigma.

"The school was presented to the students as *a marriage*," said teacher Judy Lazina. "The students were committed to try, and we, as their teachers, offered them whatever help they needed."

Steve Farleigh, former student.

"Dee was a creative pragmatist. He came up with a special privilege that helped sell the school to his students. Here is what he did.

"Almost all of us kids smoked, and Dee knew that. Dee must have been thinking that if the privilege to smoke would give us an incentive for staying in school, then why not? Besides, the school was isolated from all the other schools in the surrounding area. The smoking privilege was restricted to a designated location outside the back of the school building, and a trash can was made available to discard our cigarettes. Specific times were designated for smoking, and these times were not to be abused. If they were, the punishment was that the privilege was withdrawn for a period of time."

One of the most compelling stories to come out of Dee's experience at the Northern Catskills Alternative School is the story of Jeffery Foote, a deaf student, and his teacher Amy Hinkle Taylor. Ms. Taylor was Jeffery's teacher at the Northern Catskills Occupational Center before he was transferred to the alternative school.

Teacher Amy Hinkle Taylor.

"When I first met Dee, I was an itinerant teacher of the deaf at the Northern Catskills Occupational Center where I was working for BOCES (Board of Cooperative Educational Services). At the time I was working with Jeffery Foote, who within two months after birth, was diagnosed to be deaf. I worked with him in a special class setting at the Center, which was located just a short distance from Dee's alternative school.

"Dee was in and out of there regularly, meeting with different teachers as well as students who were taking classes there. That is where Dee met Jeff and seemed to feel that his needs would be better served in the alternative school setting. Dee seemed to have a way of detecting potential in people and was all about helping people make the best of opportunities. He was also very good at making some of those opportunities happen. Dee convinced the powers-to-be to allow Jeff to move to the alternative school. Jeff went through the interview process, like all the other kids, and was chosen to fill one of the Stamford Central School District slots at the school. So, while he was at the alternative school, I then began to work with him there. During the times I was scheduled to work with Jeff, I did so, both as a teacher and interpreter. I also worked with Dee and the other alternative school teachers to coordinate instruction. In addition, I was allowed to do group sign language instruction for the staff and students, to better facilitate communication between Jeffery and the other teachers and students. When I was teaching in other locations, Jeff would have work assigned either from myself or from the other teachers, or taking physical education with Dee.

"One day Jeffery expressed an interest in a cochlear implant. This is a surgical procedure, which, if successful, could give him usable hearing. I told Dee about it, and he immediately took up the challenge and was able to help secure a grant that made this surgery possible. Most likely Jeff's family themselves would not have been able to afford the costly surgery. Jeffery underwent the procedure and it was successful. Dee was there even to help with transportation to and from Jeff's doctor's appointments.

"I remember how Jeffery jumped when he heard a fire siren go off for the first time," said teacher Julie Lazina.

"But Dee did not stop there," Amy continued. "He helped arrange for Jeffery, me and himself to visit NTID-- the National Technical Institute for the Deaf, which is part of the RIT College (Rochester Institute of Technology in Rochester, New York). Talk about opportunities, Jeff was able to meet students, sit in on classes, and talk to professors. Dee was wonderful at showing the kids what was available to them and helping them see a way to get it.

"Jeff did eventually go on to attend NTID but he did not complete the program there. I last heard from Jeff in 2008. He called from his home in Florida. He was excited to let me know that he was back home after spending time in Russia."

Testimonials by students, parents, faculty and staff regarding their alternative school experience.

The success of the Northern Catskill Alternative Program, conducted by Dee and his staff, is best revealed from testimony from students, graduates, parents of former students, faculty and staff.

Jim Adair, former teacher at the alternative school.

"Dee was a leader by example. He was always on the go, never resting by idly when things needed to be done. He let the staff do their own thing, by allowing them to take ownership of their programs and classes, but was always interested in the staff tying things together to keep the family setting that we worked so hard to establish, and the kids bought into. He believed in fitness and athletics. All students had to participate in some aspect of athletics at their home school. He would routinely go to their games/contests and watch them participate. We didn't have report cards for grades. What we did was to close school for the last two days of each ten-week marking period, and went around to the school districts that we served and had half hour parent/student/staff conferences. In this way, so to speak, everything was out on the table. If a student or parent failed to show, the student could not return to school until this meeting was held. It didn't take long to have perfect attendance at these meetings. Dee would go to student homes daily if they were absent, to try and bring them to school. Many working parents gave him a key so he could enter their homes and get them up and ready for school. He even got a couple of kids up by dumping water on them in bed. I wish I could have been there to see that. We wouldn't be able to get away with that now," said Jim Adair.

George Coromilas, former student (Age 30, Seattle, Washington).

"I was a student at the North Catskill Alternative School for the last three years of my high school career (1993 through 1996). The circumstances surrounding my selection to attend the school was because my grades were slipping, and when I was in ninth grade I failed math and science. I had to make up classes if I wanted to graduate on time, so the alternative school was an option. I also felt that my teachers of my home school were very judgmental. While in high school, I socialized with everyone and never really got into much trouble. I think because of my outgoing personality, the way I dressed and my habit of coloring my hair different colors, gave my teachers the impression that I was up to something and considered a troublemaker, which I wasn't. Prior to attending the alternative school, I was a little unsure about attending. However, I knew it was my best opportunity to make up my failed classes, but I wasn't sure why I was approached. At first, I thought my high school was trying to get me out, which upset me because I was never a bad kid or terrible student. My grades definitely needed improvement, but I wasn't a lost cause. I really wanted to graduate on time with my class of 1996. After meeting with my high school counselor and Dee about the concept of the alternative school, I decided to give it a shot.

"The first time I met Dee was in my guidance counselor's office. Our initial meeting went something like this:

"I know you're a wise-ass by just looking at you," was the first thing Dee said to me. "I thought that was funny, since we had just met. So, I asked him, 'why would you say such a thing?'

"Because I was a wise-ass as a youth myself, and I can tell one when I meet one," he responded.

"Strangely enough, I liked Dee's honest and upfront approach. I knew he wasn't a fake person and that he was honest and sincere with his feelings. I respected that in a person.

"My attitude toward the alternative school soon changed. The perception of the alternative school, in the minds of most people, was that the students were troublemakers or students with learning disabilities. That wasn't the case. The students attending the school were from all over the county, and most of us were just misunderstood kids. We were just like Dee when he was a kid, upfront and honest people who wanted to do our own thing. We just needed some more direction, and Dee knew that. The experience taken from the school changes your life. It opened my mind to the way people look at others. My teachers at the school focused more on my needs. My home school teachers never seemed to focus on me, and get to know me and the issues I was dealing with in and out of school. Dee and his staff of teachers really wanted me to succeed. If I hadn't gone to the alternative school, I probably would have never played sports, which was mandatory for all students attending the school. I played basketball and also had a very successful tennis career in high school. That experience was priceless. Dee always had a way of connecting with me and other students. I've never forgotten the number of times Dee would drive to a student's house and pick them up if they didn't show up for school. Dee would hunt them down and bring them to school, if he knew they were screwing off. Dee always knew what to say to a student that was out of line, trying to make Dee or the other teachers look bad. Dee would hold his ground, and his response would always stop them in their tracks. I think the students were taken aback because this old guy was sharp, and always seemed to know what to do or say.

"I will never forget the time Dee took me on a tour of his house. All of his awards, medals and accomplishments were something special. I would have loved to have grown up with a friend like Dee. He would do anything for his students and friends. I'm not sure if I will ever encounter another person in my life like Dee DaBramo. I want his energy and success when I'm an older man. I have not seen Dee in several years, but think about him from time to time. I will never forget him or his favorite quote that I still use and love – *'It's not what you say, it's how you say it.'*

"Socially, as a result of my alternative school experience, I became more open-minded and felt that everyone deserved a second chance. Academically, upon graduation from the school, I went to SUNY Cobleskill for two years to study Hotel/Restaurant Management. At present, fifteen years later, I'm Director of Sales and Marketing for Marriott in Seattle, Washington. I own my own condominium, and there are plans in the making to get married soon. If I hadn't attended the alternative school, I'm not sure what my life would be like today."

Lawrence Fancher - Former Transportation Supervisor for the Gilboa-Conesville School System.

"As interim superintendent and as principal of the Northern Catskills Alternative School, Dee emphasized that every student would be treated the same. To him, it didn't matter if they were good kids or bad kids, or whether they were smart or if they struggled academically, this rule applied. He disciplined them all equally and gave them all the same opportunities. He pushed them to do what he thought they were capable of doing and made it very clear what his expectations were.

"Dee also supported his staff and their decisions. I remember an incident one day when a student, traveling with his class to Grand Gorge, misbehaved, and I made the decision to punish him by requiring him to ride the regular bus to Gilboa for thirty days, rather than being suspended from school for five days. For a high school student, who was a licensed driver, it was a greater punishment to have to ride the bus into school than being suspended from school. Dee said he absolutely agreed and he made sure the student rode the school bus to Gilboa every one of the thirty days.

"Even after Dee retired, he continued to help the Gilboa-Conesville students. On several occasions when Dee heard that there were students looking to attend his alma mater SUNY Cortland, he would call ahead to various staff members at the college and make all kinds of arrangements for their visit. He and I would take a small busload of kids and drive to the college. It was not just your everyday college visit. Upon arrival Dee would give them the grand tour of the campus -- describing the history behind each building, telling them of the wonderful exploits of the athletic teams, and where the best hangouts in the town of Cortland were. To top off each visit, he arranged for a visit with the college president."

Testimonials regarding the effectiveness of the Northern Catskill Alternative School.

The following testimonials come from a video tape recorded on March 26, 1990 at a Nothern Catskill Alternative School gathering led by Dee DaBramo. The participants included district administrators, alternative school teachers, parents, students enrolled at the school and graduates of the school.

High School Counselor.

"One of our main objectives in education is to have children succeed. If we don't try to fulfill that aim, we are a failure. Many times children cannot succeed in what we call the normal or traditional classroom. When they don't, we have to provide them with an alternative education. I think the alternative education in Grand Gorge is the most incredible school and a most incredible experience for both students and teachers. I know I have learned a lot by just visiting the school. I think that some kids have problems in the regular school because they just don't fit the mold as a regular kid in a regular classroom. When the bell rings, they are always a little bit late, they've left their book in their locker or they don't have their homework. They meet failure upon failure upon failure. The result is they get very discouraged, angry and often lose their temper. They often have personality conflicts with some of their teachers. Alternative education gives them an opportunity to wipe the slate clean and start afresh. They are placed in a good environment that is very similar to an elementary school classroom environment where there are no bells, consequently they can't be late. They can't forget their books, because their books are in the classroom. They don't have a lot of personalities to encounter with their teachers, because there are just a few teachers at the school. They are given a goal when they first arrive, and they can see a way out of their dilemma. I am very pleased to be a part of all that."

A father of a student.

"My son spends part time at the alternative school. From my observations, I've been amazed at the degree of flexibility that exists and are still able to run the school and get things done. I attribute the reason for this to the fact that Dee has surrounded himself with quality people, and he is willing to accept their opinions. From my observation, it appears that decisions are made from the bottom up and not imposed from the top down. In this way, everyone-- the teachers and the students-- get involved in the conduct of the program. For me, this is one of the mainstays of the program. The other thing is about Dee himself. He looks amazingly disorganized with all his running around (laughter), but in fact he's not. When its time to get everything together, Dee pulls all the strings, ties all the knots and everything seems to fall into place."

A mother of a student.

"I'm a mother of a child that can be classified as bright. A few years ago my daughter was not making the grades she was capable of. She had some health problems that resulted in an emotional problem. At first, when my daughter was recommended to attend the alternative school, I was not very happy, and Dee and I locked horns. I argued that she was bright and should be doing well.

"But she's not doing anything," he pointed out.

"It took some doing, but Dee finally convinced me to enroll her in the alternative school. It took so much work and patience, but Dee and his staff turned that girl around. My greatest thrill came two years later when my daughter received her senior ring. She said to me, 'Mom, if it wasn't for the decision made two years ago, this would not have happened.' I have to give Dee and his staff all the credit for that. I truly believe in my heart that Dee and his staff eat, sleep, breathe and live for these children that come to this school. The other thing that they did for our daughter was they restored her sense of her self-esteem and self-worth, and you can't put a price on something like that. Thank you very much."

A first-year female student.

"I'm a first-year student at the alternative school. It has offered so much to me. It has opened doors for me that I never thought would be opened to me. It has offered a family group that I really don't have, and this has helped me care and grow in many ways."

Dee interrupts at this point in the conversation. "This young lady has a grandfather in Georgia and an aunt in California and that is all she has. The staff recently purchased a ticket for her to visit her aunt in California."

A female student.

"Before I came to the alternative school, please excuse my language, I was a *bitch*. I hated everybody. I hated the teachers. I got mad at them and swore at them and would run out the door. The alternative school really helped me overcome that. I'm getting better grades than I was. I was going to drop out of school when I was sixteen, but they helped me not to do that. Next year I'm going to BOCES (Board of Cooperative Education Services) to study to become a teacher. I really want to thank Mr. DaBramo and the teachers for helping me."

Jeffery Foote's mother.

"My name is Donna Foote, and my son is deaf. When I first came here from New Hampshire, many of the schools there were lousy. They never taught my son. When he came here he had maybe a second grade education, and he was at level with kids younger than himself, and he felt way out of place and was not doing very well at all. Then he went to visit the alternative school. Amy, his other teacher, brought him there. I have always told people that my son was smart, but I couldn't figure out why my son wasn't learning. When he went to the alternative school, he was equal to the other kids his age. They had problems just the same as him. He learned that he could help them learn sign language, and he could learn things from the other kids, from DaBramo and his teachers. In two years he has gone from a second grade education to a seventh grade level. Next year he is going to finish and graduate, with hopes of going to college. He is going to go to RIT (Rochester Institute of Technology). Not only hope, he's going to go and it's only because of the alternative school. Jeff has gone to many schools, but none of them helped him at all like the alternative school. If you see other deaf kids that need the help, send them to the alternative school. They work wonders. I can't say enough about it."

Camp Independence.

The story of the origin, philosophy and operation of Camp Independence is best told by Naomi Yavne.

"I met Dee in 1978, when he interviewed me for a position in one of the departments for which he had responsibility in the Mamaroneck School System. In working with him during that first year, I learned a great deal about him-- his involvement with special needs populations and especially with regards to his association with the Special Olympics Program.

"I met his close friends, Jay and Pat Sherlach and their three sons, one of whom (Matt) had Down's syndrome. It was through his involvement with the Sherlachs over the years that Dee met many people involved with group homes for the developmentally disabled, as well as the folks who helped to run Camp Smith on the estate of Jean Ann Kennedy Smith in Pawling, N.Y. This was the program for handicapped adolescents/adults in Dutchess County that Dee and the Sherlachs started, with the generous assistance from Jean Ann Kennedy Smith the sister of the late President John F. Kennedy and Eunice Kennedy Shriver. Because of Dee's involvement in all these areas, people were always calling his house for advice and/or to bring people up to his country house for evaluation.

"Aside from sending Dee to every state in the U.S. and Italy to promote the Special Olympics, Eunice Shriver called many times to ask for his help with friends/associates who were having difficulties. Dee's home was like living at Lourdes, in France, where people come to be healed. That may sound like an odd analogy, but a really true one. There was something very magical and restorative about the house and property in Conesville, and Dee was always able to extract the best from everyone who would arrive, no matter what the issue."

Camp Independence

Camp Independence staff and campers at Dee's home at Conesville, New York. (Photographs courtesy of Dee DaBramo. Graphics by Tess Kean.)

Author's Note:

Lourdes, in France, is a city near the grotto of Massabielle, a Catholic shrine, where reportedly in 1858, the vision of the Virgin Mary was repeatedly revealed to a French peasant girl, Bernadette Soubirous. As the story goes, she was instructed by the Virgin Mary to drink from a previously undiscovered spring in the grotto which had surprisingly healing powers. The site is also known as the Miraculous Cave, where thousands of mostly Catholic pilgrims visit each year.

"Dee was always bringing students/teachers from Mamaroneck up to the country house to go camping on the 88-acres that he owned, and his family spent a great deal of time there, as well," Naomi continued. "I think that he decided that there needed to be a place for people to actually stay comfortably, as his restored 230-year-old house was quite small. The recreation barn was the first of the two barns to be built. The second floor of the building housed four bedrooms (bunk rooms sleeping about 14-20), two tile bathrooms that each had two toilets, two sinks and showers, and the lower level which had a full kitchen and a large space for a dining area, with couches, pool table, juke box, etc. and a handicapped-accessible bathroom. This building was built with the help of his sister Sadie, her husband Bill, and some of Dee's children, as well as other family and friends. It was built over a period of months, primarily on weekends, as everyone was working during the week. When completed, everyone who would come up to visit would stay there. After awhile, Dee would have students/staff from the alternate school that he ran in Mamaroneck come up and stay in the recreation barn, if the weather was too inclement for camping. The second barn for equipment storage was built in the late 1970s by the same groups of people, and I believe that it was somewhere in that time-frame that we

Recreation Barn and Storage Barn at Camp Independence (Courtesy of Peter Fox)

began having discussions about running a summer program for handicapped youth and adults from group homes. His intent was not so much to make money, but to do something fun and worthwhile during the summer vacation months away from school that would allow us to be at home in the mountains in the summer.

"It was in 1980 that Dee and I moved in together, and I believe that was the first year of the camp. Initially, it was a pretty informal program. We ran the camp with a young man, Dave Warren, whom Dee had hired at Mamaroneck to teach physical education. Dave was newly married and his wife, Jeanie, would come and visit on weekends. Dee's daughter Shelly was also helping to run the camp. I spent much of my time cooking, cleaning and doing laundry! Eventually, we decided that we would not have more than ten campers at a time, so that we could better focus on each individual's needs. We had both male and female campers. We would have a daily program which included arts and crafts, outdoor education, life skills, working in the vegetable garden, chores and daily exercise/swimming/picnicking at the pool in Mine Kill State Park. The evenings were filled with barbeques, movies, and trips to local events. Usually, campers would stay from one to two weeks each, although we had two teenagers, Chris and Matt Shelach, who spent the entire five weeks with us each summer. They were from Pawling, and their parents knew Dee and Dave well and trusted them implicitly. Matt Sherlach even came one summer as a junior counselor. We had special guests who came and worked with the campers in both the arts and in the outdoor education programs. The population we served included those with physical handicaps, Autism, Tourettes, Down's syndrome, as well as those who had been de-institutionalized and had major issues as a result of what they had been exposed to in those facilities.

"Again, it was the quality of the program, not the quantity of the population that was important to Dee and to all of us. In 1985, Dee and I were married at the Conesville house after our camp session was over.

"Camp Independence ran until 1989, when Dee and I divorced, not because we did not love each other, but because I really wanted to have a family (I was 39, he was 65) and we knew that he could not see his way clear to embark again on that path at that age. It was an incredibly difficult decision for both of us! Camp Independence will still always be a wonderful memory of the incredible experience that I had the good fortune to have shared with him."

Politics in the Catskills.

In 1990, Dee was encouraged by Lawrence Fancher to run for Conesville Town Supervisor on the Democratic ticket. Lawrence was Transportation Supervisor for the Gilboa-Conesville School System when Dee was the interim superintendent and principal of the Northern Catskills Alternative School.

"I had three reasons why I wanted Dee to run for Town Supervisor," said Lawrence. "First, because of his knowledge and experience in local government administration that he brought with him from Mamaroneck as a Village Trustee and Police Commissioner. Second, because of his connections with so many different politicians at the county and state level, and third, because he was very well-liked by the people of the community. For these reasons, I thought he had a good chance of winning. When I asked him to run, he questioned whether or not he should do it, because he was so busy and wasn't sure if he would have the time to do a good job. He finally relented and ran for the office. One of the major issues facing the community at the time was a lack of summer activities available for our children, including pre-teens and teenagers," said Lawrence. "Living in a rural area like ours doesn't provide these kids with much to do in the summer months to keep them occupied and out of trouble. The outcome of the election was that Dee won, much to his shock and surprise. He could not believe that the people in the town actually voted for him. The reaction of the community to his victory was quite the opposite. Everyone was pleased that he had won and they knew he would do his best to make sure that the community got what they needed."

I asked Lawrence to describe Dee's approach to solving problems that confronted the community.

"Dee was a mediator," he said. "Once he was elected as Town Supervisor he became part of the Board of Supervisors for Schoharie County. It was to this board that he brought the concerns of the people of Conesville. Our town's concerns became his concerns and he debated them vigorously with good logic and reason. If the powers-to-be couldn't provide him with the information he needed to plead our case, he seemed to always manage to find someone who could."

Then I asked Lawrence how Dee went about using his influence as Town Supervisor to help the kids in the community.

"One of the first things Dee did was to address the community's concern regarding a summer program for the kids," said Lawrence. "He did this by establishing the Conesville Summer Co-Op Camp modeled after the one he established in Mamaroneck when he worked there. The program provided the children in the towns of Conesville, Gilboa and Blenheim the opportunity to participate in a structured program, based around reading, math, and the arts, while also providing them with the opportunity to participate in swimming lessons at Mine Kill State Park. The Summer Co-Op program ran for the entire month of July and gave the children the opportunity to practice their academics for an extended part of the year, rather than the kids just sitting at home and watching television. It also kept them physically fit, which was something Dee believed in strongly as well. Dee was able to accomplish this mission by applying for grant funds, using his connections with various members of county and state government officials."

David Avitablile, reporter for the Stamford, N.Y. weekly newspaper, *Mountain Eagle*, describes the program in his article, <u>3R's, Dog Paddle Meet In Co-Op Camp Program</u>, August 7, 1990.

Most children do not like to go back to school during the summer months, but that is not the attitude of the 150 kids involved in the "Summer Co-Op Camp" at Mine Kill State Park and the Gilboa-Conesville Central School.

The camp is the brainchild of Conesville's Town Supervisor Emilio DaBramo. It combines half-days at the park pool with half-days of instruction at the school. The program, starts on July 9 and will run through Aug. 10.

Over 150 children from kindergarten through sixth grade are split up into two groups. At the school, they are given courses in reading, writing and math, and at the pool they learn to swim. The camp, which has received two state grants worth $14,000, seems to be a hit with adults and students alike.

Byron Brandow, an 11-year old freckled-faced sixth grader, said he likes the camp because, "Its fun at the school, you learn new things. There's none of the tests you have to study for. Teachers also give more attention during the summer than the regular year."

The son of Park Sports Director Connie VanValkenburg also said he likes the program. "I like it at Mine Kill," said 7-year-old Adam, "you learn how to swim and do back floats."

Assemblyman Paul Tonko, who helped secure a $10,000 state grant for the program, was on hand Tuesday to talk with the youngsters.

"His (DaBramo's) idea is unique and is not covered in the (state) process," Tonko said. Tonko added that the camp, run for children from Blenheim, Gilboa and Conesville, is an excellent idea, and noted, "The students are having fun. The children get to improve their social networking, and transportation is provided to the school and to the pool."

DaBramo said he got the idea because kids should have something to do for the summer. "The school is there and has all the facilities, and the program is a nice way to use high school leaders over the summer."

In addition to the pool, the program, which is five days a week, also includes sports and field trips. Students have already visited I-88, Great Escape and Deer Run (for bowling) and are planning a cruise on Lake George and a visit to the House of Frankenstein.

End of Article.

Aside from his many rewarding accomplishments at the alternative school and as a Town Supervisor in Conesville, life had its downside as well. On November 28, 1994, during the Thanksgiving weekend, Dee's oldest sister Aida suffered an aneurysm and passed away.

"I have always admired my dear sister Aida for her kindness and intelligence," said Dee. "She was dedicated to her family, her husband Maynard, daughter Julie and grandson Zachary, and, of course, loyalty to our mother Josephine, our father Michael, and our sister Sadie and to me. Her passing leaves a hollow space in my heart."

The family Dee grew up with was now reduced to two, his sister Sarah (Sadie) Casey and himself.

A year later, on October 19, 1995, Celeste DaBramo, Dee's first wife, passed away at age 67, after first battling breast cancer and then cancer of the palate.

"She suffered terribly from the disease with strength and dignity," her daughter Shelly told me. "Her final year was at a nursing home in Mamaroneck. She was an ardent golfer all her life, and as a resident there, she would often be seen putting golf balls with her putter," Shelly added admiringly.

Honors and Awards.

1992 – Healthy American Fitness Leaders Award (HAFL)

Dee was nominated for the Healthy American Fitness Leaders (HAFL) Award for 1992, by Dr. Richard O. Keelor, the former member of The President's Council for Physical Fitness and Sports, on which Dee served as an advisor and clinician. He was duly honored at the Eleventh Annual Healthy American Fitness Leaders Awards banquet on Saturday, September 26, 1992 at the Ritz-Carlton Buckhead Hotel in Atlanta, Georgia, with nine other inductees. The Master of Ceremony that evening was Dorothy Hammel, the 1976 Olympic Gold Medal winner in the women's individual figure skating event. The HAFL program, sponsored by the Allstate Life Insurance Co., administered by the United States Junior Chamber of Commerce and conducted in cooperation with the President's Council, annually promotes physical fitness and health awareness in America.

1994 Honorary Degree of Doctor of Humane Letters from SUNY Cortland.

"On Sunday May 15, 1994 I received a most unexpected, but my most coveted award of my life," said Dee. "I was presented with an honorary degree of Doctor of Humane Letters at SUNY Cortland's 1994 Commencement.

The citation delivered by then President Clark, of SUNY Cortland, read as follows:

> "Emilio "Dee" DaBramo, you returned from World War II wearing four Battle Stars, four air medals and the Distinguished Flying Cross to wear a green freshman beanie in a company of veterans who invaded this College, changing it as much as it changed you.
>
> "From your graduation to your current calling as principal of an alternative school, your career of 50 years has been characterized by the courage of leadership, the commitment of service, and the charisma of an enthusiasm that never dies.

"As war hero, college athlete, teacher, administrator, advocate for the disadvantaged, and fitness guru, you have demonstrated that old-fashioned virtues of courage and service to others, when buttressed by sound mind in a sound body, can transform the landscape of opportunity for those who have less. The State University of New York and its College at Cortland are proud to award you the degree of Doctor of Humane Letters."

Dee, donned in cap and gown, delivering the keynote address to the SUNY Cortland Senior Class of 1994 after receiving his Honorary Doctor's Degree of Humane Letters from SUNY Cortland, the first in the history of the college.

Dee's Address to the graduating seniors of the Class of 1994.

"As I stand here this afternoon, I cannot believe my good fortune in having all the friends and family who made this day possible for me. When President Clark wrote me a letter several months ago to tell me about this degree, I didn't write back to him for a month. I thought someone was pulling my leg. Then, when I called Laurie Barton, his secretary, she told me that it was true.

"This degree really belongs to all the teachers and friends I have had over the years. Only in the United States could such an honor come to a person with my background. I was born in Italy, and my parents brought me to this country when I was three years old. We eventually settled in Stone House, New York, where we lived in a house with no water, lights or an inside toilet. Those were

the great years because they taught me about all the advantages I did have. Like parents who loved me and made education a priority for me. One thing my daddy always said was 'that you can't pay enough for education.' He was a man who worked on the railroad with a pick and axe, but he sure had his priorities straight.

"In my elementary days, I went to a one-room school house for eight years in Poughquag, N.Y. I had the same teacher, Pansy Baker, for all those years. Since I didn't speak English at first, Miss Baker made Dick Wooden, a seventh grade student teach me how to speak English.

"After elementary school, I went to Pawling High School. I graduated in 1941 after failing two grades. I had a 65% average, and one of the few times I made my teachers smile was when I walked off the stage with that diploma. Then I went into the Army Air Corps for three years and a half and served in the European theater. I completed 31 missions.

Those war years were a valuable part of my life. The war taught me to be unselfish and to give to others in a way that I had not known before. That experience pushed me in the direction of serving others.

"Since I was the first soldier discharged in my hometown, I pictured a homecoming celebration that was a little different than the one I actually had. When I got home, I found out that my girlfriend had gotten married. That night I went out and had a little too much to drink. Later that night when my mother found me drunk on the porch, she cried. The next day she went to my high school principal to complain how the war had ruined her son. She told Mr. Norton: 'My son, he use to be a nice a boy, but now he is a bum. He drinks and the war ruined my Emilio.' So, Mr. Norton told my mom to send me to see him. When I got there, Mr. Norton told me to go to college and become a teacher. So he picked up the phone and called Dr. Smith, who was President of Cortland College. Dr. Smith immediately accepted me over the phone, and I started college two days later, with thirty-five other discharged World War II veterans. So here I was, back in the U.S.A. for only a week. Within twenty four hours, my mother called me a bum, and within a week, I was a Cortland student.

"Part of the adjustment for me was learning how to study again. Dr. Anthony Tesori, one of my Cortland professors, made me study in the town library for two hours a night. Fred Holloway was my soccer coach, and he gave me - -and all the other verterans- -the best counsel we ever received as we tried to readjust to civilian life. One quick story. Within our first twenty days at Cortland, we had a soccer game at West Point. On the way, we stopped in Newburgh, N.Y. for a bathroom break. Actually it was a gin mill and when we went in, we decided to have a beer before we boarded the bus. Now we were all combat veterans who had seen some pretty rough times and we were not babes in the woods. Fred Holloway came in to get us and he saw us drinking. He went to the bartender and ordered us all one more drink. Naturally, we thought we had one heck of a coach here to buy us a beer. That evening he called a team meeting at West Point and he gave us some straight talk: 'Boys, I am proud of all you did for your country, but the war is over. There can be no more drinking on this team.' And that was it. We never did that again. That is what we call respect.

"And that was a start of a great life. Cortland is where it all began for me. Here it is 49 years later, and I still love the place that means so much to me. As I look at this year's graduating class, I wish you all the support and friendship I have had over the years. Each of you is as capable of earning an honorary doctorate as I was. All you need is the willingness to donate your time to others and to lend a hand to those who need your help.

"I hope you stick together and that you keep your Cortland contacts. You never really succeed alone. You always succeed when you are a member of a team and surround yourself with people better than you are. Congratulations graduates. As one alumnus to another, I am proud to have you in my ranks.

"The people I need to thank are just too many to list. I do, however, want to recognize my family - -Michael, Debbie, Shelly and Jim. And I would also like to thank President Clark for being such a good friend and a good guy. I also want to wish him the best in his retirement.

"I can't be sure, but I think that somewhere up in heaven there is a lady with an Italian accent who is saying, 'That's a my son. I knew America would be good for us.'

Honors and Awards.

1999 - Certificate of Conspicuous Service to Human Kind - from the New York State Legislature.

On May 7, 1999, New York State Senator James Seward presents Emilio "Dee" DaBramo with a special legislative certificate for Conspicuous Service to Human Kind. (Courtesy of the Mountain Eagle).

The End

POSTSCRIPT

Dee's educational philosophy mirrored that of the professional staff at SUNY Cortland (known then as Cortland State Teachers College) during the 1940s and 50s when Dee and I were students in attendance there. Our indoctrination was quite simple.

As a teacher, your job did not end with the ringing of the bell at 3 p.m. signifying the end of the school day, in much the same way as the lives of the kids you were charged to teach and nurture did not end at 3 p.m. or begin at 8 a.m. You were encouraged to meet their families by visiting their homes and establishing a communication with them. You were encouraged to help troubled kids who were socially, culturally or economically deprived, or a product of a broken home. You were the purveyor of knowledge, a coach, a guidance counselor, a social worker, a community volunteer and, in some cases, even a parent in absentia. The teaching profession was portrayed as a twenty-four hour, seven-day- a-week obligation. In other words, a teacher should NEVER GIVE UP ON A KID.

Dee recognized the logic of this philosophy, based on his experience of growing up as an Italian immigrant child in a world of caring people-- his loving parents and sisters, his elementary school teacher, Pansy Baker, his first English tutor, seventh grader, Dick Wooden, his high school coach Cliff Wynkoop, and his high school principal Earl W. Norton, all of whom never gave up on him. The logic of this philosophy was further reinforced by his experiences in World War II, and his very close association with the crew of the B-24 Bomber, *The Bad Girl,* and the deep feeling of camaraderie the crew felt toward each other. Having learned the value of camaraderie, it became the hallmark of his leadership style which he transmitted to his staff members and to his students, along with his straight talk, no-nonsense and honest approach when dealing with them.

His other endearing leadership qualities were his outgoing personality and his *audacity*. His audacity was key to his persona as a great salesman. He was never afraid to think of the impossible, or ask for the impossible if it was to benefit the kids. His frank approach was-- if you don't ask for the sale, you will never get it. During his career he asked for thousands of volunteers to help run his programs for kids, and he got them. He asked for funding for his programs for kids, and he got it. As a result, untold thousands, and perhaps millions of kids benefited from his audacity, here in the U.S. and internationally.

"His audacity, at times, was very frustrating and even irritating to his superiors," one supervisor said. "He often made unilateral decisions on projects he felt deeply about without consulting with his supervisors. I remember one time he called me after-the-fact and I got so angry I ripped the telephone off the wall. I must admit though, that his logic was good and his actions always benefited the kids," he concluded.

I believe that Dee's contribution to the welfare of the mentally and physically challenged individuals will live in perpetuity. His work with the Special Olympics has been the catalyst for creation of other organizations dedicated to them as well, such as the National Center for Accessibility, the National Alliance for Accessible Golf, the National Center on Disabilities and Access to Education and many others.

What I fear the most is that the successful scheme he designed for alternative school students, as chronicled in this book, will die on the vine. Why? First, an effective alternative school program, as he designed it, requires small class sizes, individualized learning programs, with one-on-one relationships between teachers and students. This all costs money, and sadly, I am not sure the American taxpayer is willing to bear the cost, in spite of the fact that they espouse the importance of education to our national interest, national security and well-being.

Second, Dee and his staff demonstrated that the teachers and administrators must be dedicated to insuring that the kids in their charge succeed, no matter what it takes to get the job done. Again, NEVER GIVE UP ON A KID. This, of course, precludes the fact that the job requirements are twenty-four hours a day, seven days a week. I am not sure that the present employee/employer environment in our educational system will allow this to happen.

Third, the cost of training a teacher in our institutions of higher education has become increasingly more costly and out-of- reach for the average middle-class family household. Dee came from a poor family. If it had not been for the fact that he was a recipient of the World War II G.I. Bill, he may never have gone to college. What a loss that would have been to our society.

Fourth, our colleges and universities are forever raising the academic bar for admission. Dee had a high school average of slightly above 65%. In addition, Dee knew what it took to deal with *street-smart* kids because as a youth, he was one of them. It is safe to say, that because he had this experience, it was a valuable prerequisite for becoming an effective teacher in an alternative school environment. If these kids are not given the opportunity to attend college, what will happen to the potential "Dee DaBramos" of the future, or do they fall under the *theory of diminishing returns.* Will they be excluded from higher education without someone reviewing the extenuating circumstances that precluded them from meeting the stringent requirements for admission? Are our colleges and universities reverting back to being elitist institutions, as they were before World War II when only the very brightest, or the richest, or the well-connected students were admitted? Approximately eleven-million WWII Veterans took advantage of the G.I. Bill and many of them were not the very brightest, the richest or the well-connected. The economic, social and cultural impact of that program on our nation was astounding and still reverberates today.

The lessons drawn from the story of Dee's life tell me that our institutions of higher education have a strong **moral obligation** to re-examine their admissions policies and procedures for better evaluating the potential of students from socially, culturally and economically deprived neighborhoods and families. Dee recognized this moral obligation when he helped to initiate the *Project Opportunity Program* at SUNY Cortland as early as 1967. Perhaps the state universities should set up a**lternative colleges** within the structure of the existing institutions to aid these students, giving them a fighting chance to succeed and expand Dee's philosophy of NEVER GIVE UP ON A KID.

Researching and chronicling the events that defined the life of this extraordinary man has been a joyous and exciting adventure for me. From the prospective of a former elementary school science teacher, the sheer magnitude of what he accomplished as an educator, through his devotion to the kids he was charged to educate and nurture into becoming caring and productive human beings, has been an awe-inspiring experience.

From my perspective, his life story should be a must read for every *practicing educator* and every *aspiring teacher candidate* studying at our colleges and universities today. They would certainly draw inspiration from it.

ACKNOWLEDGEMENTS

Organizations:
2nd Air Division Memorial Room, Norfolk, England
    Derek S. Hill, Trust Librarian
    Judith A. Jerome, Fulbright American Trust Librarian
Amenia, N.Y. Historical Society
Brockport, N.Y. Historical Society
    Eunice Chestnut
Fort Schuyler Marine Academy
    Richard Corson, Librarian
Mamaroneck, N.Y. Historical Society
    Gloria Putts
Maritime Association of N.Y. South Street Sea Port Museum
    Norman Brower
Pawling Free Library
    Patricio Dadato and Bob Riley
Sandy Hook Pilots, Staten Island, N.Y.
    Janet Helman
Scarsdale Public Library
    Leni Glaber
U.S. Airforce Historic Research Agency, Maxwell Airforce Base, Alabama,
    Archivist Dixie Dysart, Captain William Butler, Sergeant Bird
U.S. Airforce Museum Research Division, Wright Patterson Air Force Base, Dayton, Ohio.
    Public Affairs Office -Diane Bachert

Individual collaborators:
Jim Adair
Edward Banker
Tom Burns
Debbie DaBramo Buckley
Jim DaBramo
Michael DaBramo
Sarah (Sadie) DeBramo Casey
Kevin Callagy
Teresa Capaldo
Angelina Cannizzo
George Coromilas
Helen Davis
Antoinette Esposito
Lawrence Fancher
Joseph Farleigh
Steve Farleigh
Gail Farwell
Peter Fox
Art Friedman
Frank C. Fuson (Pilot)
Grace Haake
Allen Hall
Robert M. Hogan
Dowd Jamerson
Maurice L. Jamerson
Dr. Richard Keelor
William Kotowitz (Co-Pilot)
Lou LiFifriere
Julia Lazina
Charles H. and Sally Miesenzahl
Leo McEnroe
Sandy Morley
Ernest Mott
Nick Nicaloto
Shelly (DaBramo) O'Malley

Suzi Openheimer
Joe Orosz Jr.
Carole Welsly Philips
Frank Pia
Marion Reynolds
Amand Ross
Kyle Rote Jr.
Calvert E. Schlick Jr.
U.B. Simoneaux (Crew Chief)
Amy Hinkle Taylor
Diana Teti
Evelyn Tomkins
Fielding L. Washington (Bombardier)
Ralph Whitney
Dick Wooden
Cliff Wynkoop
Naomi Yavne

Reference Publications and Photographs:
- Army Air Forces Technical School, Sioux Falls, South Dakota, U.S. Army Publication
- 458th Bombardment Group IV, written by George A. Reynolds.
- The Mission, by John Tartaro, (Self-published. Copyright, John Tartaro 1966)
    - Excerpts from the text pages and photograph of The Old Mission
- They Laughed When I Said We'd Teach Flycasting, School Management Magazine, March 1968 issue. (No author or copyright)
- Cortland College, An Illustrated History, by Leonard F. Ralston, Cortland College Alumni Association, 1991.
- 8th A F News, Journal of the Eighth Air Force Historical Society. Article: Coombe House was a Flak Farm, by Ann Newdeck ARC, 27 January, 1944.
    Photographs:
    - Entrance to the Coombe House Hotel.
    - Front view of the Coombe House Hotel
    - Map showing the location of Coombe House.

Newspaper Articles:

<u>Chapter 9 Mamaroneck</u>
Thank you to Cindy Royal, Senior Managing Editor, Journal News for granting permission for the use of following articles from The Daily Times:
- Article, <u>Community School Is Designed For Everyone</u>, by Paul Byrne and staff photographers, Wednesday, March 26, 1969 issue of The Daily Times.
- Article, <u>Apple Students Praise DaBramo</u> by Robert Viagas, Febuary 14, 1979 issue of The Daily Times.
- <u>Mamaroneck High School's APPLE Program Celebrates 10th Anniversary</u>, by Melissa Klein, The 1987 issue of The Daily Times.
- Editorial headlined, <u>200 Attend Surprise Party for DaBramo</u>, 1979 issue of The Daily Times.
- Editorial headlined, <u>DaBramo Cites Youth Programs</u>, March 15, 1972 issue of the The Daily Times.
- Editorial headline, <u>DaBramo</u>, March 1974 issue of The Daily Times.
- Article, <u>DeBramo Bids Mamaroneck Farewell</u>, by Mary Bauer in the August 22, 1980 issue of The Daily Times.
- Letter to the editor, <u>Dee Was a Doer</u>, by Allan Scott in the September 4, 1980 issue of The Daily Times.

<u>Chapter 10 The Special Olympics</u>
- Article, <u>Personal Rewards for a Public Man</u>, by Mary Jayne McKay in the November 1, 1975 issue of the Daily Times.

<u>Chapter 11 Life after Mamaroneck</u>
- Thank you to Liz Page, Editor of The Schoharie & Delaware Edition of the Mountain Eagle newspaper for granting permission for the use of the following article and photograph:
    - Article, <u>3 R's, Paddle Meet In Co-op Camp Program</u>, by reporter David Avitablile in the August 7, 1990, issue of The Schoharie & Delaware Edition of the Mountain Eagle.
    - Photograph from The Schoharie & Delaware Edition of the Mountain Eagle May 7, 1999 issue showing - NYS Senator James Seward presenting Dee DaBramo with the N.Y. State Legislative Certificate for Conspicuous Service.

Special Thanks to:

- Arnold Rist for introducing me to Emilio "Dee" DaBramo and for his liaison with him in arranging for this book to be written.
- Sarah DaBramo Casey for sharing with me the events of her brother's childhood, early family life and his career, without which this book could not have been written.
- Shelly DaBramo O'Malley for her many years of collaboration with a persistent author.
- Julie Czerendo for access to Dee DaBramo's war-time letters and early life photographs that were passed on to her by her mother; Aida DaBramo Stevens.
- Mildred J. Hennessy (my wife) for her editorial expertise and encouragement throughout the process of preparing the manuscript for this book.
- David Emmert for his editorial assistance.
- Kathy Weller for her editorial assistance.

Made in the USA
Middletown, DE
30 April 2022